AF412189

COMPARATIVELY QUEER

Comparatively Queer

Interrogating Identities across Time and Cultures

Edited by
Jarrod Hayes, Margaret R. Higonnet,
and William J. Spurlin

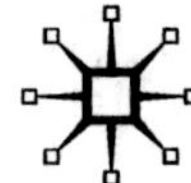

COMPARATIVELY QUEER

Copyright © Jarrod Hayes, Margaret R. Higonnet, and William J. Spurlin 2010.

An earlier version of Marie-Paule Ha's essay in this collection appeared as "Double Trouble" in *Signs* 34 (2): 423–49 © 2009, University of Chicago Press. We are grateful to the University of Chicago Press for permission to print this essay in its original form, which was published in revised form in *Signs*.

A portion of Anjali Arondekar's essay in this collection appeared in her book *For the Record* © 2009, Duke University Press. We thank Duke University Press for permission to reprint this excerpt.

First published in 2010 by PALGRAVE MACMILLAN® in the United States—a division of St. Martin's Press LLC, 175 Fifth Avenue, New York, NY 10010

Where this book is distributed in the UK, Europe and the rest of the world, this is by Palgrave Macmillan, a division of Macmillan Publishers Limited, registered in England, company number 785998, of Houndmills, Basingstoke, Hampshire RG21 6XS.

Palgrave Macmillan is the global academic imprint of the above companies and has companies and representatives throughout the world.

Palgrave® and Macmillan® are registered trademarks in the United States, the United Kingdom, Europe and other countries.

ISBN: 978-0-230-10436-5

Library of Congress Cataloging-in-Publication Data

Comparatively queer : interrogating identities across time and cultures / edited by Jarrod Hayes, Margaret R. Higonnet, and William J. Spurlin.
   p. cm.
  ISBN 978-0-230-10436-5 (alk. paper)
   1. Queer theory. 2. Gender identity in literature. 3. Literature, Comparative. I.
  Hayes, Jarrod. II. Higonnet, Margaret R. III. Spurlin, William J., 1954-

  HQ76.25.C664 2010
  306.76'601–dc22   2010009104

Design by Scribe Inc.

First edition: October 2010

10 9 8 7 6 5 4 3 2 1

Printed in the United States of America.

To the memory of Eve Kosofsky Sedgwick,

whose work inspired so many

CONTENTS

Acknowledgments

This collaborative project has had its own queer comparative history, crossing the borders of four continents and those of three professional organizations in the humanities. One site of genesis was the Modern Language Association (MLA) Division for Comparative Studies in Twentieth-Century Literature, which sponsored the session at the 2004 MLA Convention in Philadelphia titled "Comparatively Queer." The editors would like to thank the members of the division's executive committee who served with Jarrod Hayes and Margaret R. Higonnet that year and participated in the conceptualization of that session: Henry Sussman, Silvia Nagy-Zekmi, and Natasha B. Barnes, as well as the panelists of "Comparatively Queer": Neil C. Hartlen, Jana Evans Braziel, and Seri I. K. Luangphinith.

Another point of origin was the Gender Studies Committee of the International Comparative Literature Association (ICLA). Margaret R. Higonnet and William J. Spurlin presented this volume of essays to the committee for discussion alongside other comparative gender projects it has sponsored. This resulted in the ICLA sessions "Articulating Gender" in Hong Kong (2004), "Comparative Gender Studies Today" in Venice (2005), and "Changing Concepts of Sexuality, Gendered Ways of Knowing" in Rio de Janeiro (2007), as well as panels the committee sponsored at American Comparative Literature Association meetings. The editors thank their colleagues who participated on those panels for their input and advice on this volume.

We would also like to thank Bradley Epps, who has offered support for this book from its beginnings, and Luba Ostashevsky at Palgrave, New York, and William E. Cain for their advice and support.

Finally, we would like to thank Brigitte Shull and Lee Norton at Palgrave in New York and Colleen Cantrell at Scribe in Philadelphia for their kind support and patience and for keeping us on task and especially all ten of the contributors collected herein for their hard work, patience, suggestions, and dedication to this project over the past five years.

J. H., Ann Arbor
M. R. H., Storrs
W. J. S., Brighton

COMPARING QUEERLY, QUEERING COMPARISON

THEORIZING IDENTITIES BETWEEN CULTURES, HISTORIES, AND DISCIPLINES

JARROD HAYES, MARGARET R. HIGONNET, AND WILLIAM J. SPURLIN

WHAT DOES IT MEAN TO COMPARE? THE ANSWER TO this question is often taken for granted: highlighting both similarities and differences between what is being compared. The comparative essay is one of the most common of undergraduate writing exercises, but when one notices how frequently students use arguments that go something like "A and B are both alike and different," one realizes that the key question is not what *is* a comparison but *when* is a comparison worth making. How many teachers have found themselves pointing out to students that, of course, A and B are both alike and different; if they were not different at all, B would *be* A. If they did not have anything in common, what would be the point of comparing them? A strong comparative argument thus needs to be more specific than simply stating that A and B are both alike and different; it also needs to assert *how* they are alike and different and *why* these similarities and differences are relevant. The heart of comparison, one could then say, lies somewhere *between* almost totally different but not quite *and* almost the same but not quite; analyzing what exactly lies in this in-between could be said to be the work of comparison and comparative studies. Yet while one might think comparison is essential to comparative studies, at least one well-known comparatist has argued otherwise. In his response to the American Comparative Literature Association's 1993 decennial "Report of Standards"—the Bernheimer report—Peter Brooks writes, "The answer [to the question "What do you compare?"], I recall, began with a mumbled admission that you really didn't *compare* anything. You simply worked in more than one literature, studying literature without regard to national boundaries and definitions" (Bernheimer 97–98).

Comparatively Queer: Interrogating Identities across Time and Cultures, however, takes the opposite position and seeks to put comparison back in comparative studies as one way of queering the field. Indeed, by the end of our collection, we hope to convince our readers that its title is queerly redundant. If queer is always queer in relation to the normative, it is only queer in historical and cultural context. If queer differs from context to context, it might nonetheless be considered a concept capable of crossing both time and cultures. But if we are going to allow the queer to travel in such a way, we should deploy it comparatively. For this reason, the crossings implied in the subtitles of our introduction, and the collection as a whole, bridge both historical and geocultural contexts, and in so doing, they also breach disciplinary boundaries that might otherwise inhibit them. The primary interdisciplinary encounter of *Comparatively Queer,* of course, is the one between comparative literature and queer studies. *Comparatively Queer* brings together chapters that are *both* comparative *and* queer, that not only take a comparative approach to queer studies but also seek to queer the field of comparative studies. Furthermore, *Comparatively Queer* works across the varied and multiple points of intersection of these two fields, thereby strengthening their interdisciplinary potential. And crossing queer and comparative studies across disciplines will challenge and destabilize the frequent Anglocentric biases of both fields as well as the frequently presentist assumptions of queer studies—which finds its historic beginnings in the Anglo-American academy—and the Eurocentric nationalisms of comparative studies. A queer comparative studies, in short, can interrogate not only temporality itself and history as a stable record of the past but also the very borders of the "national" as the basis of literary comparison and "literature" as a discrete category unaffected by the multiple cultural contexts through which texts are produced and received.

CROSSING CULTURES

The key to queering comparison and comparing queerly, we will argue, lies precisely in the "in-between" that these crossings create. As this collection will make clear, it is no coincidence that theorizing such "in-betweens" has been important to both postcolonial and queer theory. Homi K. Bhabha, for example, defines "colonial mimicry [as] the desire for a reformed, recognizable Other, *as a subject of a difference that is almost total but not quite*" (86). The subject defined through this mimicry "is not the colonialist Self or the colonized Other, but the disturbing distance *in-between* that constitutes the figure of colonial otherness—the white man's artifice inscribed on the black man's body" (45; emphasis added). The space between "not quite" and "not" in the "not quite/not white" (92), like the difference *between* mimicry ("a difference that is almost nothing but not quite") and its double, menace ("a difference that is almost total but not quite"; 91), reveals the complex structures of violence that bind colonizer and colonized and imbricate each within the other. Furthermore, Bhabha's in-between can also be a productive concept for *queer* comparative studies; indeed, it parallels Judith Butler's discussion of the excess that distinguishes copy from "original" (always already a copy of some prior "original")—the excess that lies *between* them, one could say—in the performance of gender norms. Reading Bhabha back through Butler, then, one could also say that the subject of Bhabha's mimicry is always already defined in the comparison between some imagined, though never totally accessible, colonial original and its imperfect copy as performed by the colonized. Exploring the queer potential of this in-between will be the task of this collection.

Beginning at this nexus of postcolonial and queer, *Comparatively Queer* seeks not only to include work in postcolonial queer studies but also, through postcolonial studies, to transform areas of study conventionally thought of as far removed from questions of colonization and decolonization. For example, in its longtime investment in comparisons of national literatures, comparative literature has tended to maintain traditional borders instead of fully interrogating them. In contrast, *Comparatively Queer* seeks not only to cross these borders but also to turn them into an object of study in their own right. As such, this collection may be situated in relation to a number of ongoing intellectual developments in comparative literature. To an outsider seeking to understand these trends, the field has the benefit of requiring a decennial "Report of Standards." The report, led by Charles Bernheimer in 1993, broke with its predecessors by declining to set standards that could be enforced and, instead, described the status of the field and outlined some of its recent transformations. This report also acknowledged an increasing tendency to challenge the Eurocentric biases of previous reports and of the field as defined therein. Indeed, the "nation" at the basis of "national literatures" was recognized as a European construct as comparatists looked further and further beyond the borders of Europe, in part due to the influence of postcolonial studies that was already being felt. "Comparative literature" was thus increasingly replaced by the more interdisciplinary "comparative studies," which could involve more than comparisons between different national or linguistic contexts, since the literary was no longer seen as a necessary determining aspect of the field:

> The space of comparison today involves comparisons between artistic productions usually studied by different disciplines; between various cultural constructions of those disciplines; between Western cultural traditions, both high and popular, and those of non-Western cultures; between the pre- and postcontact cultural productions of colonized peoples; between gender constructions defined as feminine and those defined as masculine, or between sexual orientations defined as straight and those defined as gay; between racial and ethnic modes of signifying; between hermeneutic articulations of meaning and materialist analyses of its modes of production and circulation; and much more. These ways of contextualizing literature in the expanded fields of discourse, culture, ideology, race, and gender are so different from the old models of literary study according to authors, nations, periods, and genres that the term "literature" may no longer adequately describe our object of study. (41–42)

The word *between* occurs no less than seven times here, thereby stressing the comparison in comparative literature well before Brooks could try to remove it. Furthermore, the Bernheimer report expands the in-betweens that the field might consider to be its objects of comparison, including those associated with gender and sexuality as worthy objects of study.

Already in 1985, Alice A. Jardine made *comparativism* a key term alongside *feminism* in *Gynesis: Configurations of Women and Modernity*. Contemporaneous with the drafting of the Bernheimer report, a group of feminist scholars were considering further the importance of comparative studies, as it was being redefined, to gender studies. Margaret R. Higonnet collected their reflections in *Borderwork: Feminist Engagements with Comparative Literature*. Although the Bernheimer report considered lesbian and gay studies just as important to the definition of comparative studies as gender studies, in the more than 15 years since the report was released, there has still been no queer parallel to *Borderwork*. *Comparatively Queer* seeks to fill this void. The title *Borderwork* alludes to, among other things, Chicana feminist works like Gloria Anzaldúa's *Borderlands/ La frontera: The New Mestiza* (1987) and Cherríe Moraga's *Loving in the War Years: Lo que pasó por sus labios* (1983). For Anzaldúa and Moraga, the notion of border crossing inspired innovative theorizations of identity at the intersections of race, ethnicity, nationality, and gender. The border, here, becomes most relevant in its being breached, and the borderland defined through this breach, we will argue, can also become a queer alternative to the "national" in the "national literatures" that have conventionally served as the basis for defining comparative literature as a field.

Following in Anzaldúa and Moraga's border-crossing footsteps, queering comparative studies can continue ongoing efforts to decolonize literary and cultural studies while questioning the imperialist gestures of these disciplines in the West. In other words, when "the empire writes back" in *Comparatively Queer*, it not only forces the metropole to sit up and listen but also *re*writes our ways of understanding European and Anglo-American cultures and histories. Indeed, if comparatists are expected to work *in* multiple languages, Anzaldúa and Moraga open up ways of working *between* them. By writing in an in-between language (Spanglish), they resist not only both "national languages" separated by the border they cross but also the nationalities naturalized in and through them. In fact, the potential parallel between crossing national borders, crossing borders between categories of identity, and crossing those within any given category of identity (i.e., between hetero- and homosexuality) served as the initial inspiration for this collection. For *Comparatively Queer* developed out of a set of three sessions sponsored by the Division on Comparative Studies in Twentieth-Century Literature at the 2004 Modern Language Association (MLA) Convention—"Comparative Approaches to Identity Studies"—which sought to consider not only the importance of comparative studies to fields like lesbian and gay studies, women's studies, African American studies, ethnic studies, and so on but also the validity of comparing different categories of identity and the sometimes different, sometimes similar, approaches to the study of identity in the aforementioned fields. "Comparatively Queer," in fact, was the title of the session that sought to highlight comparative approaches to queer studies within the rubric for the three sessions as a whole. As our thinking developed out of that session and into this collection, we have come to see border incursions that recognize, but nonetheless challenge, borders as crucial to a queer theory of comparison that also crosses over to such fields as Africana and ethnic studies in the study of sexualities.

Whereas the Bernheimer report seemed to limit the contribution of comparative studies for gender and sexuality studies to a comparison between masculine and feminine, or between gay and straight, *Borderwork* demonstrates how feminism can rupture the categories themselves and the disciplines that constitute them as objects of study. Similarly, in contrast with the Bernheimer report's understanding of lesbian and gay comparison as occurring *between* categories of sexual identity, *Comparatively*

Queer asserts the necessity of historicizing these categories and comparing the same categories across cultures. In other words, comparison must also be *internal* to the categories themselves. Unlike Frantz Fanon's understanding of comparison as separating races and therefore as fundamental to racialization (see Shih 1349–52), queer comparison not only separates but also joins. Likewise, if Bhabha's in-between is not found between colonizer and colonized as two discreet categories, but is rather internal to the colonial subject as an embodiment of a subjectivity shared by both colonizer and colonized, this subjectivity is transformed by the colonial encounter. Indeed, there can be no colonizer or colonized prior to colonization, since both are created as subject positions by colonization itself. À la Butler and Bhabha, then, the in-between that is Anzaldúa and Moraga's borderland is not a discreet entity separating two discreet categories; it binds the categories and transforms them analytically in a move that might be described as queering. Given this parallel, what might be the queerly comparative implications of the fact that Bhabha's in-between is not a discreet entity separating two discreet categories?

Comparison thus results in an in-between that transforms what it is presumed to separate and join, and it is the potential for this transformation to queer that this collection seeks to explore. Following Higonnet's assertion that "gender studies . . . should always be comparative" ("Comparative" 155), *Comparatively Queer* demonstrates that queer studies as well will always benefit from comparative perspectives. Indeed, this volume proposes modes of queering *as* comparing, and vice versa; we are, after all, "going both ways" (an expression not without its own queer implications!). If the vernacular use of the expression "comparatively queer" might suggest to some "*only* queer in comparison with the not-so-queer," or "*only* relatively queer" when "queering" is understood as a mode of reading, then "comparatively queer" never represents such a second best but rather the potential for each term to enhance the other.

Furthermore, the parallels between different kinds of comparison as well as the in-betweens they set up might be related to the concept of intersectionality, which has become key in the field of queer studies, as many have critiqued the whiteness and masculinist biases of many definitions of queer. This concept can help us to understand how categories such as sexuality, gender, race, ethnicity, nationality, and religious affiliation and acculturation overlap and inflect one another in any given individual and within the social field. In *Inessential Woman: Problems of Exclusion in Feminist Thought* (1988), for example, philosopher Elizabeth V. Spelman goes a long way toward theorizing intersectionality when she writes, "Reflection on the experience of Black women also shows that it is not as if one form of oppression is merely piled upon another. As Barbara Smith has remarked, the effect of multiple oppression 'is not merely arithmetic'" (123).[1] In other words, the category of woman may very well signify quite differently for African American women as opposed to white women; for African American women, gender may thus be inseparable from the racialization that conditions their womanhood. To use a working definition of women based only on white women's experiences because, *in comparison with* African American women (comparison à la Fanon), white women are oppressed only because of their gender and not because of their race, would thus be a fallacy in its "merely arithmetic" understanding of the coexistence of multiple categories of identity. The contestation of terms like woman that arose out of such theorizations of intersectionality is precisely one source of inspiration for Butler's work in *Gender Trouble,* in which she proposes that such challenges to the definition of gender should be seen not as frustrating, but as a catalyst for, further theorizing.

Making more of the trouble caused when such conflicts are fostered is one of the goals of *Comparatively Queer* because making trouble of the sort Smith, Anzaldúa, and Moraga have long made might also be considered a comparative act of the sort we seek to advocate.[2] The title of an early collection in black women's studies—*All the Women Are White, All the Blacks Are Men, but Some of Us Are Brave* (Hull, Scott, and Smith)—suggests that both patriarchal and racist discourses (as well as male antiracist and white feminist ones) erect a border between gender and race in thinking (or not thinking) black womanhood. If understanding the borderland as a queer in-between means that there are more than two ways to cross a border, the intersection of the four identificatory terms in their title adds up to more than their sum. Returning to the ruptures inscribed across such borders by African American feminists like Smith (who were the first to insist on recognizing intersectionality) can thus allow us to rethink comparative studies in a way that will not only contribute to its further theorization in relation to queer studies but also develop new tools for understanding what it means to compare, for the theorization of intersectionality highlights the necessity for an additional type of comparison: comparisons between various categories of identity.

Likewise, the chapters in "Crossing Cultures," or the second part of this anthology, move across and in between cultural, national, and sexual borders while simultaneously producing new sites of heterogeneity and difference. Addressing the inescapability of gender analysis in queer studies, Marie-Paule Ha takes Judith Butler's critique of the ontological status of gender categories one step further by locating the additional "trouble" that occurs when the discursive practices that produce gender in Hong Kong come from two conflicting sets of cultural practices. In her chapter "Double Trouble: Doing Gender in Hong Kong," Ha makes the case that the study of gender in Hong Kong, and in other postcolonial contexts, must always remain comparative in order to distinguish configurations of gender that arise from indigenous cultural histories and those that reflect the influences of Western scholarship, thus avoiding the mere deployment of Western theories of gender and queer in local contexts or the reduction of indigenous knowledge about gender to the Western conceptual matrix that makes indigenous systems of gender intelligible to Westerners. Both strategies repeat the imperialist gesture and enact new sites of discursive colonization. Ha argues that the study of gender in Hong Kong will always already produce a hybrid space of theorization, that is, a space "in between," informed by Western biomedical models derived from the conceptual matrix of sex-gender-sexuality (which locates sexual difference in bodily genitalia), and by the Chinese cosmological model where sexual differences are not reducible to biology or anatomy but are made legible in the shifting, fluid variations and relative predominance of yin and yang as vital processes within the body. Bringing Butler into comparison with gender studies in Hong Kong, then, has implications not only for a culturally heterogeneous notion of gender performativity but also for the performativity and queering of cultural identity as well, always already situated relationally *in*, and negotiating *between*, Chinese and Western narratives of gender.

While work on queer globalization often attempts to make postcolonial and non-Euro-American forms of queerness more visible, such legibility is often an extension of Western gazes that read non-Western, same-sex desires as queer. Thomas J. D. Armbrecht points to the consequential fallacy in such thinking insofar as it reduces all Western queer identities politically, and rather uncritically, to self-sameness, thereby erasing different trajectories of queer cultural politics *within* the West. Taking France and the United States as cases in point and being careful not to polarize queerness in these two nations, Armbrecht opens a new comparative queer space that recognizes differences surrounding such cultural points of contention in France and the United States as same-sex marriage and gender parity. He argues that the PaCS legislation, which legalized civil partnerships between same-sex partners in France to afford them the same legal rights as married heterosexual couples, and *parité*, which sought to rectify women's underrepresentation in the French government through enforced electoral gender parity, both of which were passed into law in

1999, served to rupture the oppositional border between French universalism and American communitarianism as democratic national ideals in each nation, respectively, for addressing human differences. While giving legal redress to the disadvantage of women in the political sphere in France marked women as a distinct group to ensure the same forms of social political, and economic access typically afforded to men and comes remarkably close to American strategies of particularism, the French government's attempt to dissolve the hetero-homo opposition through PaCS legislation reaffirmed its commitment to universal equality through the erasure of social disparities, even though the government had to have recognized, as Armbrecht argues, the particularity of same-sex relationships as previously lacking legal status. While the struggles for gay marriage and partnerships have taken a different political trajectory in the United States, shaped more by religious and moral arguments than is the case in France, Armbrecht suggests that there also may be similarities to the extent that hegemonic power in both countries rests on "a dogmatic faith in a particular expression of heterosexual culture" (166), which needs to be challenged and can result in multiple intersections of comparative queer analysis within the West, especially around the categories of nationality and sexuality.

Bianca Jackson compares the texts of two Indian writers in diaspora—Suniti Namjoshi and Vikram Seth—both of whom make use of the animal fable form as a way not only of codifying sexual alterity but also of queering their own marginality as diasporic writers in English marked by sexual dissidence. Their use of beasts, according to Jackson, cannot be reduced to a metaphorical trope but is a way of identifying alternative subjective realities besides the one portrayed via the heteropatriarchal order. Namjoshi's fables addressing gender and sexuality restructure the inherited world through the depiction of animal and queer coalition ("lesbian-feminist wrens" and "'badge-wearing dyke' mice"; 180) and the possibilities of emergent utopian cultural systems written to undermine the authenticity of the dominant order; yet it is interesting that her fables remain more or less unknown outside of India despite the current trend toward transnationalism in both queer and postcolonial studies. Vikram Seth, whose work is well known in India and internationally, also challenges, in his bestial writing, a strict demarcation between the everyday and the phantasmatic and suggests the possibility of an egalitarian alliance between animals and humans. Yet his invented worlds of coexistent humans and animals construct a residual system of the dominant social order, and his texts refuse to develop a space for sexual alterity on the inside or outside of heteronormativity. The pressures of a heteronormative social world defeat Seth's homosexualized beasts, most evidently in his rewriting of "The Monkey and the Crocodile" story from the *Panchatantra* and his homoerotic retelling of the Greek myth of Arion and Dolphin. While both authors queer the Cartesian boundary between humans and animals in order to create alternative worlds or "in-between spaces" for those marginalized by the hegemonic social order, both also reinvent Orientalist strategies of representation that assume all queers, whether animal or human, and all ways of queering remain the same. Both authors, according to Jackson, in different ways, emulate the hegemonic, hierarchical framework of heteropatriarchy rather than creating textually a credible, posthumanist alternative world.

Finally, questioning the very categories of comparison themselves, James Penney simultaneously challenges dominant assumptions of comparative work that assume the crossings of cultural travelers like French writer and playwright Jean Genet either dynamize or dissolve borders between different cultural systems. Taking a cultural-comparative approach, Penney shows that Genet's engagement with the Arab-Muslim world, in the wake of a history of European Orientalism and exoticism of the Middle East, is reflected in his witnessing of the events surrounding the massacres of Palestinian refugee camps in Beirut in September 1982. Penney's analysis of Genet's *Prisoner of Love* demonstrates that the borders that Genet transgresses are not those between cultures, races, ethnicities, socioeconomic classes, languages and dialects, and sexualities, typically celebrated as sites of subversion in comparative and queer studies. Rather, what interested Genet about Palestinian resistance and other forms of revolt as political movements, according to Penney, was their impossible status within the political situation in which they erupt; that is, their uncovering of the repressed, unconscious element of the sociopolitical context from which they are forcibly excluded and therefore "cannot be thought" within available systems of cultural inscription. What this means for sexual difference, for Genet, is that it signals not a claim for recognition within a liberal political economy but, as Penney notes, "the terrain of the unthinkable, the unintelligible, the excluded, and for this reason plays a privileged role in his assault on hegemonic power and its properly metaphysical pretensions" (200). This assault fits in with Genet's larger revolutionary project that would resist the domestication of the Palestinian cause to the familiar Western tropes of fixations on territoriality, nationhood, and integration, as this would compromise its radical potential. Genet's transgressive sexual, political, discursive crossings, then, not only explode hegemonic centers insofar as they violate the frontiers of Western identity formation (white vs. black, male vs. female, hetero vs.

homo, etc.) but also occur at the very *borders of intelligibility*, rather than between the categories themselves, which implies even further speculation on the very boundaries that implicitly set up the terms by which cultural comparisons are produced.

CROSSING TIME

Comparatively Queer extends crossing cultural borders to the crossing of time in historical approaches by drawing on pre- and early modern studies for fresh approaches to the past and bringing chapters in contemporary comparative studies together with the pre- and early modernist chapters that comprise "Crossing Time," or the first part of this collection.[3] *Comparatively Queer* thus elaborates on the insight of such works as Carolyn Dinshaw's *Getting Medieval: Sexualities and Communities, Pre- and Postmodern* (1999) and Glenn Burger and Steven F. Kruger's *Queering the Middle Ages* (2001), both of which looked to postcolonial theory for methods of approaching the past. In particular, Dinshaw, though critiquing Bhabha's othering of the Middle Ages, finds that his "concept of 'affective writing' proves very fruitful for a queer project such as [hers], especially as it set up the possibility of contact between linguistic fragments across time" (21). By arguing in favor of "constructing a community across time" (34), which would involve "a queer historical touch" (3), she fosters "a consistent impulse to make contact, even finally a desire for bodies to touch across time" (3). What Dinshaw develops as a queer methodology for medieval studies becomes, in our collection, a methodology for comparative studies in and across all periods. As in her "getting medieval" as a form of cruising the past, *Comparatively Queer* puts different moments in *touch* with one another in an erotics of looking at the past.[4] An erotics of comparison can best be discerned herein when our chapters are read as allegories of reading, that is, allegories of comparatist praxis. In Penney's reading, for example, Jean Genet may be thought of as a kind of comparatist when his desire results in a number of cross-border incursions. One way of reading this volume more queerly and comparatively could also be to transgress the very categories that we, as editors, have instantiated through crossing *both* time *and* cultures in order for particular chapters to be in touch with each other. In their chapters for this collection, for example, Carla Freccero's and Bianca Jackson's zoophilic identifications might be read as analogous of the erotic possibilities of queer comparison.

One might argue that such an erotics has constituted an integral component of lesbian and gay studies from its inception. In efforts to prove that lesbian and gay sexualities not only were "natural" but also existed across broad historical, geographical, and cultural contexts, contemporary lesbian and gay activists and scholars sought roots in a long historical tradition. However, in spite of the temptation to find proof only of their own identities in other times and places (a crossing of time and cultures for evidence of lesbian and gay desire that would actually result in very little comparison), crossing time often revealed more differences than similarities, thereby leading to theories of sexuality as culturally and historically constructed and transforming queer historiography into a comparative practice. While it might be tempting to construct a narrative of progress that would present an increasingly comparatist approach to queer historical studies, it is also possible, within what a number of queer theorists have begun to call a queer temporality, to see such an erotics of comparison at work in the earliest scholarship in lesbian and gay studies.[5] For example, Lillian Faderman describes her own desire to read Emily Dickinson as a lesbian at the origin of her study *Surpassing the Love of Men: Romantic Friendship and Love between Women from the Renaissance to the Present* (1981). Crossing time, however, resulted in denaturalizing the historical and cultural contexts within which she wrote and that constituted her framework or point of view: "By the time I finished gathering my material, however, I realized that something was wrong: Although Dickinson had written the most passionate and sensual pronouncements of love to Sue Gilbert in the 1850's [*sic*], there was never any suggestion that she felt the need to be covert about her emotions. If I had really uncovered a lesbian relationship, why could I not find any evidence of the guilt and anxiety, the need to keep secrets from family and friends, that I thought were inevitably associated with homosexuality before the days of gay liberation?" (15). Her research project might thus be characterized as *not* having found what she sought (sexuality or homosexuality), which instead resulted in the historicization of her topic and her initial desire. Homosexuality and, more generally, sexuality had been "invented" and the history of their invention could be written.[6]

Likewise, John Boswell's 1980 assertion in *Christianity, Social Tolerance, and Homosexuality* that gay people could be found throughout history led constructionists to turn him into a sort of straw man representing all that was wrong with essentialism. Nonetheless, in examining the correspondence in Boswell's papers, Dinshaw describes such a "community across time" in the relation among Boswell, his many readers, and the desire he elicited among them for the Middle Ages (Dinshaw 22–34). In fact, although those on the constructionist side of the essentialist-constructionist debate have cast Michel Foucault's *History of Sexuality* (1976) as the polar opposite of Boswell, Foucault figures prominently among the many admirers of Boswell whose letters Dinshaw examines. Bringing Foucault in touch with Boswell is thus surely one of Dinshaw's more surprising and provocatively erotic gestures of comparison.

While medievalists have been queering the Middle Ages for some time now, scant comparative attention has been paid to premodern intellectual history along queer lines and the new kinds of comparisons that are thereby made possible. Addressing this lacuna, Kofi Campbell, whose chapter begins this collection, contests Foucault's assertion that homosexuality, as a discursive cultural phenomenon in the Middle Ages, did not exist. More importantly, Campbell argues for a relationship between the growth of European vernacular languages in medieval Europe (indeed a prerequisite for the existence of Western comparative literature), which threatened the hegemony of Latin, and the simultaneous social emergence and proliferation of nonheteronormative gender and sexual performativities. While Latin and normative genders and sexualities are linked in medieval culture, given that any confusion of genders in Latin is nearly impossible given its inflections, the rise of the vernaculars and less rigid grammars, according to Campbell, enabled the textual representation of the confusion and ambiguity around gender and sexual meanings through the use of gender-neutral nouns and new spaces of textual and sexual indeterminacy that subverted the previous semantic and sexual order. In his analysis of three medieval texts, Campbell reshapes the boundaries of comparative literature by resisting national boundaries and exclusive literary analysis in order to move between other disciplines and cultural discourses, while challenging some of the presentist biases of comparative studies and the Anglocentric assumptions of queer studies.

Moving beyond strict historical periodization and particular national borders, thereby creating new spaces of alterity and supplementarity, Carla Freccero, in her chapter "Figural Historiography: Dogs, Humans, and Cynanthropic Becomings," queers temporality through examining particular "topoi," including figures, affects, metaphors, metonymies, and intertextual allusions, that (re)signify *across* historical eras but in ways that are more promiscuous and errant than linear, thereby undercutting master narratives of linearity and causality through which the past is normatively recounted. Beginning with the figure of the devouring dog that symbolizes the historical trauma of New World conquests by Europeans in the late fifteenth century, Freccero traces the repetition of this figure historically, culturally, and intertextually in a succession, or rather, in a fusion, of Old and New World meanings. In addition to acknowledging how trauma saturates the past, her queering of temporality and spatiality raises new implications for comparative queer work by questioning linear, teleological, and reproductively heteronormative notions of time generated from progressive understandings of history, usually marked by a process of relative stability and rupture, by looking instead at what *persists, survives, fades, and wanes through and across time.*

Susan S. Lanser's comparative approach makes a compelling case for the breadth of public interest in "sapphic subjects" in early modern culture. Lanser's chapter traces the rise in discursive representations of female homoeroticism between 1600 and the later social and philosophical shifts instantiated by such movements as the Reformation and Enlightenment in seventeenth- and early eighteenth-century Europe, which engendered a wide range of attitudes and responses beyond public scorn to include, for example, titillation, sympathetic explanation, and celebration. "Mapping Sapphic Modernity" insists that same-sex female relations became increasingly salient not only in early modern literary and cultural history but also within broader social, legal, economic, and religious discourses that were implicated in the production of modernity itself; in this regard, the chapter is not merely a history of sexuality in early modern Europe, but instead makes a compelling case for the *sexuality of history.* Lanser crosses specific times and social locations on the larger map of early European modernity, assembling a range of distinctive discursive and narrative genres in order to theorize the multifarious purposes the representation of female homoeroticism can serve and to demonstrate the variety of ways in which female homoeroticism disrupted both gender norms and the larger economies within which the heteronormative gender order was imbricated.

In focusing on circus and fair sideshow performances in Europe and the United States from the turn of the century until just before World War II, Francesca Canadé Sautman, in "'Fair Is Not Fair': Queer Possibility and Fairground Performers in Western Europe and the United States, 1870–1935," opens a new space of comparative queer work by stressing the ongoing tension between the locality of the sideshow performances and their constant movement across national borders, rendering the national origins of the performances indeterminable. Furthermore, just as the bodies of the performers were often marked by gender ambiguity (such as bearded women, hermaphrodites, female athletes, and androgynous male acrobats) and exhibited and displayed for their non-normative traits, Canadé Sautman marks queer space as that which is not reducible to a single recognizable category but always already "in process, shifting, and redeployed in contact with other instances or moments of queer potential" (92). Canadé Sautman also makes the case that the performers were neither confined to the fringes of normative socialization nor merely passive objects of the normative gaze. Rather, the sideshows often played actively on societal notions of the taboo for economic gain by enticing spectators to come to the fairgrounds. At the same time, the performers had to negotiate and maintain a space within the hegemonic, such as bearded women like Madame Clementine Delait, who appeared conventionally feminine in all other aspects except for her beard, was normatively sanctioned through marriage and its attendant social position, yet nonetheless created a transgressive space for queer possibility, both challenging *and* maintaining gender and social norms. This chapter, then, locates queer not in contrast to the normative social world but in the *tension between* transgressions of gender, sexual, national, linguistic, and class boundaries and the desire to overcome social marginalization. In this complex social-historical context, Canadé Sautman locates queerness as a space to be (re)negotiated "within its own professional space vis-à-vis the compelling pull of normative socialization" (99).

Finally, moving to the twenty-first century but looking back to related cultural antecedents, Anjali Arondekar addresses critically the overdetermined and problematic history of comparative studies that has relied on the Eurocentricity of normative categories that form the very basis of comparison. Shifting the comparative lens to a politics of comparison grounded at the conjunction of South Asian studies and queer studies, Arondekar analyzes the ideologies of temporality and causality that surround the historiography of sexuality in postcolonial India. "Time's Corpus: On Sexuality, Historiography, and the Indian Penal Code" exposes the ways in which the colonial record is invoked juridically and politically in postcolonial present-day India both to mark and erase radical histories surrounding enacted same-sex desires. Citing the petition filed by the Naz Foundation, an HIV/AIDS prevention nongovernmental organization in Delhi, against the Indian government in 2001 that declared the since-repealed antisodomy statute of the Indian Penal Code, Section 377, not only a violation of rights to equality, freedom, and life as guaranteed by the Indian Constitution but also an impediment to HIV/AIDS outreach, Arondekar demonstrates how the petition aimed to rupture dominant historical narratives in India that located homosexuality not in the Indian past but as a colonial, Western import. By providing archival evidence of indigenous same-sex acts as tied to an "authentic" Indian past through appeals to history as a site of recovery and legitimacy, such rhetorical arguments, instantiated in the legal discourse surrounding the petition and by its supporters, according to Arondekar, "merely invert[s] the language of historical ontology" (119), thereby reinventing the colonialist gesture insofar as the decriminalization of sodomy is conflated with India's entry into progressive modernity. More important, given the larger shifts in recuperative historicizing at work in contemporary India (operating between the acknowledgement of divergent historical temporalities and spatialities, on the one hand, and narratives of the past that attempt to stabilize homogeneity and externalize difference, on the other), Arondekar asks how a historiography of sexuality in postcolonial India can be situated discursively and comparatively in struggles for contemporary legal reform to the extent that such a historiography remains attentive to the political exigencies and pitfalls of reading the past, maintains the radical indeterminacy of (homo)sexuality, and records uncertainty as a radical condition of (re)readings of the past and present as a way of resisting the stabilization of the historical corpus.

If queer studies denaturalized the contemporary sexual subject in crossing time, casting queer historical studies as a comparatist practice allows us to understand this subject (including the queer scholar himself or herself) as an *object* of comparison as well. For example, what is the relation between the contemporary lesbian and Lanser's "sapphic subjects"? Indeed, the subject of comparison (in Lanser's case, the comparatist who crosses time to examine early sapphic modernity) might also be understood as actually being partially constituted *through* comparison and the resulting denaturalization. The power of comparison to generate queer subjectivities has interesting implications that have yet to be theorized. One consequence of this seemingly "inverted" (and we use this word queerly) cause-and-effect relationship has been that queer histories often look a lot like narratives of progress, in which "self" comes after "other" not just in its genesis but also in the narrative articulated through comparison. The explicit object of comparison (the "other" in time or culture) and the implicit one (i.e., the subject of comparison—"homosexuality as we know it today," as the cliché goes) are often ordered in a narrative sequence that looks a lot like a coming-out story. And in this coming-out story, even contemporary cultural others are associated with a prior time that is also thought of as being more primitive. In this model, queer history becomes a narrative of development, of civilization, and therefore of colonization. By coming out, the contemporary "lesbigay" subject leaves the dark continent of her past behind; by becoming homosexuality, same-sex desire does the same. A number of scholars have pointed out the parallel between the narratives of the civilizing mission and those of psychological development, but it should give one pause that in Freudian models of sexual development, nonnormative sexualities are what is relegated to this primitive past. In other words, in the coming-out model of lesbian and gay history, the homosexual has merely taken the place of the colonizer-heterosexual in narratives of both economic and psychosexual development. Queer studies could thus still use a little queering itself, which, like the queering of comparative studies, needs to involve decolonization. One starting point for this decolonization, we argue, requires making the subject of comparison explicit as comparison's object as well.

An additional point of departure might be located in the interdisciplinary spaces that underlie this collection's queer theory of comparison. Indeed, it is our view that interdisciplinarity should involve much more than drawing on two or more disciplines for the purposes of literary and cultural inquiry. Crossing the boundaries between disciplines should "go both ways" to interrogate the very disciplines it brings together. Likewise, crossing the boundaries between disciplines in queer approaches to interdisciplinarity might be thought of as similarly betraying the very disciplines they cross in the spirit of *double*-crossing that makes "comparative" queer and vice versa. If either queer studies or comparative studies could ever have been considered pure disciplines, *Comparatively Queer* diffuses their always already fictional purity as well as any separation that our claim to cross them must provisionally assume.

Taking this idea further, the collection ends with an afterword by Valerie Traub that draws connections between the chapters and raises larger implications for work operating at the ongoing, shifting nexus of the comparative and queer. Traub's response, by "coming *after*" (215), sharpens the crossings and intersections occurring *within* and *between* the chapters in this volume. This afterword is informed by the broader epistemological and ethical questions of what it means to compare and the extent to which comparisons are worth making given the shifting contours of comparative studies, queer studies, and the broader shifts in our understandings of nation and national belonging, race, language, ethnicity, gender, and sexuality. And perhaps beyond the scope of this collection, Traub raises important implications concerning the efficacy of comparativism, queer or otherwise, in a changing academic and institutional context and within the shifting contours of knowledge production in an ever-shifting transnational world.

NOTES

1. The citation of Smith is taken from "Notes for Yet Another Paper on Black Feminism, or Will the Real Enemy Please Stand Up" (see Smith).
2. Marie-Paule Ha's chapter in this collection *explicitly* makes such trouble.

3. Predecessors for using the concept of crossing in transcultural and transhistorical work include Amer's comparative study of "love between women" in French and Arabic medieval literatures and Babayan and Najmabadi's study of "Islamicate sexualities" "across temporal geographies."

4. As Traub also makes clear, however, "such desires, while deeply felt and potentially productive, can obscure the ways that historical difference can provide us with critical resources and understandings otherwise unavailable" (334). *Comparatively Queer* recognizes and hopes to negotiate both these desires and their dangers.

5. On queer temporalities, see Edelman; Halberstam; Jagose; Freeman; Bravmann.

6. In spite of the comparison that Faderman's crossing time led to, more recent work has revealed both similarities and differences between romantic friendship and lesbianism she may have neglected (see Traub; Marcus). For a fuller picture of the richness of scholarly inquiry that Faderman initiated, see also Castle; Vicinus.

WORKS CITED

Amer, Sahar. *Crossing Borders: Love between Women in Medieval French and Arabic Literatures*. Philadelphia: U of Pennsylvania P, 2008.

Anzaldúa, Gloria. *Borderlands/La frontera: The New Mestiza*. San Francisco: Aunt Lute, 1987.

Babayan, Kathryn, and Afsaneh Najmabadi, eds. *Islamicate Sexualities: Translations across Temporal Geographies of Desire*. Cambridge: Center for Middle Eastern Studies of Harvard U, 2008.

Bernheimer, Charles, ed. *Comparative Literature in the Age of Multiculturalism*. Baltimore: The Johns Hopkins UP, 1995.

Bhabha, Homi K. *The Location of Culture*. London: Routledge, 1994.

Bravmann, Scott. *Queer Fictions of the Past: History, Culture, and Difference*. Cambridge: Cambridge UP, 1997.

Burger, Glenn, and Steven F. Kruger, eds. *Queering the Middle Ages*. Minneapolis: U of Minnesota P, 2001.

Butler, Judith. *Gender Trouble: Feminism and the Subversion of Gender*. New York: Routledge, 1990.

Castle, Terry. *The Apparitional Lesbian: Female Homosexuality and Modern Culture*. New York: Columbia UP, 1993.

Dinshaw, Carolyn. *Getting Medieval: Sexualities and Communities, Pre- and Postmodern*. Durham: Duke UP, 1999.

Edelman, Lee. *No Future: Queer Theory and the Death Drive*. Durham: Duke UP, 2004.

Faderman, Lillian. *Surpassing the Love of Men: Romantic Friendship and Love between Women from the Renaissance to the Present*. New York: Morrow, 1981.

Fanon, Frantz. *Black Skin, White Masks*. Trans. Richard Philcox. New York: Grove, 2008.

Foucault, Michel. *Histoire de la sexualité*. Vol. 1. Paris: Gallimard, 1976.

Freeman, Elizabeth, ed. "Queer Temporalities." Special issue of *GLQ* 13.2–3 (2007).

Halberstam, Judith. *In a Queer Time and Place: Transgender Bodies, Subcultural Lives*. New York: New York UP, 2005.

Higonnet, Margaret R., ed. *Borderwork: Feminist Engagements with Comparative Literature*. Ithaca: Cornell UP, 1994.

———. "Comparative Literature on the Feminist Edge." Bernheimer 155–64.

Hull, Gloria T., Patricia Bell Scott, and Barbara Smith, eds. *All the Women Are White, All the Blacks Are Men, but Some of Us Are Brave: Black Women's Studies*. New York: The Feminist P, 1982.

Jagose, Annamarie. *Inconsequence: Lesbian Representation and the Logic of Sexual Sequence*. Ithaca: Cornell UP, 2002.

Jardine, Alice A. *Gynesis: Configurations of Women and Modernity*. Ithaca: Cornell UP, 1985.

Marcus, Sharon. *Between Women: Friendship, Desire, and Marriage in Victorian England*. Princeton: Princeton UP, 2007.

Moraga, Cherríe. *Loving in the War Years: Lo que pasó por sus labios*. Boston: South End, 1983.

Shih, Shu-mei. "Comparative Racialization: An Introduction." *PMLA* 123.5 (2008): 1347–62.

Smith, Barbara. "Notes for Yet Another Paper on Black Feminism, or Will the Real Enemy Please Stand Up." *Conditions* 5 (1979): 123–32.

Spelman, Elizabeth V. *Inessential Woman: Problems of Exclusion in Feminist Thought*. Boston: Beacon, 1988.

Traub, Valerie. *The Renaissance of Lesbianism in Early Modern England*. Cambridge: Cambridge UP, 2002.

Vicinus, Martha. *Intimate Friends: Women Who Loved Women, 1778–1928*. Chicago: U of Chicago P, 2004.

PART I

CROSSING TIME

CHAPTER 1

QUEER FROM THE VERY BEGINNING

(EN)GENDERING THE VERNACULAR IN MEDIEVAL FRANCE

KOFI CAMPBELL

THE FIELD OF COMPARATIVE LITERATURE HAS BEEN THE SITE of an intensifying struggle for both self-definition and validation. This struggle can best be observed in the dialogue in two collections of essays published under the auspices of the American Comparative Literature Association (ACLA): *Comparative Literature in an Age of Globalization* (2006) and *Comparative Literature in the Age of Multiculturalism* (1995) (see Saussy; Bernheimer). While each provides an ACLA ten-year report on the state of the discipline, the latter prints three reports to the ACLA and a range of responses to them. Any discussion of the history and definition of comparative literary studies must begin with Henry Remak's famous definition of the field: "Comparative Literature is the study of a literature beyond the confines of one particular country, and the study of the relationships between literature on the one hand and other areas of knowledge and belief, such as the arts (e.g. painting, sculpture, architecture, music), philosophy, history, the social sciences, religion, et cetera, on the other. In brief, it is the comparison of one literature with other spheres of human expression" (3). Jonathan Culler essentially dismisses the latter part of this formulation, suggesting that comparative literature should be concerned precisely and only with literature, rather than "with the other spheres of human expression." For Culler, those other spheres are properly the work of cultural studies, and in fact, he suggests that cultural studies are the purview of literature departments. "French literature," he suggests, "is obviously a part of French culture, so let French departments become departments of French studies to examine it in this way. But it is also part of literature in general, and to study it as such . . . is the task . . . of comparative literature" (121). Let literature departments study culture, he argues, and "let us become comparative literature at last" (121). But it seems to me that the two cannot be separated; as Culler argues, French literature is a part of French culture, but the reverse is also evidently true: French culture is a part of French literature. It is one of the earliest lessons of literature scholars, traditional or comparative, that no text exists without context, without a history of social significations and inheritances, or without culture in other words. There is no way to study literature without culture, and it seems to me that Culler's arguments do not solve the problem of separating comparative literature from traditional literature studies—it simply makes comparative literature specialists into comparative cultural theorists, which they already are. Indeed, it will be my argument in this chapter that the interconnected nature of literature, language, and culture has existed from the beginnings of the growth of comparative literature, beginnings we can locate in the growth of the European vernaculars that have formed the basis of a comparative literary criticism for so long.

On the other side of this debate, Charles Bernheimer, in the introduction to *Comparative Literature in the Age of Multiculturalism*, argues for a renewed emphasis on collaboration, rather than for a clamping down of disciplinary boundaries. He suggests that collaboration "could well reach beyond literary fields to include interested colleagues in such departments as history, anthropology, sociology, music, art history, folklore, media studies, philosophy, architecture, and political science" (13). Indeed, he notes, to seek such a cosmopolitan approach is "not to abandon literature as an object of study [which Culler seems to fear] . . . but rather to suggest a fundamentally relational and dynamic approach to cultural forms, including literary texts" (13).

This expansion and evolution of the fields of comparative literature and cultural studies necessarily entails some reconsiderations. It is no longer sufficient, for example, to limit comparative literature to the study of literature "beyond the confines of one country," particularly at a time when, in the words of David Ferris, "the field reflects the increased presence of literatures other than those of its classical European past" (80). Thus, as writers such as David Damrosch demonstrate, the study of postcolonial literatures is in many ways inherently a comparative literary practice, although often dealing with texts from the same nation, and even the same language. Because the two sets of cultures are different and produce a different literature, they can fruitfully be the subject of a comparative criticism. It is equally obvious that the study of Latino literature in the United States or First Nations writings in Canada, even when in English, are properly objects of comparative literary and cultural criticisms. Owen Aldridge's reconsideration of comparative literature fruitfully moves us away from the dogmatic focus on national boundaries that has characterized a great deal of the history of comparative studies: "Briefly defined, comparative literature can be considered the study of any literary phenomenon from the perspective of more than one national literature or in conjunction with another intellectual discipline or even several" (1). Aldridge, too, embraces a comparative literary practice that compares literature to other disciplinary objects, thus enabling, perhaps even inviting, cultural criticism.

Embracing this paradigm, this chapter discusses three texts produced in the same country, across two languages, in conjunction with the history of another intellectual discipline, queer theory. This chapter is thus most closely aligned with the thought of Susan Bassnett, who writes that "comparative literature involves the study of texts across cultures, that it is interdisciplinary and that it is concerned with patterns of connections in literatures across both time and space" (1). Bassnett articulates an aspect of comparative literature that is far too often ignored—its temporal aspect. While much of the debate over comparative literature and its nature is concerned with questions of nation, language, and the past up until about the early nineteenth century, scandalously little attention has been paid to the premodern intellectual histories out of which both comparative literature and queer studies have evolved. Jan Walsh Hokenson puts it best when she laments that "truly global intercultural conceptions of literary history, diachronic and synchronic, still elude us" (64).

This concern has been probed in depth by Caroline D. Eckhardt, who points out that medieval literature as a whole is nothing if not comparative, containing, referring to, and engaging in dialogue with numerous sources both insular and continental. For example, she notes that Chaucer's "Parlement of Foules" interacted with texts from three languages and several different nations and cultures. Sarah Kay, too, notes that "theories of intertextuality of one kind or another have dominated the critical scene in medieval French studies since at least the 1960s" ("Sexual Knowledge" 69). Because their works usually comprised varied sources, Sylvia Huot argues that "the conventional romance narrator of the twelfth and thirteenth centuries mediates between his audience and a real or posited pre-existent text or texts, usually identified as books and often in Latin" (84); this characterization is also true of the authors of those texts, and thus medieval authors were, essentially, comparative literary scholars, analyzing, interpreting, and incorporating into their own works themes, sources, images, styles, histories, names, and so on, often from several texts in several different languages. Yet, despite the fact that medieval literature is inherently comparative to a degree unmatched by most contemporary objects of comparative literary study, Eckhardt notes that the study of comparative literature today is still "frequently a presentist discipline" (141). She offers much painstakingly collected data to demonstrate the small part medieval studies has played in comparative literary studies—for example, over a period of 15 years, medieval studies comprised two percent of papers at ACLA conferences, four percent of ACLA prizes, about five percent of articles published in the journals *Comparative Literature* and *Comparative Literary Studies*, and around nine percent of dissertations (144). With exquisite litotes, Eckhardt notes that, within the field of comparative literature, "the representation of medieval studies has not been extensive" (144).

Eckhardt's work demonstrates a lack, the remedy of which offers exciting possibilities for the field of comparative studies, which I hope to demonstrate through my examination of the perceived relationships between the inception of the European vernaculars (a precondition for the existence of a Western comparative literature) and the inception of nonnormative sexualities and genders. By focusing on the specifically medieval emergence of European vernaculars in this way, I hope to queer both the study of comparative literature and queer studies. I wish to suggest, contra Culler, that the study of comparative literature is inevitably bound up with cultural discourses and has been so from the very beginning. My analysis is also based on the possibilities for a comparative literary practice not across national lines but across cultural ones, as proposed by Bassnett. Finally, I wish to demonstrate that the greater inclusion of medieval studies within the field can open up new areas of inquiry and lay bare some of the historical processes that accompanied the rise both of the possibilities of a comparative literature and of nonnormative sexualities within the European imaginary. I hope as well to queer queer studies in two important ways. First, queer studies focused on postmedieval eras (as is the case with the vast majority of work in queer studies) have also been slow to recognize the importance of the medieval to their projects; while many medievalists have engaged fruitfully with queer and gender theories and the history of sexuality,[1] queer theorists focused on more modern eras have resisted looking back to the medieval, ever since Foucault's assertion that homosexuality as a discursive cultural phenomenon (as opposed to individual homosexual acts) did not exist in the Middle Ages, an assertion strongly and ably challenged by many medievalists. This chapter will show that medieval French writers thought and worried and theorized about homosexuality a great deal, at a time when such thoughts were supposedly "impossible"; indeed, they focused not only on discrete homosexual acts but also on a social phenomenon they perceived as sufficiently widespread to endanger their heteronormative cultural framework. Second, postmedieval queer studies in North America have had an undeniably Anglocentric vision[2]—by focusing on French texts I hope to demonstrate, to scholars working on queer studies in postmedieval contexts, the possibilities inherent in a comparative queer studies as well.[3]

This chapter, then, will focus on the perceived relationship between the growth of the European vernaculars (a necessary condition for comparative literary practice) and the proliferation of unorthodox sexualities and genders in three French medieval literary works. This chapter, it should be noted, uses not a comparative linguistic approach but a comparative literary and cultural one. Because my comparisons are thematic and my texts largely unfamiliar to nonmedievialists (not many of whom will be familiar with Latin and Old French), I examine them largely in translation to show how their authors pictured the relationship between linguistic and sexual queerness and between the rise of nonnormative sexualities and the very possibilities of a comparative literature.

The chapter is divided into three sections. The first discusses Alanus de Lille's *De Planctu Naturae* (*The Plaint of Nature*) and Jean de Meun's *Roman de la Rose*, works that contain polemics against nonnormative sexualities; whereas Alanus also argues against the rise of the vernaculars, de Meun welcomes the linguistic and creative indeterminacy they offer. Both represent a tradition that conflated language, genealogy, sexuality, and gender, and a direct line of influence can be traced from Alanus to de Meun. The second section considers the *Roman de Silence*, a manuscript that, while isolated physically from the other two, is thematically similar to them and participates in the same tradition of conflating sexuality, genealogy, and language. I then conclude with some thoughts on the ways in which these texts relate to present understandings of queerness and comparative literature.

Vernacular Indeterminacy, Vernacular Power

Alanus de Lille was a scholar generally acclaimed by his contemporaries as a genius of profound intellectual range and learning, both of which are demonstrated in the way he synthesizes his society's discursive linking of sexuality with language into a theory of degeneration. Alanus was both a master of the arts and, in the words of Barbara Newman, "a theologian profoundly concerned with the relationship between the 'queen of sciences' [rhetoric] and her handmaids" (66). He was also deeply concerned with questions of orthodoxy in society and religion (Newman). Upon his retirement, he became a monk at Cîteaux.

Alanus's *De Planctu Naturae* begins with a dreamer falling asleep; as he sleeps, Nature personified appears to him and begins to lament the things that have begun to fall away from perfection in the world. The poem resolves itself immediately into a polemic against homosexuality; it begins, "I turn from laughter to tears, from joy to grief, from merriment to lament, from jests to wailings, when I see that the essential decrees of Nature are denied a hearing . . . when Venus wars with Venus and changes 'hes' into 'shes' and with her witchcraft unmans man." And, a paragraph later, "the active sex shudders in disgrace as it sees itself degenerate into the passive sex. A man turned woman blackens the fair name of his sex" (Alan of Lille 67–68).

For Alanus de Lille, language and sexuality are intricately bound together because all patterns of gender, sexuality, and language originate with Nature. He approaches his discussion through the figures of Venus and Nature, a Nature whom Alanus, unlike his predecessors in the tradition, sexualizes in such a way that she becomes more suitable as the übermatrix of heterosexuality (see Newman 67). When God created the universe and all living things, he assigned Nature the job of ensuring the continuation of every species by ensuring that "like things . . . should be produced from like" (145). Thus language, too, should remain faithful to its original image, which for Alanus, is Latin. Nature, though, soon tires of her job and appoints Venus to take her place. It is when Venus, too, tires of her job and has an affair to pass the time that man begins falling away from the rules laid down by Nature. Here we begin to see most clearly Alanus's conflation of sexuality and language.

Nature, describing the delegation of her role to Venus, explains that she taught Venus the art of grammar and also "which procedures in the art of Grammar she should adopt . . . and which she should reject as irregular and unredeemed by any excusing figure" (156). Venus was to be guided by the rules of grammar in her construction and perpetuation of the sexual union and the procreation of species. Nature's plan centers on two genders, the masculine and feminine, that comprise the domain and limits of both sexuality and language for Alanus.

Alanus most often uses grammatical metaphors to describe man's deviation from the sexual and gender roles laid down by Nature, and specifically homosexuality. According to Alanus's construction, man's role is the active and woman's the passive. Grammatically, the man is the subject of a sentence and the woman is the object. The active must never be allowed to become passive or vice versa—the roles of man and woman must never be interchanged. Gender and language for Alanus are ways of ordering the world and each other; the relationship between the sexes is crucial to his understanding and explication of language, at the same time that language and grammar are instrumental in discussing the relationship between sex, gender, and sexuality.

This conflation of language and sexuality perhaps comes about as a result of what R. Howard Bloch refers to as "the coincidence of the linguistic and the social" (*Etymologies* 18) at this period in history, noting that there was "a long and respected Latin and vernacular tradition according to which Nature, writing, and sexual difference are allied" ("*Silence*" 83). Language and humanity in the milieu of *De Planctu* were considered connatural and inextricably linked. Language, a necessary condition of human society, was held to be proper only to man. Refinement of speech was synonymous not only with rhetorical excellence but also with reason itself. Further, man himself was the reflected image of the natural universe whose laws he embodied. Therefore, if language was synonymous with man as a social being, clearly Nature should somehow mirror that fact, and it therefore makes sense that Alanus and Nature both use language, and by extension grammar, to help understand and explain the world and its workings. As Bloch puts it, for Alanus, "the natural order equated with the social order rests upon an essentially linguistic model" (*Etymologies* 20).

However, the linguistic model to which Alanus refers is a fallen one. When Venus turns her attention away from man, both sexuality and language degenerate; sexuality falls away from the heterosexual ideal, and language from its Latinate ideal. For Alanus, Latin is the perfect language because the confusion of genders is almost impossible due to its highly inflected nature. The growth of the vernaculars, however, threatened the place of Latin as the dominant language. The vernaculars brought with them less-rigid grammatical rules and therefore greater possibilities for the confusion of genders and meaning. Language, in this fallen and "decadent state can no longer lead fallen man back to harmony with Nature and Nature's God" (Newman 67). As Maureen Quilligan puts it, language in its fallen state "makes it impossible to conceive of the proper place of sexuality within the divinely ordered chaos" (172). The possibilities of confusion and lack of strict determination seem to unsettle Alanus most. Bloch observes astutely that Alanus seems "more perturbed by the notion of irregularity than by any specific linguistic or sexual derogation," and that ultimately, it is "the mobility of poetic language and of sexual identity . . . that represents for Nature the most potent threat to the straightness . . . of grammar and to the continuity of lineage" (*Etymologies* 135–36).

De Planctu continually stresses this relationship between genealogical structures and linguistic and sexual models. When Nature hands over her responsibilities to Venus, she endows her with two instruments of order: orthography, or correct writing guided by the rules of grammar, and orthodox sexuality—symbolized by the hammer and anvil. Both aid Venus's primary function, the continuity of the species: proper sexual intercourse provides continuity of lineage and is synonymous with correct writing and grammar, both inherently excluding deviation from what is proper. Nature herself says to Alanus,

> Since the plan of Nature gave special recognition, as the evidence of Grammar confirms, to two genders, to wit, the masculine and feminine . . . I charged the Cyprian [Venus], with secret warnings and mighty, thunderous threats, that she should, as reason demanded, concentrate exclusively in her connections on the natural union of masculine and feminine gender.
>
> Since, by the demands of the condition necessary for reproduction, the masculine joins the feminine to itself, if an irregular combination of members of the same sex should come into common practice, so that the appurtenances of the same sex should be mutually connected, that combination would never be able to gain acceptance from me . . . For if the masculine gender, by a certain violence of unreasonable reason, should call for a gender entirely similar to itself, this bond and union will not be able to defend the flaw. (156–57)

Desire, then, must always be subject to reason, represented by grammar, lest it lead us away from the perfect paradigm of Nature. Bloch argues that Alanus theorizes that desire—which is indiscriminate and disruptive of hierarchy—and linguistic ambiguity—the mixing of meanings and the break with intelligibility—are coterminous principles that cause and reflect equally the subversion of a traditional order, both semantic and social (*Etymologies* 136). Sexual degeneration, mirrored in the linguistic degeneration of the vernaculars, disrupts the continuity of lineage, which is one of *De Planctu*'s primary concerns. The very possibility of a comparative literature is figured as degenerate and as a threat to the continuation of mankind.

This correlation is also of primary concern to Jean de Meun's continuation to Guillaume de Lorris's *Roman de la Rose,* a text that complicates Alanus's binary gender conception. The *Rose* is an allegorical dream narrative, in which the Lover (Amant) finds his way into a garden, falls in love (or more properly lust) with a rose that he sees reflected in a pool, encounters several characters who represent different aspects of the rose and others who represent various human qualities, and in the end plucks his rose, accompanied by sexual imagery of a much more explicit and obvious nature than the phrase that precedes this one. Unlike Alanus's text, which has been described as a homosexual narrative in its suppression of the masculine (see Kay, "Sexual Knowledge" 72), the *Rose* is a text very much focused on the joys and woes of heterosexual sexuality; although, as Simon Gaunt notes, "the apparently straight narrative . . . turns out to be unbelievably camp, while the allegorical embodiment of the Rose alternatively as a castle that one enters through the back door, or as a sanctuary in which one has to kneel down and kiss relics at times leaves one uncertain not only as to the gender of Amant's partner, but also as to whether one is reading about sodomy or oral sex rather than the vanilla sex that Nature and Genius seem to encourage" (*Retelling* 100).

De Meun's continuation is, as Newman puts it, "a vast, sprawling edifice that both dwarfs and deconstructs the original" (98). Inherently comparative in its interpretation and rewriting of the original text and in its reinterpretations of the original source materials, the continuation itself is largely composed "of translations and adaptations of two famous Latin philosophical dream-vision texts, Boethius's *De Consolatione Philosophiae* and Alan of Lille's *De Planctu Naturae*" (Kay, "Women's Body" 212) and "draws substantially on a thirteenth-century academic polemic by William of Saint-Amour, concerning Joachim of Fiore and his prophetic mode of historiography. Translations and reworkings of Ovid provide a further important ingredient" (Kay, "Sexual Knowledge" 71). Thus, de Meun performs a comparative analysis and reexamination of these source texts, synthesizing them into a theory of desire, language, religion, identity, and of course, sex.

As in *De Planctu*, homosexuality here is a crime against Nature because it does not result in procreation, and therefore is a threat to the continuation of lineages. The figure of Genius polemicizes against homosexuality as a form of narcissism, and he rages against homosexuals because they are so blinded by pride that they "despise the straight furrow of the beautiful, fecund field . . . and go off to plow in desert land where their seeding goes to waste" (324). Again in this text sexuality is associated with language, and specifically with a language fallen away from its ideal; this association is normally portrayed through three paired images representing male and female sexuality as active and passive, respectively: a stylus and parchment, a plow and field, and a hammer and anvil. For Genius, homosexuals are those who "do not deign to put their hands to the tablets to make a mark" (322) and he exhorts the people gleefully to "Plow, for God's sake, my barons, plow and restore your lineages . . . Remember your good fathers and your old mothers . . . Don't let yourselves be overcome. You have styluses; think about writing" (324–26).

And as in *De Planctu*, a specific event causes the degeneration of both language and sexuality. Jean de Meun moves from a prelapsarian golden age before the existence of sexual and linguistic difference to a fall visualized through the castration of Saturn. Saturn's son Jupiter cut off his testicles "as though they were sausages, and threw [them] into the sea" (113). From the point of this castration onward, we are told, language and sexualities proliferate and disseminate into multiplicity. Both the proliferation of sexualities and the proliferation of languages and meanings represented by the vernaculars represent a falling away from the ideal, when all things and their names enjoyed a one-to-one correspondence. Sexuality and language are again conflated, and as Bloch notes, "the break in genealogy that castration causes, the physical disruption of the continuity of lineage, is directly associated with a radical problematization of the nature of verbal signification . . . Saturn's mutilation entails a break in genealogical continuity, a disruption . . . that is indissociable from semiological dispersion, a break with the fixity of signs implying, in turn . . . indiscriminate sexuality" (*Etymologies* 138, 140). This conflation can be seen most clearly in the debate between the Lover and Lady Reason. The association of sexuality with the vernaculars is the reason the debate between the two, what Bloch calls "a drama of desire and seduction," can be couched in terms of an argument about linguistic propriety (*Etymologies* 138).

The fact that Reason and the Lover are debating Reason's use of the words *viz* [prick] and *coillons* [balls] points "to the close identification of the directness of a proper appellation and the continuity of generation" (Bloch, *Etymologies* 139). The Lover chastises Reason for using such a crude word. She responds that she can call things by their proper names because, since everything in God's creation is part of his divinity, there can be no harm in using the proper name for a thing. The conflation of proper sexuality and proper language is represented perfectly here; the word *coillons* "possesses grammatical rectitude and is the very instrument of generation; the straightness of proper signification and of linear descent are conjoined" (Bloch, *Etymologies* 139).

The vernacular in this work is clearly associated with the possibilities for confusion inherent in a fallen language. The Lover and Reason argue over the multiple meanings a word may have and the multiple words that may be used to refer to the same thing. Reason complains that women go around referring to testicles as "purses, harness, things, or prickles, as if they were thorns . . . One should not take whatever one hears according to the letter" (136). Meaning, in other words, like sexuality, has disseminated and proliferated to the point that both are utterly confused. The indefinite nature of the vernaculars, and language in general, is reflected in Reason's highly ambiguous discourse itself. On the one hand, she affirms the importance of linguistic propriety: she says, "How would I dare not to name the works of my Father properly?" But, on the other hand, she maintains the ultimately contingent nature of all verbal signs: she says, "Although God made things, at least he did not make their names; . . . not, at least, the names that things have now" (135). She simultaneously supports a doctrine of names proper to things and one of pure convention or arbitrariness. She is inconsistent in thought and behavior, representing the state that was so horrifying for Alanus, namely indeterminacy.

Again, this degeneration of language, represented in the proliferation and confusion of meanings inherent in the vernaculars, is conflated with the degeneration of sexuality from its heterosexual, procreative ideal. Where *De Planctu* displays an anxiety over the growth of vernaculars, though, the *Rose* seems to welcome the semiological dispersions they offer. While Saturn's castration entails a disruption of lineage, the break with the fixity of signs it represents becomes a source of creativity for de Meun, and he uses the possibilities offered by the vernacular to drive his text. The very allegory of the rose, and of the Lover's sac, walking stick, and plucking of the rose, are made possible by the proliferation of meanings—puns, double entendres, gender-neutral names, and so on—inherent in the vernaculars. The text itself, Bloch argues, is a "directionless, never-ending, ever-supplemental, seemingly tumurous, multiform . . . text that, like Faux-Semblant [False Seeming], is difficult to pin down because it incarnates the very undefined principle of semiotic and sexual indeterminacy, free-floating desire, the abrogation of the rule of family and of poetic form" (*Etymologies* 141).

In the *Rose* the vernacular becomes a positive source of creativity and linguistic play at the same time that it is used to undercut the courtly conception of love subscribed to by the Lover. Both the *Rose* and *De Planctu* conflate sexuality and language and associate degenerate sexuality with degenerate language. The idea of the vernacular in both texts works to create the concept of normative sexuality by hearkening back to a time when both sexuality and language were unfallen and when all things and their names enjoyed a one-to-one correlation. The *Rose*, because it displays a more tolerant attitude to the vernacular, if not to deviant sexuality, is able to go a step further and use the idea of the vernacular to create the category of normative masculinity as well. Jean de Meun moves beyond

Alanus's simple man-woman binary by discussing more fully the idea of the eunuch. For Alanus, the eunuch was effectively a nonentity, a neutral grammatical construction. For de Meun, the eunuch is a third term fully realized in itself, introducing a split within the male term of the binary, which produces the eunuch as an offshoot of "man."

Genius says of the eunuch, "We are certain that castrated men are perverse and malicious cowards because they have the ways of women" (329). The eunuch is not only not-man but also womanish. This has an important resonance because, throughout this text, it is stressed not only that women are inferior to men but also that language and creativity are specifically male prerogatives. Procreation, potency, language, and power all come together in Genius, thereby conflating themselves into a purely masculine matrix. Nature, for example, has a great deal of power, but she remains dependent on Genius, and he has definite authority over her; at one point he commands her to remain within her forge. Only in the figure of Genius, under the sign of the male, do language, power, and procreation come together, and so the category of normative male defines itself here against women, homosexuals, and eunuchs.

These two texts, then, have several things in common. Both acknowledge the potential fluidity of gender and sex roles. While Alanus calls for strictly defined genders and sexuality, the very existence of homosexuality forces him to acknowledge the possibility that these roles can be subverted, as, indeed, can linguistic realities; he himself cannot, of course, write his text without recourse to the passive tense and without linking male grammatical terms to male grammatical terms, as is in fact proper (he . . . his, Natura . . . her, etc.). Likewise de Meun, while lamenting the homosexual's predilection for plowing barren fields, must accept the fact that Nature's plan can be subverted through the exercise of free will. De Meun, however, does not exhibit the same anxiety with regard to the vernacular that Alanus does. While using the possibilities of the vernacular to promote a normative concept of heterosexual love, he employs those same possibilities and potential confusions to lend energy and creativity to his text.[4] For de Meun, writing in the vernacular, the possibilities of a fallen language are also a source of excitement rather than simple anxiety.

PERFORMATIVE LANGUAGE AND THE PERFORMANCE OF SILENCE

By the time the *Roman de Silence* was written, then, there was an established literary tradition that saw genealogy, sexuality, and language as intricately interconnected. *Silence*, written by someone who self-identifies as Heldris of Cornwall, continues to interweave these concepts, and Bloch in fact suggests that this romance "reads in many places like a vernacular version of Alain's *De Planctus [sic] Naturae* which its author most certainly knew" ("*Silence*" 84). Newman agrees that Heldris, whoever she was, "knew *De Planctu Naturae* and may have known the *Roman de la Rose*" (123).

At the beginning of this story, the King makes a law that women will no longer be able to inherit. This challenges the laws of primogeniture, and it is with this threat to genealogical institutions that gender confusion enters the poem. Silence is the first child born to her parents, and in order to protect her inheritance, they decide to disguise and raise her as a boy. She goes through life as a man until the end of the tale, when the king recognizes her for what she is and takes her as his bride. At this point he repeals his unjust law, and proper genealogical progression is reassured.

The success of Silence's disguise is due primarily to two factors, namely clothing and language. One of the ways in which this text is unusual is in its denial of sex as the essential essence of a person. Here we see Nature arranging and making her materials even before she turns to fashioning Silence's physical body, intimating that there is an essence that precedes and exceeds the body, prior even to the inscription of sex.[5] The physical body, rather than being the determinant of sex and gender, is nothing more than a covering according to Nature herself. Newman suggests that this view of gender construction posits that, in fact, "Silence's core identity cannot or does not change, but a new dress and a makeover suffice" to determine her gender in socially acceptable terms (127). On top of the initial corporeal covering, then, Silence's parents place more coverings, albeit coverings inappropriate to her "true" sex. Silence's father says, "We will have her hair cut short in front, have her wear garments split at the sides and dress her in breeches" (Heldris 97). He subscribes to a fairly fluid view of gender construction in that he is confident that he can make Silence into a boy and that, if they ever really have a boy, they can turn Silence back into a girl.

Linguistically, her disguise is accomplished through her name. Her parents call her Scilentius, rather than Scilentia. In *Silence*, as in the *Rose*, the author revels in wordplay and the proliferation of meanings made possible by the vernacular. Her father declares, for example, that if necessary they will change Silence's name back from Scilentius to Scilentia; he says, "And if by any chance his real nature is discovered, we shall change this -us to -a, and she'll be called Scilentia. If we deprive her of this -us, we'll be observing natural usage" (99). A pun here occurs on the word "us," which translates roughly as modern French "usage," which means something like "habit" or "way of being" or "nature" (descended from Latin *usus*). The pun is immediately evident in the original, which reads

"Se nos li tolons dont cest -us / Nos li dontons natural us" (98). In other words, by removing the masculine ending "-us" from her name they will also remove a certain "us," or a way of being, and replace it with another "us," the "natural" and "correct" one. Silence's confused gendering is underscored here both by the possibilities of linguistic artifice and sexual artifice. The confusion inherent in a fallen language and fallen sexuality become conflated again in constructing deviant sexuality; Silence's "-us" represents both.

Such double meanings, puns, and linguistic play are everywhere in this text and continue to mirror Silence's confused sexuality with its confused elements. Later in the poem, after Nature has once again lamented that Scilentius's "-us" is contrary to Nature's "us," she tries to convince Silence to give up the whole game. Silence, though, has been too effectively gendered as male by this point, and she realizes that she cannot easily become a woman. Her disguise is accomplished through both linguistic and sartorial conventions, and her reply to Nature plays upon both. She replies to Nature, "Donques sui jo Scilentius, / Cho m'est avis, u jo suis nus" (118). These verses can be translated as either "Therefore I am Scilentius, as I see it, or I am no one" or "Therefore I am Scilentius, as I see it, or I am nude." Because her identity as Scilentius is constructed partly through the clothes she wears, the stripping of that identity would leave her both physically naked—"nude"—and figuratively and discursively naked—"no one."[6] The time has not yet come to return to her "true" gender, and so she must remain as Scilentius or literally become no one, a being without gender or place, a being without even the linguistic privilege of a name.

Fallen vernacular language and gender also interact in other very interesting ways in this text, which underscore not only their identification with one another but also the potential for fallen language and false meaning to disrupt the work of Nature. Nature's work is described as an act of writing, a literal inscription of Silence's features and gender upon her body. The narrator tells us, "Nature designed and drew a pair of little ears . . . Then with her thumb she forms the space between the two eyes beautifully . . . and traces a well-turned visage and colors it most beautifully" (91). Her work mirrors the orthography performed by Alanus's Nature, and like that Nature's work, her work is also ruined by the caprices of man.

Through language the rupture with Nature occurs, and through language that rupture is, seemingly, made whole again at the end. Silence's father explains his plan to hide Silence's gender to the midwife and orders her to proclaim that the child is a boy regardless of its true sex; because he will be among the guests, he himself will not know the child's true gender until later. The midwife does so, proclaiming to the assembled company that the child is male. This is a performative statement in that it initiates Silence into her culture's sexual discourse as a boy, but it is a subversive one in that it is, according to societal norms, false. At this point Silence's father is perhaps more aware than anyone of the importance of gender and language in creating the culturally intelligible subject. Until he knows for sure whether it is a boy or a girl, the child remains an "it," a source of anxiety for him, suspended on the edge of his linguistic matrix and on the verge of entry, but as yet unknowable. Thus the falseness of the utterance both creates and underscores the instability of the child's queer gender.

A second performative utterance, which does not appear to be one on the surface, signals Silence's reinscription into a framework of normative gender roles. Robert Omar Khan suggests that, at the end of the romance, "the protagonist abruptly adopts the female gender role conventionally associated with her biological sex," but her adoption of that role is anything but abrupt (77). After Silence has captured Merlin, a task that only a woman may perform, Merlin tells the king that she is indeed a woman. The king orders Silence stripped, and when he sees her naked, exclaims, "We see clearly that you are a woman" (309). This seems a simple statement, but as Peggy McCracken notes it is immediately undercut by the fact that Nature has to take three days to refinish Silence's body. McCracken observes with characteristic astuteness that this description of Nature's work recalls her earlier "writing of the feminine features on Silence's newly created form and suggests a literal reinscription of gender on the body" (532). She argues that, "ultimately, Silence's body signifies 'female' [only] because the king says it does, not because it demonstrates an inherent truth" (535). In other words, the king's statement "We see clearly that you are a woman" is performative in that it reinscribes Silence into society as a woman when it is clearly *not* obvious that she *is* a woman. The fact that Nature takes three days to remake her into a woman attests to this fact. Gaunt notes too that the removal of the "-us" ending from Silence's name represents "a castrating gesture" ("Significance" 207), thus also suggesting that, in the linguistic terms of the text, she is in fact regendered rather than simply having her true gender revealed. As with the nurse's earlier utterance, it is the king's performative that creates Silence's gender. Thus Silence's gender status is again and irrevocably bound up in language and its possibilities.

Bloch, in fact, argues that this text, especially the figure of Silence herself, is almost entirely an allegory for the process of vernacular writing. He points out that she is very much attracted to poetry from an early age and excels easily at it and that Nature, in inscribing Silence's features, "reproduces the movement of the author, whose own corpus of inscription is coterminous with the feminine body of romance" (85). The story's maintenance of a false name associated with sexual inversion also mirrors the field on which written romance was played out. The romance, Bloch argues, "is written in the interstices between nature, an assumed propriety of names, sexual difference, and the rule of primogenital inheritance, on the one hand, and, on the other, the ruses of language expressed as artifice or hiding (including silence), transgression of grammatical property, sexual inversion, and the deflection of a proper succession" (87). Cross-dressing romances such as this one, then, are based on the tension between orthography and normative sexuality, on the one hand, and the proliferation of meanings inherent in the vernaculars and fallen sexualities, on the other.

Bloch goes on to suggest that "silence represents the systematic refusal of univocal meaning" exactly as the vernaculars do (88). And, exactly as a romance or allegorical story does, Silence "wears other clothes and takes other names in defiance of Nature" (88). The important thing is not whether Nature or truth lies beneath Silence's clothing or the text's surface, but rather the very incongruity of the relationship between the body and the things that cover it, including a fallen language—this is directly representative of the relationship between vernacular poetry and the truth it purports to represent, between Silence's outer appearance and her true gender, whatever *that* has become by the end of the text.

CONCLUSION

In all three texts, then, we see a tradition of conflating language, genealogy, gender, and sexuality, a tradition that easily lends itself both to comparative literary studies and to the problems and issues of queer studies. Gaunt has written that *Silence* "appears to engage deliberately with problems that interest modern theorists," a statement that also applies to *De Planctu* and the *Rose* ("Significance" 19). All three texts, in fact, lend themselves almost extraordinarily to readings based on Judith Butler's *Gender Trouble: Feminism and the Subversion of Identity* (1990) and *Bodies That Matter: On the Discursive Limits of "Sex"* (1993), works that remain important for the ways in which they synthesized the history of European and North American feminist work into a gender theory of performativity and performance, a synthesis that lent considerable impetus to the rapidly expanding discourses of queer studies.

For Butler gender is a repeated social performance fundamental to the process of identity creation. Gender is a performance in that it is accomplished primarily through the forced reiterations of norms. This is not to say that gender is something over which the individual has full control; rather, it is through being assigned a gender that a particular subject is called into existence and assigned a primary societal identity. Therefore, "gender proves to be performative—that is, constituting the identity it is purported to be . . . Identity is performatively constituted by the very 'expressions' that are said to be its results" (*Gender* 25). Gender occurs through the internalization and repetition of normative behavior over time, a repetition that then fixes itself as the natural order.

It is this very repetition, of course, that the first two works I have examined call for repeatedly. In those texts, proper language is determined precisely by what Butler calls its "iterability," its proper repetition over time; they view any variance from that repetition as degeneration, as they view any variance from normative sexual roles as degeneration. They both long for a world in which, as Alanus puts it, "like things should proceed from like." Yet, as Butler argues, the very fact that normative roles require continual repetition opens up the possibilities for subversion, and particularly for parodic repetitions that question normative representation. Thus, Silence is able to effectively mime a gender that is not "natural" to her; she repeats normative masculine behavior, but her repetition is subversive. Likewise, the vernaculars in these texts mirror the poetry and order of nature. However, the "fallibility" of Latin grammar, the possibilities for its rules to be subverted into gender-bending roles and for queer purposes (indeed, for Latin itself to become a "homosexual text" as has been argued in relation to *De Planctu*), and the very fact that queer identities *do* exist all demonstrate that all constructions are precisely constructions and not natural. These subversive repetitions underscore that "gay is not to straight as copy is to original, but rather as copy is to copy. The parodic repetition of the 'original' . . . reveals the original to be nothing other than a parody of the idea of the natural and original" (*Gender* 31). Indeed, "the persistent possibility of disruption and rearticulation" (*Bodies* 8) is what seems to bother Alanus and de Meun, and leads to the confused ending of *Silence*.

As this chapter has demonstrated, then, both comparative literature and queer studies have something to gain from a deeper engagement with medieval studies. Apart from the very comparative nature of medieval literature itself, its concerns with questions of gender and the relationships among languages allow us to view these issues at an earlier stage and in a different context. All three of these texts offer rich fruit for examination in their discussion, indeed their very linkage, of sexuality and comparative language.

All three texts are defined in large part by how they negotiate that relationship. While *De Planctu* does not bother to recuperate the fallen language and the fallen sexuality that it mirrors, and while the *Rose* finds a way to separate the two and thus recuperate the vernacular but not degenerate sexuality, *Silence* simply does not bother to separate them and thus ends on a more ambiguous note than either of the other two works. *Silence*, like the *Rose*, revels in the possibilities offered by the vernacular and is filled with all kinds of linguistic play and confusions. In the end, it does not try to recoup one and exclude the other. It therefore ends on a discordant note because it comes out of a tradition in which the reinscription of a heterosexual paradigm was par for the course, and the figure of a cross-dressing woman who retained significant aspects of her manhood, or at least refused to accept fully her womanhood, was perhaps culturally unintelligible.

Silence is most definitely not easily reinscribed into a heterosexist paradigm. The emphasis on the construction of her role as a man makes it painfully obvious that a similar process must take place before she can be a woman again. Silence hints at this fact earlier in the narrative, lamenting that she would have no idea how to play the role of a woman in intercourse because she has been a man for so long. She says, "I have a mouth too hard for kisses, and arms too rough for embraces. One could easily make a fool of me in any game played under the covers, for I'm a young man, not a girl" (125).[7] Furthermore, the text shies away from many of the romance conventions that typically end such a story. Silence is not the happy bride, pleased to be married to the king and to reassume her feminine "us." In fact, she shows neither happiness nor unhappiness, but merely does as she *must*, which is not necessarily as she *would*. In fact, she has already told us that she would prefer to remain a man because men have the better lot in life. A marriage ceremony and wedding night are also conspicuous by their absence, and Silence's body remains unviolated at the end of the text, even by the king. Silence does not simply slip into the role of the romance heroine; she remains strong and silent. From the time that Nature remakes her into a woman, Silence does not say another word. This is, perhaps, her only possibility of resistance to the heterosexual law to which she must now bow; in assuming a unitary identity, she is simultaneously deprived of the joys of language. In refusing to replace itself firmly within the heterosexual paradigm, this text denies itself the possibility of a satisfying conclusion. Instead, both its sexually ambiguous heroine and the vernacular with which she is identified fade finally into silence, into the vernacular and sexual indeterminacy of the text itself.

Notes

1. See, for example, Lochrie; Lochrie, McCracken, and Schultz; Zeikowitz; Sturges; Dinshaw; Frantzen.
2. There are, of course, exceptions to this general rule. Notable among them are Boellstorff; Provencher; Hayes; Patton and Sánchez-Eppler.
3. Again, medievalists have long challenged this Anglocentric vision. See, for example, Amer; Howie; Burgwinkle.
4. On these connections see especially Hult.
5. Strikingly, but beyond the scope of this discussion, Nurture also enters this poem later. Newman notes that although Nature is a stock figure in this literary tradition, "no text prior to *Silence* constructs 'Norreture' [Nurture] as an allegorical character" (123).
6. For several other examples of the ubiquitous word play in this romance, see especially Cooper.
7. For an excellent reading of this passage, its construction of a passive sodomitic sexuality, and its representation of "homosexual panic," see Clark.

Works Cited

Alan of Lille. *The Plaint of Nature*. Ed. James J. Sheridan. Toronto: Pontifical Institute of Medieval Studies, 1980.

Aldridge, A. Owen. *Comparative Literature: Matter and Method*. Urbana: U of Illinois P, 1969.

Amer, Sahar. *Crossing Borders: Love between Women in Medieval French and Arabic Literatures*. Philadelphia: U of Pennsylvania P, 2008.

Bassnett, Susan. *Comparative Literature: A Critical Introduction*. Oxford: Blackwell, 1993.

Bernheimer, Charles, ed. *Comparative Literature in the Age of Multiculturalism*. Baltimore: The Johns Hopkins UP, 1995.

Bloch, R. Howard. *Etymologies and Genealogies: A Literary Anthropology of the French Middle Ages*. Chicago: U of Chicago P, 1983.

———. "*Silence* and Holes: The *Roman de Silence* and the Art of the Trouvère." *Yale French Studies* 70 (1986): 81–99.

Boellstorff, Tom. *A Coincidence of Desires: Anthropology, Queer Studies, Indonesia*. Durham: Duke UP, 2007.

Burgwinkle, William. *Sodomy, Masculinity and Law in Medieval Literature, France and England, 1050–1230*. Cambridge: Cambridge UP, 2004.

Butler, Judith. *Bodies That Matter: On the Discursive Limits of "Sex."* London: Routledge, 1993.

———. *Gender Trouble: Feminism and the Subversion of Identity*. London: Routledge, 1990.

Clark, Robert L. A. "Queering Gender and Naturalizing Class in the *Roman de Silence*." *Arthuriana* 12.1 (2002): 50–63.

Cooper, Kate Mason. "Elle and *L*: Sexualized Textuality in *Le Roman de Silence.*" *Romance Notes* 25.3 (1985): 341–60.

Culler, Jonathan. "Comparative Literature, at Last!" Bernheimer 117–21.

Damrosch, David. "World Literature in a Postcanonical, Hypercanonical Age." Saussy 43–53.

Dinshaw, Carolyn. *Getting Medieval: Sexualities and Communities, Pre- and Post-modern.* Durham: Duke UP, 1999.

Eckhardt, Caroline D. "Old Fields, New Corn, and Present Ways of Writing About the Past." Saussy 139–54.

Ferris, David. "Indiscipline." Saussy 78–99.

Frantzen, Allen J. *Before the Closet: Same-Sex Love from "Beowulf" to "Angels in America."* Chicago: U of Chicago P, 1998.

Gaunt, Simon. *Retelling the Tale: An Introduction to Medieval French Literature.* London: Duckworth, 2001.

———. "The Significance of Silence." *Paragraph: A Journal of Modern Critical Theory* 13.2 (1990): 202–16.

Guillaume de Lorris and Jean de Meun. *The Romance of the Rose.* Ed. Charles Dahlberg. Princeton: Princeton UP, 1971. Repr. Hanover: UP of New England, 1986.

Hayes, Jarrod. *Queer Nations: Marginal Sexualities in the Maghreb.* Chicago: U of Chicago P, 2000.

Heldris of Cornwall. *Silence: A Thirteenth-Century French Romance.* Ed. Sarah Roche-Mahdi. East Lansing: Colleagues, 1992.

Hokenson, Jan Walsh. "The Culture of the Context: Literature Past and Future." *Comparative Literature and Comparative Cultural Studies.* Ed. Steven Tötösy de Zepetnek. West Lafayette: Purdue UP, 2003. 58–75.

Howie, Cary. *Claustrophilia: The Erotics of Enclosure in Medieval Literature.* New York: Palgrave, 2007.

Hult, David F. "Language and Dismemberment: Abelard, Origen, and the *Romance of the Rose.*" *Rethinking the "Romance of the Rose."* Ed. Kevin Brownlee and Sylvia Huot. Philadelphia: U of Pennsylvania P, 1992. 101–30.

Huot, Sylvia. *From Song to Book: The Poetics of Writing in Old French Lyric and Lyrical Narrative Poetry.* Ithaca: Cornell UP, 1987.

Kay, Sarah. "Sexual Knowledge: The Once and Future Texts of the *Romance of the Rose.*" *Textuality and Sexuality: Reading Theories and Practices.* Ed. Judith Still and Michael Worton. Manchester: Manchester UP, 1993. 69–86.

———. "Women's Body of Knowledge: Epistemology and Misogyny in the *Romance of the Rose.*" *Framing Medieval Bodies.* Ed. Sarah Kay and Miri Rubin. Manchester: Manchester UP, 1994. 211–35.

Khan, Robert Omar. "Genealogy and Cross-Gendering in *Le Roman de Silence* and *Ariake no Wakare.*" *Arthuriana* 12.1 (2002): 76–84.

Lochrie, Karma. *Heterosyncrasies: Female Sexuality When Normal Wasn't.* Minneapolis: U of Minnesota P, 2005.

Lochrie, Karma, Peggy McCracken, and James Schultz, eds. *Constructing Medieval Sexuality.* Minneapolis: U of Minnesota P, 1997.

McCracken, Peggy. "'The Boy Who Was a Girl': Reading Gender in the *Roman de Silence*." *The Romantic Review* 85.4 (1984): 517–36.

Newman, Barbara. *God and the Goddesses: Vision, Poetry, and Belief in the Middle Ages*. Philadelphia: U of Pennsylvania P, 2003.

Patton, Cindy, and Benigno Sánchez-Eppler, eds. *Queer Diasporas*. Durham: Duke UP, 2000.

Provencher, Denis M. *Queer French: Globalization, Language, and Sexual Citizenship in France*. Surrey: Ashgate, 2007.

Quilligan, Maureen. "Allegory, Allegoresis, and the Deallegorization of Language: The *Roman de la Rose*, the *De Planctu Naturae*, and the *Parlement of Foules*." *Allegory, Myth, and Symbol*. Ed. Morton W. Bloomfield. Cambridge: Harvard UP, 1981. 163–86.

Remak, Henry H. H. "Comparative Literature: Its Definition and Function." *Comparative Literature: Method and Perspective*. Ed. Newton Stallknecht and Horst Frenz. Carbondale: Southern Illinois UP, 1971. 1–57.

Saussy, Haun, ed. *Comparative Literature in an Age of Globalization*. Baltimore: The Johns Hopkins UP, 2006.

Sturges, Robert S. *Chaucer's Pardoner and Gender Theory: Bodies of Discourse*. New York: Palgrave, 2000.

Zeikowitz, Richard E. *Homoeroticism and Chivalry: Discourses of Male Same-Sex Desire in the 14th Century*. New York: Palgrave, 2003.

CHAPTER 2

FIGURAL HISTORIOGRAPHY

DOGS, HUMANS, AND CYNANTHROPIC BECOMINGS

CARLA FRECCERO

FIGURAL HISTORIOGRAPHY

IN "LITERARY HISTORY AND LITERARY MODERNITY," AN ARGUMENT FOR defining literature as the medium that puts its own ontological status into question, Paul de Man suggests that a change is required in historical approaches to literature as these are currently understood and practiced. Such a conception of literary history, he writes, "would imply a revision of the notion of history and, beyond that, of the notion of time on which our idea of history is based" (164). For example, given that—in this hypothesis—"truth and error" exist simultaneously in the literary text and nowhere more so than when literature conveys knowledge about itself, one would have to abandon "the pre-assumed concept of history as a generative process . . . of history as a temporal hierarchy that resembles a parental structure in which the past is like an ancestor begetting, in a moment of unmediated presence, a future capable of repeating in its turn the same generative process" (164). He concludes, "To become good literary historians, we must remember that what we usually call literary history has little or nothing to do with literature and that what we call literary interpretation—provided only it is good interpretation—is in fact literary history. If we extend this notion beyond literature, it merely confirms that the bases for historical knowledge are not empirical facts but written texts, even if these texts masquerade in the guise of wars or revolutions" (165). De Man names here what has become an object of scrutiny in queer theorizations of historicism and of temporality within literary studies, that is, the lingering tendency to view history as progressive, teleological, and generative, so that metaphorically it mimes ideologies of heteronormative reproductivity, or what Lee Edelman has called "reproductive futurism" (2). The challenge, it would seem then, is to think through other ways of attending to historicity that less clumsily bioanthropomorphize temporality, on the one hand, and more closely track the rhetorical properties of figurative language, on the other. This could, in turn, give rise to a practice of comparative historical literary study that did not respect national boundaries or periodizations and that would follow, instead, the promiscuous and errant movement of figures across times and places.

The parental model of history that de Man critiques carries with it particular, and often unacknowledged, affective structures associated with the "movement of time." The future is the hope of the past and the present, it is the end or culmination of desire, and it "promises" redemption; or, alternatively, the past is what is (violently) superseded and rejected, improved upon, or revered by a filial piety that honors its legacy. Furthermore, in the interstices of grand affective narratives that cleave to genetic familial configurations live a host of other feelings, both familial and not, that follow other temporalities: longing, demand, desire, love, rage, envy, obsession, and the feeling that is not one, trauma. Affects do not obey sequence; they have histories, but they do not respect the historical injunction to move on and to get beyond. Rather, the properties proper to affect, even within the genetic narratives of history, seem better described in the language of psychoanalysis: persistence, repetition, stasis, fading and waning, sudden change.

Psychoanalysis has traditionally been the domain of such a historical endeavor through its practice of reading figural language and its affective force. The focus in psychoanalysis, however, has often been on the history of individuals and their kinship network. I want to argue that, to understand the work figures do, we must make use of phantasmatic historiographies, the temporalities of which resemble psychoanalytic understandings of time as subjectivity and affect more than they do the time of progressivist history. What would it mean, for example, to take seriously the possibility that history repeats itself, not necessarily event-wise, but in its driving affective force? To work this way historically is to "do literary interpretation," to read the "impersonal passion" figurative language conveys, and thus perhaps—and only perhaps—to work through some of the ways we continue to be haunted, at times knowingly, but also in ways we are unable to acknowledge or cannot imagine.[1]

CARNIVOROUS VIRILITY

My case study takes as its point of reference an instance of historical trauma—the conquest of the New World by Europeans—as it repeats itself through signifiers across texts and time. The figure I am following is the devouring dog—that ubiquitous companion of colonizers in the New World—as (lethal) weapon. This symptomatic figure repeats itself, changes places or displaces, travels between and among subjects and objects, and condenses in itself a whole series of New and Old World meanings, from companion to cannibal, from primitive savage to savagely civilizational. And even as I track the historicity of this figure, I want to attend to its affective echoes, to the way it haunts—one might say dogs—our footsteps.

Donna Haraway, in writing about the "ontological choreography" that configures dog-human "naturecultures," notes, "Dogs, in their historical complexity, matter here. Dogs are not an alibi for other themes; dogs are fleshly material-semiotic presences in the body of technoscience. Dogs are not surrogates for theory; they are not just here to think with. They are here to live with. Partners in the crime of human evolution, they are in the garden from the get-go" (5). At the same time, and in consort with de Man's remark that texts "masquerade in the guise of wars or revolutions," she notes the tropic force of dog stories, naming a figure of speech, "metaplasm," particularly appropriate to the material-semiotic confusion (fusing together) of the dog-human nexus (20). Dogs are a matter of ontological uncertainty: not a metaphor, a substitute, or surrogate, and at the same time, not the name of a discrete material otherness (what sometimes gets called nature). Their designation, in Haraway's words, as both material and semiotic and as "partners in the crime of human evolution," finds its tropic counterpart in colonial metaplasmic fusions and confusions that link dog and cannibal and conjoin them into sensuous and potent being (see Hulme). If, as Marjorie Garber has asserted, one dimension of the modern-day anthropomorphization of dogs is a transferential and idealizing displacement of the nostalgia for humanism, then another is an equally projective displacement of a desire to kill and ferociously consume another human, a nostalgia, we might call it, for carnivorous virility.[2]

But is displacement what is really at stake? Eduardo Kohn, in "How Dogs Dream," observes the transpecific intersubjective relating of dogs and humans among the Runa of Ecuador's Upper Amazon. He argues that the Amazonian cosmological framework allows an understanding of metaplasmic fusions that do not use "culture" or "the human" to mark difference—that do not, in other words, ontologically privilege the human as sole locus of subjectivity and agency but confer being on "life" in a complex ecology of selves (4).[3] Generalizing on this insight, he notes, "We humans live in a world that is not only built according to how we perceive it and the actions those perceptions inform. Our world is also defined by how we get caught up in the interpretive worlds, the multiple natures—the *umwelt*—of the other kinds of beings with whom we relate" (17). Intersubjectivity is thus, in part, a condition of "becoming other," and in the case of transspecies relating, this means a kind of ontological blurring. Dogs, who have the longest history of nonhuman companionate existence with humans, have excelled at the process of ontological blurring. They have learned to "become human" in ways that ensure their survival, Kohn argues, borrowing from Gilles Deleuze and Félix Guattari's phrase, "becoming animal."[4]

What of the humans in this "transspecies habitus" (7)? Humans, it is said, have strategically capitalized on canine hierarchical social organization by inserting themselves into the top position to assure canine subordination to human volition. At the same time, for humans, dogs serve a prosthetic function: they add to the human, enhancing human being while also supplementing a lack in that being. For the Runa, there is an added consciousness of resemblance: even the Quichua term for persons—the pronominal marker *runa*—and the (derogatory) term, in Spanish, for their mongrel dogs, is the same (11). They both share a relation of predator-prey, dominance-submission, with their environment and the jaguars who inhabit it, and they share a history of colonial encounters, for during the conquest Spanish ancestors of these dogs hunted these people's ancestors, these dogs whom the Ávila Runa often acquire from white mestizos nearby and who become, in turn, subservient to the Runa (11–12). The mutual entanglements of dogs and humans in this ecology of selves create a need for mediation between two poles: what Kohn calls "cosmological autism," on the one hand—the loss of the ability to become other, which, for the Runa, involves the loss of the ability to hunt successfully—and, on the other, excessive merger, a becoming-dog that would entail the loss of human selfhood and its privileged position in the transpecific hierarchy (9). Figurality performs the mediation; metaphor "aligns different ontologically situated points of view" (12). The terms of comparison, dog and human, maintain their (related) discreteness even as they mutually contaminate each other on an ontological level. Tracking dog-human figurations in this manner suggests an approach that does not privilege only the human or the nonhuman as the site of subjectivity and agency but implicates both in a consequential becoming.

Cynocephalic (dog-headed) and cynanthropic cannibals have a long and strange history and participate in a transnational *translatio imperii* from East to West and past to present in the classic movement of ideological narratives of Western modernity (White). The point, not of origin, but of fusion between old and new, myth and history, and the point of a certain congealment of humanism, is a small moment, a brief text, in the history of transatlantic travel. In Christopher Columbus's *Diario* of his first voyage to the Americas, as "transcribed" or reported by Bartolomé de Las Casas, appear the following passages, separated by a space of three days, from 23 to 26 November 1492: "They said . . . there were people on it [Bohio] who had one eye in their foreheads, and others whom they called cannibals, of whom they showed great fear" (Dunn and Kelley 167), and "all the people . . . have extreme fear of the men of Caniba, or Canima, and they say that they live on this island of Bohio . . . fearing that they would have them to eat . . . And they say they have but one eye and the face of a dog" (177). Cyclops, cynocephaly, canibal, canis, carib, and of course, the Great Khan, all converge in an oneiric condensation that grafts ancient resonances onto new bodies to produce material mongrels, both human and canine.[5] Ktesias (Ctesias), Herodotus, Pliny the Elder, Solinus, Augustine, Isidore of Seville: these and more testify to the dog-headed (sometimes dog-faced) human-eating peoples at the extremities of their worlds, as does the fifth-sixth century Buddhist missionary Hui-Sheng as recorded in *Liang Shu*.[6] Dog-headed cannibals and dog-men may have begun by being assigned to India, but soon they became the inhabitants of parts of Africa, of many islands in Asia and Africa, and eventually also of the New World. European and Islamic medieval encyclopedists and travelers, from ibn Battuta, Vincent of Beauvais (thirteenth century), and Kazwini, to Marco Polo (late thirteenth, early fourteenth century), to Sir John Mandeville (fourteenth century) confirm their existence in the far more chatty ethnographic discourse of travelogues, adding details regarding their customs and character and mitigating with simile the suggestion of monstrous morphology. Vincent, whose *Speculum maius* represents a massive compendium of his world's encyclopedic knowledge, writes, in the volume called *Speculum naturale*, that there is "an animal with the head of the dog but with all other members of human appearance . . . Though he behaves like a man . . . and, when peaceful, he is tender like a man, when furious, he becomes cruel and retaliates on humankind" (126; see also Wittkower). On Andaman Island, off the coast of India, Marco Polo finds "that all the men of this island have heads like dogs, and teeth and eyes like dogs; for I assure you that the whole aspect of their faces is that of big mastiffs. They are a very cruel race: whenever they can get hold of a man who is not one of their kind, they devour him" (258). Sir John Mandeville writes, "Men and women of that isle have heads like dogs, and they are called Cynocephales. These people, despite their shape, are fully reasonable and intelligent . . . if they capture any man in battle, they eat him" (134). Columbus, who developed a mythology about his name, Christopher, also perhaps knew that sometimes St. Christopher had a dog's head; this martyred man, once called Reprebus, was a Mamaritan prisoner of war, Mamarica being a North African tribe in the province of Cyrenaica, part of modern-day Libya. Mamarica was a land of dog-headed cannibals. Reprebus served or was forced to serve in the Roman army against his own people and was baptized and later martyred as a Christian.[7] The Latin tradition soon effaced his cynocephaly and gave him the name of "Christ-bearer," but Byzantine iconography preserved his wolfish appearance. Was Columbus haunted by this strange past, too—the past of the saint best known as the patron saint of travelers like Columbus?[8]

To be a dog-headed cannibal, then, is to occupy the periphery of an observer's known world; but to be a dog-headed cannibal is also to display hostility to strangers—those who originate from beyond the borders of one's known world. Dog-headed cannibals connote war, battle, an enemy relationship, and a virility untainted by heterosociality (i.e., they are males who live among males). And this devouring doggishness has affinities with both sides of the colonial encounter, as the Hawaiian legend of Kaupe, the Olohe demigod who assumed the form of a dog and who cannibalized as he colonized Oahu, Maui, and Hawaii until he was defeated and became, instead, a ghost-dog, also suggests.[9] The merger of dog and man produces a carnivorous virility able both to reason and to ferociously attack and consume the enemy.

NEW WORLD ENCOUNTERS

In *Sodometries*, Jonathan Goldberg recounts the story of Balboa's massacre of 40 Panamanian Indians of Quarequa who are accused of "sodomy" by delivering them as prey to his dogs (180–85). The passage, from Peter Martyr, describes the sodomitic Indians as "contagious beasts," and, as Goldberg demonstrates, their slaughter effects a division between "good" and "bad" Indians—those who descry sodomy and those who practice it. And yet in a passage preceding this moment in the text, all the Indians are likened to nonhuman animals and slaughtered accordingly, "in pieses as the butchers doo fleshe," thus remarkably mirroring the countless contemporary woodcuts that illustrated cannibal dinner preparations as outdoor butcher shops and open-air barbeques (182).[10] Columbus also brought dogs, and there are reports that European public markets sold human body parts to furnish dogs with a taste for human flesh in preparation (Schwartz 163; see also Varner and Varner). This last detail may come from Las Casas's famous description of the practice of using dogs against Native Americans, occurring throughout his account and culminating in another textual inspiration for New World cannibal illustrations:

> As has been said, Spaniards train their fierce dogs to attack, kill, and tear to pieces the Indians . . . The Spaniards keep alive their dogs' appetite for human beings in this way. They have Indians brought to them in chains, then unleash the dogs. The Indians come meekly down the roads and are killed. And the Spaniards have butcher shops where the corpses of Indians are hung up, on display, and someone will come and say, more or less, "Give me a quarter of that rascal hanging there, to feed my dogs until I can kill another one for them." As if buying a quarter of a hog or other meat. (*Devastation* 127–28)

Did these cynanthropes know the apocryphal stories of Saints Andrew and Bartholomew among the Parthians, where the cannibalistic cynocephalic man—Abominable—is converted to Christianity and in the process has his "nature" tamed, only to be commanded to unleash it later against his compatriots in Bartos, whom he slaughters, disembowels, and devours (White 22–25, 197)? It is worth remembering too that the medieval order of the Dominican monks were folk-etymologically referred to as the *canes domini* or hounds of God, to which François Rabelais so playfully alludes in punishing a proud lady and a roasting Panurge with the pursuit of many eager hungry dogs.[11] God as dog is copilot here, but in disavowal; to pursue the holy work of empire one must be cannibalistic and doglike, eradicating the devouring and savage doggishness in and of the other.[12] Dog is the *pharmakon*, the poison that is also the cure. It will take a marginalized European in the New World, Jean de Léry, to recognize the mechanism of displaced abjection in the accusers:

> During the bloody tragedy that began in Paris on the twenty-fourth of August 1572 . . . the fat of human bodies (which, in ways more barbarous than those of the savages, were butchered at Lyon after being pulled out of the Saône)—was it not publicly sold to the highest bidder? The livers, hearts and other parts of these bodies—were they not eaten by the furious murderers, of whom Hell itself stands in horror? Likewise, after the wretched massacre of one Coeur de Roy, who professed the Reformed Faith in the city of Auxerre—did not those who committed this murder

cut his heart to pieces, display it for sale to those who hated him, and finally, after grilling it over coals—glutting their rage like mastiffs—eat of it? . . . So let us henceforth no longer abhor so very greatly the cruelty of the anthropophagous—that is, man-eating—savages. (131–33)[13]

Sophie Menache argues that canines are demonized throughout monotheistic clerical doctrine because they compete with God for human allegiance, on the one hand, and recognize humans as their (godlike) masters, on the other (2). Like God, they mediate, for humans, a relation to another world, one that is only sometimes subordinated to cultural institutions; they are a shuttle between worlds, "life" and "death," occupying the threshold between home and wild, the domestic and the savage (Serpell 254).[14] They embody, even as they figure, an ontological uncertainty. Indeed, for Vanita Seth, anthropomorphic nature—and, I would add, zoomorphic humanity—testify to an agency and a subjectivity that are not exclusively human (she calls it "the world of nature"; 79). She locates this phenomenon in the premodern, pre-Enlightenment world before humanism, where gods, zoomorphs, wild men, nature, and humans share what Eduardo Viveiros de Castro calls a "multinaturalist framework" of disparate but commensurable being. Columbus and the conquerors after him seem poised on this threshold between the literal and figurative; but the humanism-in-disavowal that would pit cannibalistic dogs against dog-headed cannibals in the New World intimates that spectral cynanthropes have not ceased to haunt this scene.

PRESA CANARIO

Among the territories colonized, with difficulty, by the Castilian crown in the fifteenth century, was an archipelago off the northwestern coast of Africa now called the Canary Islands, inhabited by a group of people related to the Berbers who came to be known as the Guanches.[15] Pliny, who located a race of "dog-men" (*canarii*) in western Africa, called these the Fortunate Isles, and identified one of them as Gran Canaria, attributing the name to the presence of huge dogs (Pliny, book VI, chap. 37, 491). The history of these dogs is a transnational one, too, and it follows and crosses paths with the trails of the dog-men, participating in an equally phantasmatic story of origins and nomenclatures. They were probably descendants of the ancient Molossians, themselves sometimes thought to be descendants of the Tibetan mastiff, of whom it was said that they were "trained to attack men of a strange race" (Leighton 512). They migrated with the Molossi, a once-barbarian Greek group, from Thessaly to Epirus and later became part of the Roman Empire. Molossian is also the breed-type for what are called in English mastiffs, descendants of ancient guard and war dogs from Asia or the Middle East, drifting westward and metaplasmically mating, in the Middle Ages, the domesticated—*mansuetus*, accustomed to the hand—to the folk-etymological "massive" and the term for mongrel in Old French, *mestif*.[16] According to a breeder Web site, "one Canarian legend relays how the Guanche warriors sent their fierce dogs down to the beachheads where it is claimed these dogs massacred the marauding invaders."[17] It took nearly a century for the Spanish to conquer the fiercely resistant people of the Canaries; the islands in turn became a relay first for the Spanish, then for the English traveling across the Atlantic. They also became single-crop cultivation sites—first for sugar cane, then, when the Caribbean market outstripped their production, vineyards for the Spanish wine trade with England. Spanish and English dogs mixed with the dogs of the Canary Islands, producing one of the mastiff breeds that is today known as the Perro de Presa Canario, the Canarian dog of prey.[18] "Holding" or "guarding" Molosser-type mixed-race dogs, these *perros de presa* are thought to combine the indigenous island herding dog of Fuerteventura—the Perro de Bardino Majorero—with Spanish cattle-guarding mastiffs (Presa Español) and English bulldogs (Alano Español, from the English Alaunt) used in the American conquest.[19] In the course of the sixteenth century, these dogs appear as subject to legislation in the municipal councils of several of the islands; the *perros de presa* are threatening livestock, or there are too many of them, or they are running free. Various documents from 1501 to 1737 order that they be tied up or exterminated with impunity (with the exception of those used for guarding the home or by farmers for guarding livestock) and that every dog of prey be registered with the court (Torres).[20]

These centuries also saw the development of dog-fighting matches, introduced to the Canaries by the English. The matches used mongrels that combined the island dogs with English "Bandogges" and "Tiedogs" (thought to be the predecessors of bulldogs and mastiffs). Dog fighting continued legally until the 1940s when the dogs of World War II—German Shepherds, Great Danes, and Doberman Pinschers primarily—also made their appearance on the islands, along with Generalissimo Francisco Franco. The opposition to Franco's regime and its eventual decline brought movements to reclaim lost cultural traditions, and beginning in the 1970s and culminating in 1982 and 1983 with the autonomization of the Canary Islands, a Club Español del Presa Canario was formed to recover, protect, and develop the breed, winning exclusive rights to represent it to the Real Sociedad Canina de España and thus to the Fédération Cynologique

Internationale (World Canine Federation) that recognizes and certifies the Perro de Presa Canario breed to this day. Thus these mestizo dogs were forged in a crucible of colonial encounters, enlisted to defend and conquer and cannibalize one another in "civil" wars until they were swept up into a national movement for independence and liberation, when their "race" is fixed and given an identity, and when they also began to participate in the commodification of Third-World culture for First-World consumption. Immigrants to North America and descendants of those immigrants, Presa Canarios are conscripted to infuse civilization with a certain virilizing savagery, as the following story in this history of haunted and haunting ontologies suggests.

DOGS OF WAR

On 26 January 2001, two Presa Canarios, a dog and a bitch named Bane and Hera, attacked Diane Whipple in the hallway of her Pacific Heights apartment in San Francisco, where she lived with her partner, Sharon Smith. The bites to her larynx, combined with the loss of one-third of her blood, caused her death within hours of the six-minute attack. Bane and Hera were originally owned by various proxies for Pelican Bay State Prison inmate Paul Schneider, a member of the Aryan Brotherhood, whose plan was to become a dog breeder from his cell where he was serving time for armed robbery and attempted murder (Jones; see also Bretches). The breeder name was "Dog O' War," cofounded by Schneider and Dale Bretches, inmate since 1979 and author of an e-book, *Dog O' War*, which is a memoir, an account of Presa Canario breeding, and a commentary on the San Francisco case. The dogs' caretakers were Marjorie Knoller and Robert Noel, residents of the same apartment building floor as Whipple and Smith, adoptive parents of Paul Schneider and lawyers who specialized in bringing lawsuits on behalf of inmates against the California Department of Corrections for its inhumane treatment of prisoners.

Although this was not a unique event—other dogs have attacked and mauled people resulting in death—it was one that immediately generated an archive, both legal and cultural, marking a traumatic moment in the recent U.S. history of dog-human relating, and it brought attention and notoriety to this little-known breed. Some parties in the case make the argument that these animals are genetically predisposed to attack and kill. Most cultural commentary, however, familiar by now with the disconcertingly close resemblance between species sociobiology and racism, adopts a liberal humanist position that, on the one hand, polices the ontological boundaries between canine and human, and, on the other, maintains a contradictory distinction between "nature" and "nurture" that testifies eloquently to the fetishist's famous phrase, "I know, but nevertheless . . ." (Mannoni).[21] For example, some fault the dogs' handlers and caretakers for their negligence and failure to train their animals and simultaneously condemn the practice of deliberately raising dogs for their capacity to fight (Millan 174–78; Jones). Aphrodite Jones, the "true crime" author who also brought notoriety to the Brandon Teena murder, dedicates her book to Diane Whipple and concludes her narrative with a plea for animal protection (364–65), while Cesar Millan, the "dog whisperer," writes, "I've said before that pack leaders are born, not made. Red-zone dogs are just the opposite—made, not born. Humans create dogs to be red-zone monsters. We started thousands of years ago by breeding dogs to be fighters, selecting them for certain characteristics and matching them up with a similar mate . . . We breed these dogs to be warriors, but under their armor, they're simply dogs with more powerful weapons than other dogs. They don't begin life as dangerously aggressive . . . Though fighting is in their genes, they need guidance to bring this instinct out" (178–79). These discourses point to a conundrum of dog-human "natureculture": the inability definitively to articulate the boundary between nature and culture (animal and human) in the history and agency of this companion species relation. They posit an originary and "natural" innocence followed by a genetic fall due to human intervention—a kind of diabolical eugenics project that produced organic "warriors" or fierce, "killer" dogs. They also, to different degrees, argue against genetic determinism by positing a decisive role for "nurture," or human cultural intervention, into instinctual potentiality. Nurture—the thing that is to blame, as Millan's statement makes clear—is also the cure for what nurture has genetically produced. Like Montaigne and Rousseau, these arguments occlude, even as they intermittently recognize, the always already thoroughly contaminated category to which any dog—and any human civilization—belongs.

The doubly supplemental and fetishistic logic that says that culture must be added to nature to enhance it but also to repair a deficiency in nature resulting from culture, on the one hand, and that the animal prosthetic that supplements a lack in the human also produces an excess, on the other, testifies to the work of a symptom, or what Slavoj Žižek describes as the ideological symptom par excellence. This symptom is a recognition, a knowledge that is refused, not as a matter of belief, but in practice (31–33). He notes that subjects in capitalism know very well that "money is in reality just an embodiment, a condensation, a materialization of a network of social relations" (31) but argues that "in their social activity itself, in what they are *doing*, they are *acting* as if money, in its material reality, is the immediate embodiment of wealth as such.

They are fetishists in practice, not in theory. What they 'do not know,' what they misrecognize, is the fact that in their social reality itself, in their social activity—the act of commodity exchange—they are guided by the fetishistic illusion" (31). This abstraction of human subjectivity and agency into the commodity relation—a real abstraction—characterizes human activity under capitalism and constitutes the fantasy that animates or anthropomorphizes commodities. Jean-Joseph Goux, who, like Žižek, links a psychoanalytics of subjectivity to capital, further argues that this subject is archaically masculine, originating in the exchange of women as gifts that founds the principle of exogamy-instituting social relations.[22] In this animating fantasy of commodity fetishism, the subject is detached, displaced, and abstracted into the commodity as the site of an idealized objectification that preserves the subject from consumption and use in the process of exchange while memorializing the loss of corporeality, transmuting it into value in the "sublime" object. These commodities, however, also have a subjectivity and agency of their own; in their embodiment they are not only (but also) the animate vessels of an agency that inhabits them from elsewhere. The (dog-)commodity fetish, then, can be seen to mark a desire—and a longing—for an embodied and unalienated masculine subjectivity, one that refuses to sacrifice carnivorous virility in exchange for symbolic power and that consumes rather than being subsumed.[23] Like Montaigne's "savages" ("Of Cannibals" 150–59) and the cynanthropic cannibals inhabiting the peripheries of civilization, the merger of human and dog figures an embodied plenitude that phallic modernity experiences as loss.

The aporia delineated by these contradictions also recalls anthropologist Claude Lévi-Strauss's name for the boundary between nature and culture—the incest prohibition. In its character as "universal," the incest prohibition would seem to be natural; in its character as rule, however, it partakes of culture. For Lévi-Strauss, it is above all a prohibition against the fantasy of and desire for an endogamous intimacy not unlike ontological blurring, where the merging of other and self constitutes an inside against which outsiderness or alterity is measured and refused. Lévi-Strauss thus argues that symbolic manifestations of incest "do not . . . commemorate an actual event. They are something else, and more, the permanent expression of a desire for disorder, or rather counter-order" (491).[24]

The desire for an archaic counterorder, figured in the plenitude of human-dog becoming, may be one of the recognitions disavowed in humanist efforts to maintain the ontological divide between nature and culture, dog and human, in this scene of violent species merger. Traces of this recognition persist, both in the accusations of bestiality against Noel and especially Knoller, rejected as evidence in the trial, and in the jury's subsequently overturned (and later reinstated) verdict of second-degree murder, implicating both dog and human in a murderous agency and intent.[25] What thus haunts this case is the possibility that, rather than an accidental failure in the history of social relations between humans and dogs, the attack on Diane Whipple was one exemplary instance of an archaic force unleashed in and by dog-human becoming.

In *Dogs O' War*, Security Housing Unit (SHU) inmate Dale Bretches provides an account of the Dog O' War breeder project that he and his cellmate developed, autobiographically linking his life of fighting to the fighting dogs he grew up with and the breed—Presa Canario—that came to incarnate, for him, a heroic ideal. Throughout this book, a double portrait emerges: the embattled survivalism of a warrior protecting family and tribe against a world of hostile strangers, on the one hand, and the heroic individualism of a captive "gladiator" pitted against other gladiators for sport in a battle to the death, on the other. In the SHU prison, inmates form racialized tribes for protection against the guards and other racialized tribes and value strength, courage, sangfroid, loyalty, pain tolerance, and the ability to fight.[26] Schneider's description of the Aryan Brotherhood, whose motto "in for life and out by death" points to a double condition of constraint, both individual and collective, horizontal and vertical, puts this in stark and somewhat counterintuitive terms: "I'm no Nazi. I'm in prison. Prison is made up of Blacks, Mexicans, Whites. The Whites are a minority. I've grown up around Black people. They don't relate to me and I don't relate to them . . . Things are really racially divided in prison . . . I'm not a White Supremacist . . . I didn't start the Aryan Brotherhood and I'm not going to end it. I'm just along for the ride" (Jones 291). The Brotherhood creed invokes a bellicose tribalism— "I will stand by my brother / My brother will come before all others / My life is forfeited should I fail my brother / I will honor my brother in peace and war"—memorialized by the adoption of ancient Celtic, Norse, and Irish mythology and iconography in tattoos and in Pelican Bay artwork, which also prominently features Presa Canarios.[27]

The motto emblazoned on Bretches's Dog O' War breeder logo is "Courage, Strength, Loyalty"; Presa literature, including Bretches's book and Millan's, documents the tests of "gameness"—the ability to fight to the death—administered by "dogmen" to produce the combination of hardness and endurance (especially endurance of pain) that is said to mark the breed: "These men engage in a sport known as 'game testing,' throwing their dogs into a ring with another dog and culling out the ones that manage to survive but that don't perform to the breeder's standards" (Millan 179). Bretches describes the training his prison provides: "These conditions have earned the SHU a place alongside Iraq and Kenya in 1996 U.N. [United Nations] human rights report citing 'inhumane' prison facilities around the world. 'A lot of inmates who go in there become severely affected with mental illness,' says attorney Russell Clanton. 'Those who don't go mad become incredibly strong individuals'" (176–77). That strength and its challenges are what Bretches names as the point of identification between himself and the dogs: "To me there's no better high than the test of one's own gameness and abilities. One of the reasons I respect these traits in presas and pit bulls is I identify with theses [*sic*] warrior breeds. Ole' war dogs, yeah, you are the company you keep as the saying goes. Maybe that's why so many resemble their dogs" (38).

Embodiments of "bare life," achieving only intermittently, in the eyes of the state, the status of human, Pelican Bay SHU inmates inhabit concrete cellblocks with access, once daily for 90 minutes, to an area called a "dog run."[28] Noel graphically describes some of the dehumanization techniques designed to erode the subjectivity of particularly unruly and recalcitrant prisoners: "They put Paul in what's called dog status. That's where, in the cold of winter, they throw you in an unheated concrete box, with a hole in the floor as the only sanitary facility. You're there with no running water, naked, with no blankets, no mattresses, no nothing. They leave you there for three days, and the only thing they would slip through in the way of food was a tray with a pile of, literally, frozen dog shit on it" (cited in Jones, 225). This carceral performative works to transform the prisoner into pure animal embodiment, a body that matters for punitive purposes but is stripped of its status as subject and rendered unintelligible as human.[29] The animal body is, in turn, degraded—forced to eat excrement. Prison practice thus deploys the mediatory metaphorics of human-canine becoming to produce, discursively and materially, ontological uncertainty as a degradation of being. Caught up, like the Runa, in the mutual entanglements of dog and human with their shared histories of predation and oppression, dominance and submission, and unable to claim their subjectivity in human terms, the prisoners embrace a counterdiscursive version of this ontological uncertainty, transforming the "underdog" into an überbeing. Rather than issuing a plea for "humane" treatment, Bretches and Schneider refigure becoming-dog as the powerful embodiment of an archaic force articulated in the metaplasmic confusions of warrior and gladiator that join dogmen and dogs of prey. This force is nowhere better realized than in the idealized and heroic carnivorous virility of the Presa referred to as "El Supremo" Bane (Bretches 84). Like the cannibals Peter Hulme studies in the history of colonial encounters, which become an ideology concept designating fierce resistance to colonization, the devouring dog, in Bretches's description, assumes the weight of prisoners' resistance to their oppression, mediating between worlds for them and sacrificing himself in their name (see also Freccero, "Cannibalism").

If, then, the symptomatic disavowals apparent in dominant discourses concerning the case consist in misrecognizing the intersubjective relation between dog and human and in misrecognizing, as well, the degree to which the dog of prey can be understood to have absorbed a corporeal subjectivity in excess of the animal object-status to which these discourses consign it—what Kohn dubs "ontological autism"—it might also be said that Bretches and his colleagues perform the excessive merger at the opposite pole of this transpecies habitus, a subsumption of human selfhood in becoming-dog. In the one case, it is a question of the essential ferocity or innocence of the nonhuman animal and its sheer instrumentalization for human ends, and in the other it is a question of the nonhuman animal's nobility and capacity to mediate racial tribalism, traits absent from a humanity stripped of agency altogether. What results from the complex metaphoric interplay of dog and man in these accounts recalls the genealogy of cynanthropic becoming even as it labors to forge an anthrocynic being in the subjectivities of those consigned to the status of "mere" dog by a system in disavowal.

HAUNTED ONTOLOGIES

Although, because Sharon Smith was able to bring a wrongful death lawsuit against Noel and Knoller on Whipple's behalf, this case was cited as a landmark moment in securing rights and privileges for same-sex partners, the encounter was often described as queerly heterosexual. Knoller and Noel suggested at various points that Bane did not intend to attack, but was, rather, attracted to Diane Whipple and approached her as a dominant male inspecting a creature of the opposite sex. Sensationalist media reports, including Jones's, allude to evidence of bestiality between Knoller and Bane, and they allege personal correspondence describing a mythical incestuous sexual union among Noel, Knoller, and Schneider, with Bane standing in as substitute or symbol of the absent son, Schneider. The sexualization of the relationship between Bane and Knoller was cited—and then dismissed—as potential cause of Bane's aberrant behavior, while the alleged noninvolvement of Hera in the attack was also used to buttress the heterosexual reading.

Indeed, in accounts and illustrations of Presas engaged in the work of protection and guardianship, a (genetically enhanced) heteronormative masculinity is precisely what seems to be at stake. The Presa (male) is enlisted to protect women (and, as other accounts demonstrate, children) against the competing predations of strange men. Presa Web sites often display puppies surrounded by children (to illustrate their docile nature) on the one hand, and adults attacking padded men during *Schutzhund* (protection dog) training, on the other, while anecdotal accounts often turn on the seeming contradiction—reminiscent of travelers' accounts of the character of cynocephalic cannibals and saints and for which the Presa, among dog breeds, is known—between a protective, gentle, "human-like" intelligence and temperament and a ferocity toward hostile strangers (Eubanks). Sanders Kennel displays the sheer power of the (male) Presa by visually staging him in a gym, wearing a spiked leather collar and faux-dominated by an equally muscular, but very slender, Asian woman in army fatigues and ersatz combat boots; or held at leash's length and companionably seated next to an African American male bodybuilder or heavyweight lifter. He—for this Presa is of course a male—is the ideologically compensatory fetish. Freud makes the point that fetishism, the sexual valorization of a metonymic substitute for the mother's (always already) absent penis, acts as a memorial to the horror of castration, wards it off, and "saves the fetishist from being a homosexual by endowing women with the attribute which makes them acceptable as sexual objects" (206). In these photographs, the fetish is doubled: the human bodies of color already phantasmatically assume the cultural significance of embodied plenitude, even as, simultaneously, the dog prosthetically restores potency, that is, stands in—and compensates—for the symbolic castration to which those bodies are subject (see Eng). If the phantasmatic figural relations that reinscribe ontological mergings between human and dog (and that conjure the ghost of the cynanthrope) suggest both sexual and racial/tribal homosociality, Sanders Kennel offers some clues to the disavowals at work in the heterosexualization of the Presa's participation in human kinship arrangements. It suggests that the dog's masculinity, though metaphorically heterosexual perhaps, metonymically works as identification—a site of narcissistic investment.

That this fetishistic relation is linked to bodies of color on the Web site reiterates the ideological and historical affinity of dogs and dogmen in the multiple colonial encounters that haunt their ontological conjoining, effected here through the (metonymically) related metaphors of species and race. It is precisely that juxtaposition that also hints at another dimension of the disavowals in this case: the spectral appearance of the "myth of the black rapist" at the scene of the murder, uncannily accented by the ultrawhiteness of the photographs of Whipple (and the ultrablackness of Bane) that circulated in the press.[30]

On the one hand, then, there is an effort to renormativize a queer cross-species encounter through the heterosexual matrix, a matrix that, in this case, disregards species difference insofar as it signifies anything other than primitive masculinity. But to inscribe the encounter with human (hetero)sexual meaning also conjures spectral—specular and spectacular—histories of racialized power in the United States. Both transform the human-dog encounter into a potent and condensed figure of (human) sexual and racial conflict distributed across multiple cultural institutions or "state apparatuses," from the legal system, to the prison system, to the populist imagination represented by the media (see Althusser).

CODA

The figure of the cynanthrope has, in this tale, been domesticated, insofar as its hybrid and borderland ferocity—its queer pre- and postcolonial travels—becomes relegated to archaic, even mythic, genealogies of (white) primitivism, while its current-day racialization is timelessly fetishized in a present of meaning, but a present that, like the fetish, is haunted by history. In the epilogue to his book, Bretches, whose analysis of the legal case is a fascinating, if paranoid, view of San Francisco insider politics, makes a shocking remark: "And if all this wasn't poetic enough, Grin! Sharon Smith went ahead and took her cut of the two and a half million she cheated the apartment building owner out of. And got her and her newest 'life mate' pregnant! They stole my idea to use the law suit money to breed dogs!" (221). In some sense, Bretches succeeds: sales of Presa Canarios rose spectacularly in the United States after this event. But I also hear in these lines another postcolonial hybrid's wish, one whose name carries our story in it, too: "O ho, O ho! Wouldt had been done! Thou didst prevent me; I had peopled else this isle with Calibans" (Shakespeare 1.2, 349–51).

The haunted agencies and subjectivities that (finally) collided in the Diane Whipple case are not available to me—however much I might wish to understand them—and such access, were it possible, would not offer up truth, even if the native informants were to speak language for purposes other than to curse. This figural historiography is comparatively queer relative to any progressive, ameliorative rational accounts of historical process, and it reveals the pre- and posthumanist queerness at the heart of some of our affective and spectral histories. Those histories have a force and they have effects, however unrationalizable those effects may be. The rationalist disavowals of liberal humanism relative to cynanthropic becoming or anthrocynic being cannot wholly efface or evade the spectral knowledges they yield. If we are indeed partners in a crime of evolution, as Haraway insists, it remains for the living—caught between ontological autism and merger—to figure out how to survive this uncertainty.

NOTES

1. The phrase is from the title of Riley's book.
2. For carnivorous virility, see Derrida, "Eating Well."
3. In "Difference with a Difference," Seth discusses the ontological privileging of the human subject and some of its consequences for modernity (78).
4. "Through a process that Brian Hare and colleagues (2002) call 'phylogenetic enculturation,' dogs have penetrated human social worlds to such an extent that they exceed even chimpanzees in understanding human communication. Becoming 'human' in the right ways is central to surviving as a dog in Ávila . . ." (Kohn 9). For an application of Deleuze and Guattari's "becoming-animal" to Creole aesthetics—specifically in relation to human-dog becomings—in Francophone Caribbean literature, see Boisseron.
5. See Lestringant 43–55; Hulme, especially chap. 2; White 63–64.
6. See Lestringant 43–55.
7. See Woods.
8. Las Casas discusses Columbus's changing of the way he signs his surname to reflect his "mission" of bringing Christianity to the New World in *History of the Indies*: "This is why he was called Cristobal, which is to say Christum Ferens, which means the bearer of Christ" (28). Ferdinand Colón, in *The Life of the Admiral Christopher Columbus*, interprets Columbus's signature similarly and brings in St. Christopher: "And if we give his name its Latin form, which his Christophorus Colonus, we may say that just as St. Christopher is reported to have gotten that name because he carried Christ over deep waters with great danger to himself, and just as he conveyed over people whom no other could have carried, so the Admiral Christophorus Colonus, asking Christ's aid and protection in that perilous pass, crossed over with his company that the Indian nations might become dwellers in the triumphant Church of Heaven" (8).
9. See "Kaupe"; Armitage and Judd 69–70.
10. For the woodcuts, see Bry 86; Lestringant 108–9, 178–79; Léry 86, 339, 367; Thevet.
11. *Gargantua and Pantagruel*, book 2, chap. 14, 213–18; chaps. 21–22, 242–44.
12. As White puts it, "behind the bathos of Bartos, however, is a piece of ecclesiastical propaganda that depicts not only the triumph of Christianity over a backwater of the universe, but also the neat use of one monstrous or barbarian convert to destroy other barbarians" (198).
13. "Displaced abjection" is Dollimore's term (54).

14. See also White: "Just as the dog dwells on the boundary between domestication and savagery, so foreign or barbarian races have inhabited a space, in the human imagination, between the exotic and therefore fascinating, and the horrifying: animal freedom is as fascinating as animal savagery is terrifying, and the ethne of ancient and medieval mythology, geography, and historiography were as much animal races as they were human" (15).

15. See Fernández-Armesto.

16. See Anderson.

17. See *Sanders Kennels*; *Dogo Canario Club*.

18. Ibid. and "Fédération Cynologique."

19. Numerous documents of New World conquest refer to the dogs used by the conquerors as "mastiffs" and "greyhounds" (Las Casas, *Devastation*; Varner and Varner; Schwartz).

20. The translator, Bethencourt, is a descendant of Juan de Bethencourt, one of the Norman nobles who first "explored" the Canary Islands. See also *Irema Curtó Kennels*.

21. See also Freccero, "Fetishism." This is the way Mannoni describes the mechanism of disavowal at work in Freud's notion of fetishism, in a phrase uttered by one of his patients. In Freud, fetishism is a split knowledge: on the one hand, the man (boy) recognizes that his mother does not have a penis; on the other, he supplies a penis substitute for the one that is not (never has been) there. See also Lévi-Strauss's discussion of nature and culture (3–13), and Derrida's critique of the distinction in "Structure, Sign, and Play."

22. "The original *coup de force* is in the assignation of the roles by which a dissymmetry is instituted between that which becomes the agent and that which becomes the thing of the agent. *Man is the giver, woman is the gift. Man is the exchanger, woman is the exchanged.* Such is the principle of this archi-economy which is the basis for all economies (*oikos*: the household). The position of the exchanging subject, in opposition to the objects of the exchange (which are themselves people), marks a place, a function, which is not that of the 'subject' whose aporias transcendental philosophy explores, but which may involve the essence of the subject's symbolic site . . . Here we approach the originally sexed archi-exchange from which the exchange in general, including the economic one, can be conceived" (Goux 65).

23. Derrida's interview on the question of the subject in (post)modernity, "Eating Well," argues that the philosophical schema of Western subjectivity is founded on a sacrificial structure, whereby the subject consumes and gives himself to be consumed; he calls this carno-phallogocentrism. My argument is that this structure is a schema in disavowal. Goux discusses the sacrificial transition from penis (fleshly embodiment) to phallus (symbolic masculine power).

24. See Lévi-Strauss: "To this very day, mankind has always dreamed of seizing and fixing that fleeting moment when it was permissible to believe that the law of exchange could be evaded, that one could gain without losing, enjoy

without sharing . . . removing to an equally unattainable past or future the joys, eternally denied to social man, of a world in which one might keep to oneself" (496–97).

25. For a comparison between second-degree murder and involuntary manslaughter in the case, see Van Derbeken.

26. See Terhune; Davis and Shaylor; Davis, *Are Prisons Obsolete?*; Wright.

27. *Celtic Reign*; see also "Aryan Brotherhood."

28. See Agamben; Butler, *Precarious Life*. Wright notes that "inmates are kept inside their cells for twenty-two and a half hours a day. During the ninety minutes in which inmates are allowed 'outside,' each man is transferred to a larger concrete box called the 'dog run.' The dog run is an eleven-by-twenty-six-foot cell with a drain in the center and a small opening eighteen feet above their heads" (45).

29. See Butler's *Bodies That Matter* on the issue of what constitutes conditions of intelligibility. See also Scarry; and, for a description of the reduction of body to flesh under conditions of torture and slavery, Spillers.

30. For photographs of Whipple and Bane, see Van Derbeken and Hatfield; also "Multimedia Special." For myths of the black rapist see, among others, Davis, *Women, Race, and Class*; Hall; Omolade.

Works Cited

Agamben, Giorgio. *Homo Sacer: Sovereign Power and Bare Life.* Stanford: Stanford UP, 1998.

Althusser, Louis. "Ideology and Ideological State Apparatuses (Notes Toward an Investigation)." *Lenin and Philosophy, and Other Essays by Louis Althusser.* Ed. and trans. Ben Brewster. New York: Monthly Review, 1971. 127–86.

Anderson, J. K. *Hunting in the Ancient World.* Berkeley: U of California P, 1985.

Armitage, George T., and Henry P. Judd. *Ghost Dog and Other Hawaiian Legends.* Honolulu: Advertiser, 1944.

"Aryan Brotherhood: Prison Gang Profile." *Insideprison.com.* <http://www.insideprison.com/prison_gang_profile_AB.asp>. 21 May 2010.

Boisseron, Bénédicte. "A Creole Line of Escape: A Story of Becoming-Dog." *Contemporary French and Francophone Studies* 10.2 (2006): 205–16.

Bretches, Dale. *Dog O' War.* 2nd ed. Lincoln: iUniverse, 2005.

Bry, Theodor de. *Collection des grands et petits voyages.* London: Molins, Ltd., 1921.

Butler, Judith. *Bodies That Matter: On the Discursive Limits of "Sex."* New York: Routledge, 1993.

———. *Precarious Life: The Power of Mourning and Violence.* London: Verso, 2004.

Castro, Eduardo Viveiros de. "Cosmological Deixis and Amerindian Perspectivism." *Journal of the Royal Anthropological Institute* 4 (1998): 469–88.

Celtic Reign. <http://www.celticreign.com>. 21 May 2010.

Colón, Ferdinand. *The Life of the Admiral Christopher Columbus*. Trans. Benjamin Keen. New Brunswick: Rutgers UP, 1992.

Davis, Angela. *Are Prisons Obsolete?* New York: Seven Stories, 2003.

———. *Women, Race, and Class*. New York: Vintage, 1983.

Davis, Angela, and Cassandra Shaylor. "A Question of Control." *San Francisco Chronicle* 9 Apr. 2000: SC-1.

Deleuze, Gilles, and Félix Guattari. "1730: Becoming-Intense, Becoming-Animal, Becoming-Imperceptible." *A Thousand Plateaus: Capitalism and Schizophrenia*. Trans. Brian Massumi. Minneapolis: U of Minnesota P, 1987. 232–309.

De Man, Paul. 1971. *Blindness and Insight: Essays in the Rhetoric of Contemporary Criticism*. Minneapolis: U of Minnesota P, 1983.

Derrida, Jacques. "'Eating Well' or the Calculation of the Subject." *Points: Interviews 1974–1994*. Ed. Elisabeth Weber. Stanford: Stanford UP, 1992. 255–87.

———. "Structure, Sign, and Play in the Discourses of the Human Sciences." *Writing and Difference*. Trans. Alan Bass. Chicago: U of Chicago P, 1978. 278–93.

Dogo Canario Club of America, Inc. <http://www.dogocanarioclub.org>. 21 May 2010.

Dollimore, Jonathan. *Sexual Dissidence: Augustine to Wilde, Freud to Foucault*. Oxford: Clarendon, 1991.

Dunn, Oliver, and James E. Kelley, Jr., eds. and trans. *The Diario of Christopher Columbus's First Voyage to America 1492–1493*. Norman: U of Oklahoma P, 1989.

Edelman, Lee. *No Future: Queer Theory and the Death Drive*. Durham: Duke UP, 2004.

Eng, David. *Racial Castration*. Durham: Duke UP, 2001.

Eubanks, Jeanne. "Uey's Homeraised Puppies, 'Quips & Quotes.'" *The Gripper: The Official Publication of the United Perro de Presa Canario Club* 33 (2004). <http://www.uppcc.net/gripper>. 21 May 2010.

"Fédération Cynologique Internationale." <http://www.fci.be/>. 21 May 2010.

Fernández-Armesto, Felipe. *The Canary Islands after the Conquest: The Making of a Colonial Society in the Early-Sixteenth Century*. Oxford: Oxford UP, 1982.

Freccero, Carla. "Cannibalism, Homophobia, Women: Montaigne's 'Des Cannibales' and 'De L'Amitié.'" *Women, "Race," and Writing in the Early Modern Period*. Ed. Margo Hendricks and Patricia Parker. London: Routledge, 1994. 73–83.

———. "Fetishism." *New Dictionary of the History of Ideas* 2 (2005): 826–28.

Freud, Sigmund. "Fetishism (1927)." *Sexuality and the Psychology of Love*. Ed. Philip Rieff. New York: Collier, 1963. 204–9.

Garber, Marjorie. "Heavy Petting." *Human, All Too Human*. Ed. Diana Fuss. New York: Routledge, 1996. 11–36.

Goldberg, Jonathan. *Sodometries: Renaissance Texts, Modern Sexualities*. Stanford: Stanford UP, 1992.

Goux, Jean-Joseph. "The Phallus: Masculine Identity and the 'Exchange of Women.'" *differences* 4.1 (1992): 40–75.

Hall, Jacquelyn Dowd. "'The Mind That Burns in Each Body': Women, Rape, and Racial Violence." *Powers of Desire: The Politics of Sexuality.* Ed. Ann Snitow, Christine Stansell, and Sharon Thompson. New York: Monthly Review, 1983. 328–49.

Haraway, Donna. *The Companion Species Manifesto: Dogs, People, and Significant Otherness.* Chicago: Prickly Paradigm, 2003.

Hulme, Peter. *Colonial Encounters: Europe and the Native Caribbean 1492–1797.* London: Routledge, 1986.

Irema Curtó Kennels. <http://www.iremacurto.com>. 21 May 2010.

Jones, Aphrodite. *Red Zone: The Behind-the-Scenes Story of the San Francisco Dog Mauling.* New York: Avon, 2003.

"Kaupe: The Cannibal Dog Man." *Native Hawaii.* <http://www.nativehawaii .com/legends/dog_man.php>. 21 May 2010.

Kohn, Eduardo. "How Dogs Dream: Amazonian Natures and the Politics of Transspecies Engagement." *American Ethnologist* 34.1 (2007): 3–24.

Las Casas, Bartolomé de. *History of the Indies.* Trans. Andrée Collard. New York: Harper and Row, 1971.

————. *The Devastation of the Indies: A Brief Account.* Trans. Herma Briffault. Baltimore: The Johns Hopkins UP, 1992.

Leighton, Robert. *The New Book of the Dog.* London: Cassell, 1916.

Léry, Jean de. *History of a Voyage to the Land of Brazil.* Ed. and trans. Janet Whatley. Berkeley: U of California P, 1990.

Lestringant, Frank. *Le cannibale: Grandeur et décadence.* Paris: Perrin, 1994.

Lévi-Strauss, Claude. *Elementary Structures of Kinship.* Trans. James Harle Bell, John Richard von Sturmer, and Rodney Needham. Boston: Beacon, 1969.

Mandeville, Sir John. *The Travels of Sir John Mandeville.* Ed. and trans. C. W. R. D. Moseley. London: Penguin, 1983.

Mannoni, Octave. *Clefs pour l'imaginaire; ou, L'autre scène.* Paris: Seuil, 1985.

Menache, Sophia. "Dogs: God's Worst Enemies?" *Society and Animals* 5.1 (1997): 23–44.

Millan, Cesar, with Melissa Jo Peltier. *Cesar's Way: The Natural, Everyday Guide to Understanding and Correcting Common Dog Problems.* New York: Harmony, 2006.

Montaigne, Michel de. "Of Cannibals." *The Complete Essays of Montaigne.* Trans. Donald Frame. Stanford: Stanford UP, 1957. Repr. 1965. 150–59.

"Multimedia Special: The Whipple Case." *SFGate.com.* <http://www.sfgate.com/ cgi-bin/article.cgi?f=/g/a/2002/03/22/dogmaulgallery.DTL>. 21 May 2010.

Omolade, Barbara. "Hearts of Darkness." *Powers of Desire: The Politics of Sexuality.* Ed. Ann Snitow, Christine Stansell, and Sharon Thompson. New York: Monthly Review, 1983. 350–67.

Oxford English Dictionary. <http://www.oed.com>. 20 July 2008.

Pliny the Elder. *The Natural History.* Trans. H. Rackham. Cambridge: Harvard UP, 1967.

Polo, Marco. *The Travels of Marco Polo.* Ed. and trans. Ronald Latham. London: Penguin, 1958.

Rabelais, François. *Gargantua and Pantagruel.* Trans. J. M. Cohen. London: Penguin, 1955.

———. *Œuvres complètes.* Paris: Seuil, 1973.

Riley, Denise. *Impersonal Passion: Language as Affect.* Durham: Duke UP, 2005.

"Saint Christopher." *Wikipedia.* <http://en.wikipedia.org/wiki/Saint _Christopher>. 1 July 2006.

Sanders Kennels. <http://www.sanderskennels.com>. 1 July 2006.

Schwartz, Marion. *A History of Dogs in the Early Americas.* New Haven: Yale UP, 1997.

Serpell, James. "From Paragon to Pariah: Some Reflections on Human Attitudes to Dogs." *The Domestic Dog.* Ed. James Serpell. Cambridge: Cambridge UP, 1995. 245–56.

Seth, Vanita. "Difference with a Difference: Wild Men, Gods, and Other Protagonists." *parallax* 9.4 (2003): 75–87.

Shakespeare, William. *The Tempest.* Ed. Robert Langbaum and Sylvia Barnett. New York: Signet Classics, 1964.

Spillers, Hortense. "Interstices: A Small Drama of Words." *Pleasure and Danger: Exploring Female Sexuality.* Ed. Carol S. Vance. Boston: Routledge and Kegan Paul, 1984. 73–100.

Terhune, C. A. "A Question of Control." *San Francisco Chronicle* 9 Apr. 2000: SC-1.

Thevet, André. *Les Singularitez de la France Antarctique.* Paris: Maurice de la Porte, au Clos Bruneau, a l'enseigne S. Claude, 1558.

Torres, Agustín Millares. *Historia general sobre las Islas Canarias.* Las Palmas de Gran Canaria: Cedirca, D. L., 1977.

Van Derbeken, Jaxon. "Why Jury Called It Murder: Negligence, Deception Cited in Mauling Trial." *San Francisco Chronicle* 22 Mar. 2002: A-1.

Van Derbeken, Jaxon, and Larry D. Hatfield. "Jailed Lawyers on Suicide Watch." *San Francisco Chronicle* 28 Mar. 2001. <http://sfgate.info/cgi-bin/article.cgi?f=/c/a/2001/03/28/dog.DTL>. 21 May 2010.

Varner, John G., and Jeannette J. Varner. *Dogs of the Conquest.* Norman: U of Oklahoma P, 1983.

Vincent of Beauvais. *Speculum Naturale.* Nuremberg: Anton Koberger, 1486.

White, David Gordon. *Myths of the Dog-Man.* Chicago: U of Chicago P, 1991.

Wittkower, Rudolf. "Marvels of the East: A Study in the History of Monsters." *Journal of the Warburg and Courtauld Institutes* 5 (1942): 159–97.

Woods, David. "The Origin of the Cult of St. Christopher." <http://www.ucc.ie/milmart/chrsorig.html>. 1 July 2006.

Wright, Evan. "Mad Dogs and Lawyers." *Rolling Stone* 28 Feb. 2002: 42–47, 68–69.

Žižek, Slavoj. *The Sublime Object of Ideology.* London: Verso, 1989.

CHAPTER 3

MAPPING SAPPHIC MODERNITY

SUSAN S. LANSER

> Men I say may live without women, but women cannot live without men.
> —Joseph Swetnam, *The Araignment of Lewd, Idle,*
> *Froward, and Unconstant Women,* 1615

> After 1600, things were different.
> —Fernand Braudel, *The Wheels of Commerce,* 1979

IN 1566, THE GENEVA PUBLISHING SCION HENRI II ESTIENNE printed a scathing attack on modern morals known as the *Apologie pour Hérodote*. To crown his chapter "On the Sin of Sodomy, and the Sin Against Nature in Our Time," Estienne offers this "amazingly strange" tale:

> A girl from Fontaines, which is between Blois and Romorantin, having disguised herself as a man, served as a stable groom for about seven years at an inn on the outskirts of Foye, then married a girl from there, with whom she lived for about two years while working as a wine-grower. At this point, the wickedness she used in order to simulate a husband's role was discovered, she was seized and, after confessing, was burned alive. This is how our century can boast that beyond all the wickednesses of the preceding ones, it has some that are specific and peculiar to itself. For this act has nothing in common with those of the sordid ones who were called "tribades" in ancient times. (110; my translation)

This passage makes one ordinary girl's act of dressing as a man and marrying a woman tantamount to the sexual crime of the century. While he dates male sodomy back to the ancients and forward to the Pope,

Estienne chooses the marriage of two lowborn girls to represent the specific evils of modernity. Estienne's separation of the Greek tribades from his modern paysannes is all the more significant in that this text stands as the first known use of "tribade," or of any noun alluding to erotic intimacy between women, in a European vernacular. By negating the very signifier that he inaugurates, Estienne ushers female homoeroticism into print culture by dividing the two women from the only word by which they can be evoked. Moreover, Estienne introduces female homoeroticism not simply as a practice that needs to be condemned but as a story that must—and yet cannot—be told. For even as Estienne provides seemingly gratuitous details about time, place, and occupation that establish the here-and-now quality of the woman's gender transgression, the details of sexual "wickedness" remain unnamed. This brief passage thus reveals a categorical paralysis about how to explain, define, and describe what the story also purports to recount. In this way, two unnamed girls in an unnamed relationship also enter textual history as a conundrum that modernity will have to figure out.

This use of female same-sex desire to herald a new age occurs likewise in one of the first vernacular love poems from a woman to a woman printed under a man's signature, the "Dame enamourée d'une autre Dame" published in 1573 by French cleric, poet, and philosopher Pontus de Tyard. Tyard's unnamed speaker also recognizes her problem as specifically modern: because today's men lack honor, Love has "laced a knot never before seen" between the speaker and "another woman." The lady in love had hoped not only for her own happy union but also for a revision of history, providing "eternal proof that love between women could win out over centuries of male-male and male-female bonds."[1] Had this love been requited, the "dame" and her "aimée" would displace a lineage of such ancient pairings as Damon and Pythias, Aeneas and Achates, Hercules and Nestor, Cherephon and Socrates, along with male-female couples the speaker claims are too numerous to name. Here again, love between women is specifically French and specifically modern, a phenomenon whose time has come. While Estienne's girl commits the crime of the century, then, Tyard's lady promotes the love of the century; in both instances a French writer presents intimacy between females as a sign of the times. Indeed, Tyard's poem foregrounds its own need to tell by underscoring the fact that nothing happens between the two women; the story narrates what did not occur. Both writers thus instantiate a story of sapphic modernity that they immediate disallow (Tyard) or disavow (Estienne). Across the vastly different class settings, genres, and attitudes of these two texts, a cultural recognition emerges that some women might choose to forge relationships with one another.

Why might both a Protestant printer living in Geneva and a Catholic priest connected to the French court consider erotic relations between women not just modern but the very *signifier* of modernity? While biographical probing might uncover reasons for Estienne's and Tyard's particular choices, my interest here lies in reading Estienne and Tyard themselves as signs of the times. For what Estienne and Tyard proclaimed to be modern about women was actually modern about themselves: what was new was not so much a sexual formation as the recognition that a new sexual formation might intervene in history. What is also modern about Estienne and Tyard is the very distinction between antiquity and modernity that anchors their attention to female same-sex desire.

In recognizing what I will call "sapphic modernity," Estienne and Tyard were far from alone: the late sixteenth century inaugurated a burst of public attention to female homoeroticism that quickly became a French fashion and almost as quickly a broader one. In 1565 Jean Tahureau's *Dialogues* had already mocked women who loved "à la tribadique" and Jean Papon had written up a lesbian legal case. Within a decade Juan Huarte de San Juan and Ambroise Paré would describe women who allegedly "turned into men" and married women; bawdy verse about tribades would turn up in Spain; and love poems like Tyard's would appear in writings by Jean-Antoine Baïf, Estienne Jodelle, Pierre de l'Estoile, and Pierre Ronsard, often following Estienne and Tyard in positing love between women as something "strange and new" (for l'Estoile; III, 185) that will top all the loves of antiquity (for Ronsard's speaker). Long designated the *mutum peccatum*, the silent sin, sapphic sexuality becomes the focus of new discursive practices, so that transgressions seemingly by women are also, or perhaps only, the transgressions of the men who have dared to name the previously unnamed behaviors.

As a rich scholarship now testifies and as my examples below will illustrate,[2] by 1600 erotic desires, acts, and affiliations between women had already become a notable presence in the print cultures of several European languages as European poets, playwrights, physicians, scholars, scandalmongers, and travelers placed homoerotic female desires and relations before the public eye. And although a substantial body of sapphic representation will accrue over the next two centuries, the fiction that relations between women were new in form or effect if not in substance persists into the late eighteenth century.

This connection between the modern and the sapphic is no accident. In the larger project from which my chapter in this collection derives, I argue that this story of female-female desire that modernity keeps repeating is in a real sense the story of modernity itself. Across the long period of reform, revision, revolution, and reaction that is bounded by Dutch revolts in the 1560s and French revolts in the 1830s, what I call "sapphic subjects"—the multivalent term I use to describe representations of erotically inflected desires, behaviors, and affiliations between women—became a flash point for epistemic upheavals that threatened to change if not collapse the order of things. Imbued with powers and dangers that far exceeded any real challenge, indeed arguably deriving their efficacy from this very gap, sapphic subjects function as both cause and effect of a cataclysmic shift into (an always incoherent) modern order, a slate upon which modernity wrote and rewrote itself. As gay marriage today has become a charged site for concerns vaster than gays or marriage—serving variously as a stand-in, a synecdoche, or a side step—so in an earlier period intimacies between women became a site for engaging with fundamental shifts in social structures and beliefs. Sapphic subjects became linked to contests over nature and power, liberty and authority, desire and duty, human nature and human difference, and social order and social mobility: challenges to the predictable workings of the social universe that philosophical and social modernity entailed.

My discussion here focuses on the period around 1600 to ask how, where, and speculatively why certain cultures recognized—or forged—an imbrication between the sapphic and the modern and to consider the larger purposes this conjunction may have served. Asking why some locations seem to be comparatively queerer than others, I will argue that sapphic subjects draw their greatest attention in particular countries and cities and thus map differently—or not at all—on different European terrains because they confront us not only with the history of sexuality but also with history tout court. In making such a claim, I seek as well to flip the scholarly coin from the *history of sexuality* to the *sexuality of history*: from the premise that sexuality is historically constructed to the claim that history is also sexually constructed and that the large movements of societies and cultures can be read as and through sexuality.

On 18 March 1600, according to the (probably inaccurate) dating in her putative memoir, a 15-year-old Basque convent girl named Catalina de Erauso allegedly let herself out of the cloister, took scissors to her clothing, turned herself into a boy, and embarked upon a bloody colonial career in the Spanish Americas, wooing women who fancied her or whose dowries she may have coveted, until a near-fatal duel prompted her to confess her sins and her sex. With papal permission to continue in men's clothes, she returned to Europe a celebrity, wrote or dictated her memoir, was celebrated in a play, and lives on in legendry (see Pancrazio).

On 4 August 1600, William Shakespeare's acting troupe registered *As You Like It*, the first of Shakespeare's comedies to play centrally with female same-sex desire, though by no means the first instance of female homoeroticism on the English stage. John Lyly's *Gallathea* (1588/1592) had blatantly recreated the Ovidian tale of Iphis and Ianthe that Shakespeare would recast as *Twelfth Night* in 1602. By 1600, the Spanish stage had also established the convention of the *mujer varonil* who attracts other women, in a pattern that pervades the theatre of Calderon, Cubo, Cubillo, and especially Lope de Vega despite legal and ecclesiastical efforts to prohibit it.

In 1600, sections of Brantôme's gossipy *Recueil des dames*, begun in 1582, may already have been circulating among his friends at court. While harking back to classical examples in Lucian, Martial, and Juvenal, Brantôme emphasizes a here and now in which "Lesbians" are ubiquitous and imagines a lively sapphic subculture at the highest levels of French society.

In 1600 there appeared an English translation of Leo Africanus's *Descrittione dell'Africa* (1550). In what is arguably the first geographical and cultural study of Africa, Africanus (Al-Hassan ibn-Muhammad al-Fazi) describes a group of Moroccan "women-witches" with "a damnable custome to commit vnlawfull Venerie among themselues." Local wives, it turns out, are likewise "allured with the delight of this abominable vice" and are said to feign illness so that they might return to the witches for a "cure" (148–49).

In 1600 André du Laurens's *Historia anatomica humani corporis*, already in its second printing, was making its way across the European continent. Its "anatomical history" of the human body followed the example of Ambroise Paré in linking sexual orientation to the size of the clitoris, which "grows so excessively in some women that it hangs out of the opening like a man's penis, and such women play with each other and are, for that reason, called tribades and fricatrices" (223). Contemporary anatomists also speculated that women could "turn into" men after making love with other women or even before birth; Huarte de San Juan, for example, argues that excessive heat or cold children even create queer boys and girls in utero.

In the decade before 1600, the Spanish poet Fray Melchor de la Serna produced his ribald *El sueño de la viuda*, in which a widow who sleeps each night between two servants, Teodora and Medulina, finds herself directed in a dream to mount her husband, mistakes Teodora for the dead spouse, and begins making love to the sleeping maid, who then miraculously sprouts a penis. But the "manly" Teodora's affections have been fastened on the more "feminine" Medulina, and in a class-inflected triangle the two maids trick the widow to believe that Teodora's organ has disappeared, though in fact Teodora retains her penis and even impregnates Medulina.

Dutch trial records claim that Maeijken Joosten, wife and mother of four, began within a few years of 1600 to court a young woman named Bertelmina Wale. Joosten apparently convinced Bertelmina "that she was really a man, extracted a promise of marriage from her and got her into bed" (Dekker and van de Pol 59). "Abraham" Joosten and Bertelmina were married in Leiden on 8 March 1606, but in October of that year, Joosten was tried and sent into exile in what appears to be the first prosecution of a "female husband" in the Netherlands, though not in Europe as a whole (see Crompton; Robson).[3]

Between 1597 and 1601, John Donne composed his startlingly frank "Sapho to Philaenis," which renders love between women not as heterosexual imitation but, on the contrary, as an idyllic similitude between two bodies that explicitly excludes penetration. Donne's plaintive poem circulated during his lifetime in at least nineteen manuscripts and appears in the 1633 first edition of his collected poems, but its import, and even the fact of its existence, has confounded scholars from his generation to our own.

In 1601 the word "tribade" entered printed English through a poem in which Ben Jonson, in order to insist upon his "owne true Fire" of inspiration, rejects one classical muse after another, including the "Mankind Maide" Athena, while describing the three graces as a "Tribade Trine" (Chester 181). Jonson again used "tribade lust" to attack rival poet Cecilia Bulstrode for "forc[ing] a muse," effectively turning "tribade" into a misogynist metaphor.

What, beyond the happenstance of centennial dating, connects the confessions of a cross-dressing Basque adventurer, homoerotic play on the English and Spanish stage, court gossip about "Lesbians," the labeling of Moroccan diviners as Fricatrices, medical treatises linking sexuality to the size of genitalia, a Spanish burlesque about a widow and her maid, the trial of a Dutch woman for same-sex marriage, female-to-female love poems by male poets, and the first uses of "tribade" as a metaphor? I gather these examples to map a wider and deeper body of representations that rehearse—and sometimes compulsively repeat—scenarios variously alluring, analytic, and anxious implicating female-female desire as a modern phenomenon. Reaching around 1600 what sociologists might call a "tipping point," these discourses elaborate, across obvious generic differences, a logic that might explain how, to recall my first epigraph, women *can* be imagined to "live without men." In recognizing that desire might propel individuals to transgress centuries-old understandings of woman's very purpose, representations of female homoeroticism threaten to unmoor not only a gender order but also the larger economies with which that order is intertwined.

Despite an ever-increasing body of research, scholars have not yet demonstrated any clear chains of influence that might account for the new plenitude of sapphic discourse in many European settings or for its absence in others. There is scant evidence of influence across, or even within, different domains of inquiry. It is precisely this absence of manifest influence that I find significant, all the more as influence might have produced a more coherent surface of representation than do these diverse texts. My exploration therefore works through a logic not of influence but of confluence. Rather than implying causal relationships from text to text, confluence suggests a relatively simultaneous eruption of practices that, rather like symptoms of a systemic illness, are plausibly understood as manifestations of a deeper cause. Without discounting the role of the biographical or the local, I am arguing that broader forces underlie the eruption around 1600 of sapphic tropes.

We will not find the explanation for intensified interested in the sapphic in a simple story of opprobrium intensified. While Louis Crompton is right to demolish a myth of "lesbian impunity," positive representations of the homoerotic also need to be reckoned with, and not by claiming that what was not condemned must have been understood as "platonic" in its time. Early modern sapphic representations display a wide range of attitudes from prohibition to equivocal allegation, from burlesque to titillation, from neutral explanation to celebration, all of which are already represented in the examples above.

Indeed, the proliferation of both generic forms and textual attitudes suggests that, around 1600, the sapphic is a conundrum to be investigated rather than simply a practice to be condemned, for sapphic subjects confront the culture with a desire that cannot be rationalized according to an existing logic. Given a legal, religious, and social codes by which women, to evoke Aquinas, "should not have been made in the first order of things" (II, 265) except to be wives and bearers of children and in which, by the laws of coverture, woman + man = man, female-female alliances disrupt the most basic assumptions about why women exist. Small wonder, then, that the idea of a primary sapphic affinity would be epistemically confusing, a phenomenon that helps to explain the repeated assertions that the sapphic is either new or impossible. Alexander Niccholes's *Discourse of Marriage and Wiving* (1615), like Swetnam's injunction of the same year, raises the latter possibility by purporting to dismiss it when the speaker offers his sexual services to a wife whose husband is absent:

> And you, but with your Maide, left all alone.
> Where, least sad Care, or Melancholy, grieve you,
> My best endeavour's ready to relieve you.
> What Female Comfort can one woman finde,
> Within the bed with other woman-kinde? (36)

The very mention that women might find "Comfort" with "other woman-kinde" suggests a loosening of the sign "woman" from the sign "man," a rupture so radical that, as we will see, sapphic writings usually attempt to repair the very problem that they are producing. Indeed, in their efforts to make sense of the culturally nonsensical and reinstate the excluded (male) term, early modern sapphic representations reveal a pervasive practice of turning discourses about sex between *women* to discourses about women's similarity *to* or difference *from* men, their (in)ability to enjoy sex *without* men, and their imitations *of* men and attempts to pass *as* men. Brantôme's *Recueil*, for example, reveals a startling prominence of such language, which is present in most of the representations I have discussed, even when, like "Sapho to Philaenis," they claim to construct a desire that explicitly excludes men.

This epistemic confusion helps to explain why, beneath the wide range of genres and attitudes described previously, we find an insistent logic of *narrative*. Virtually all the examples I have offered, even those that seem static, inscribe or embed a story. Story can be found not only in Henri Estienne's obviously narrative account of a female husband, for example, but also in Pontus de Tyard's poem of spurned love; indeed, Tyard's poem embeds *two* narrative sequences, the failed suit of the speaker and the lineage of love in which the speaker hopes to intervene. Catalina de Erauso's memoir, itself a narrative, also incorporates subsidiary stories about her flirtations with women and her escapes from pressures to marry them. *As You Like It* and *Twelfth Night* show how love between women gets righted as men turn up to replace the women with whom other women are in love. The medical accounts offer narratives about girls who become boys after having sex with other girls, while the legal stories explain how a particular woman came to marry a woman or describe the sequence that led to her arrest. Donne's "Sapho to Philaenis" embeds both a courtship plot in which Sappho begs Philaenis to choose her rather than a man with his "rough tillage" and an erotic narrative fantasy; Serna's widow's dream is a wholly narrative account of sexual triangulation; Brantôme's chapter on "*donne con donne*" is a pastiche of narrated anecdotes about who did what with whom; and even Jonson's "*Tribade* Trine" embeds a narrative injunction: "Go . . . invent new sports." In this sense, it is fair to say that sapphic discourse in early modernity *is* story even when the discourse is also lyric poetry, medical treatise, or theatrical display.

Despite what is sometimes a recourse to the miraculous, which I will discuss later, these sapphic representations manifest a strong realist, here-and-now imperative. Like Henri Estienne's anecdote with which I opened, sapphic stories are concerned with the where and when, the who and how of same-sex relations. *Mobility* is a major trope: some settings evoke spaces of pastoral wandering; others evoke an exoticized or eroticized elsewhere. Frequently, sapphic subjects are located in "foreign" settings, usually settings marked with some cultural ambivalence, with particular countries and cities set up as carriers of sapphic sentiments to other European sites: Italy, represented as both a site of (high) culture and a zone of promiscuity; Venice as a commercial and cultural crossroads that is also teeming with every sort of foreigner; and Turkey as an imperial rival and a cultural elsewhere at Europe's edge. In this light, the attention to female homoeroticism in travel discourses and similar protoanthropological writings suggests a need for details that provide credibility for the (putatively) never-seen-before wonder that female homoeroticism represents around 1600: the new, unexpected, and unaccountable. The sapphic subject around 1600 is itself a kind of foreign country peopled by strange creatures of uncertain anatomy, morality, or psychology, often therefore figured *as* a foreign agent, but one that also affects or infects the home space and reveals its unexpected underside. Nathaniel Wanley's *Wonders of the Little World* (1673) will devote one of its chapters to 24 numbered accounts "Of such Persons as have changed their Sex," in all but one of which the sex change is from female to male and in many of which that change occurs in the wake of a homoerotic experience, thus presenting sex change as the solution to a desire perceived as anomalous but recognized through the accretion of examples as commonplace (51–54). As I will discuss later, this location of the sapphic as a kind of traveler's wonder may help to explain, or be explained by, the much greater presence of sapphic subjects in countries heavily committed to a colonial enterprise.

The need to make meaning from the "wonder" of sapphic desire seems to me to lie behind the pervasive narrative impulse in early modern sapphic representations. But there is a simpler explanation as well: the imperative of action intrinsic to all narrative also turns out to be intrinsic to the very conception of the sapphic in early modernity. Although several of the examples I have offered use words that designate sapphic persons—tribade, lesbian, fricatrice—there is little indication that these "persons" are more than the (potentially temporary) sum of their acts. Female homoeroticism is associated around 1600 with a spatiotemporal position rather than with a form of being; the "tribade" is the one who makes homoerotic behaviors a habitual practice or simply a practice for which she is known. When Brantôme talks about *donna con donna* as something women do or make (*faire*), he exposes this centrality of performance in constructing the sapphic subject; she is "made" through her actions, and in this sense she is also *self*-made. In the end, therefore, neither cross-dressing, an enlarged clitoris, nor any other characteristic can, of itself, make the sapphic subject; sexual performance grounds the term. It is worth recalling that when Estienne proclaims the "girl from Fontaines" to be modern, it is her behavior, not her "self," that he considers distinctive: "For this *act* has nothing in common with those of the sordid ones who were called *tribades* in ancient times" (110; emphasis added). In order to "make" sapphic representation, then, there must action, and so there must be narrative.

Many of these sapphic stories attempt to explain—or explain away—same-sex desire by locating it in the aberrant body, extending a confusion already evident in the classical sources from which many early modern discourses take their cue (see Brooten). Female homoeroticism thus often gets linked to clitoral hypertrophy, to hermaphroditism, to masculine characteristics such as height and strength, and to outright sex change from female to male. It is significant that the intense discursive energy expended to account for female-female desire by way of the body finds scant parallel in early modern representations of male same-sex desire; the tendency to equate all forms of sodomy and arguably all forms of sex with penetration has the queer consequence of normatizing sex between men while minoritizing sex between women. At stake is the crucial issue, implicitly under debate in early modern representations, of whether the sapphic can be restricted to a small minority of aberrant individuals or whether the possibility of same-sex orientation extends to women in general.

Most of the sapphic stories I have been describing falter at the level of causality but embrace change as a way of resolving same-sex desire. Typically, this logic of alteration turns woman + woman into woman + man. The most common resolution is the Ovidian intervention that turns a woman literally into a man through some means beyond human control. This Iphis-Ianthe scenario is present not only in obvious fictional reinscriptions such as Lyly's *Gallathea* but also in the medical accounts that describe women becoming men through the workings of an inexplicable natural process as well as in the many stories of women like Maeke Joosten who cross-dress, change their names, and are "reborn" as men. Such resolutions, it must be noted, do not explain same-sex desire, for the sex change invariably follows after that desire; indeed, in the case of *Gallathea*, it is declared irrelevant which of the two women will be changed into a man.

The widespread use of alteration plots suggests that it is not ultimately same-sex love but same-sex marriage that must be circumvented in these texts. This recognition implies a crucial disjunction between desire and institution, between the self and the social: the problem is not homoeroticism as such but the demand for its formal accommodation. In a deep sense, the acts of substitution that govern the cross-dressing scenarios of Lope and Shakespeare have a similar logic: the solution to the problem of love between women is an act of transformation or substitution whereby a woman is replaced by or revealed as a man.

It is worth pursuing the particular recourse to the miraculous in so many of these representations as symptomatic of a wider *mentalité*. *Gallathea*, *El sueño de la viuda*, and the medical stories of women becoming men all reveal the extent to which early modern Europe would rather imagine a miracle than acknowledge the seemingly more "natural" or (in Occam's sense) simpler, but far more epistemically confusing, prospect of affiliation between two fully female persons. In my examples we can find two divergent modes of this alteration plot: a comic mode, most prevalent in fictional representations, in which a woman who marries a woman is somehow in actuality marrying a man or potential man, and a tragic mode, most prevalent in legal accounts, in which a woman who marries a woman is punished with imprisonment, exile, or death.

The Ovidian scenario also resolves the tension emerging in early modernity between duty and desire. Given centuries of religious and civil injunctions that women shall be men's wives, female homoeroticism necessarily represents the ascendance of individual desire over social prescription. Around 1600, Reformation ideologies are, of course, attempting to wed the individual to the social by reimagining marriage as the product of desire. In 1560, for example, the Reformed Church of Scotland officially declared that when two young people's "hearts" are "joined," parents should not "resist" their children's preferences (MacCulloch). Sapphic writings imply that two *women's* "hearts" might be "joined," and indeed, a Scottish compilation known as the "Maitland Manuscript" that dates sometime before 1586 includes an unsigned poem, thought to be the work of a woman, Sara Maitland, that expresses the speaker's wish to seal her love for another woman with the "bond of Hymen" (see Farnsworth). The Ovidian sex change appears to restore fixity even though it is premised on an unsettling and scientifically vulnerable mutability. And if the change is either miraculous (through divine intervention) or biological (through nature's own doings), then no individual can be held accountable.

It is not surprising, then, that an irreducible intimacy between two ordinary women—women who are not in any metonymic or metaphoric sense men—is decidedly the least common resolution through which early modern Europe figures same-sex relations; the easy sliding of same-sex into sex change avoids the logic of relations between women *as* women. Such a move effectively takes the "same" out of "same-sex" relations. It is precisely in this resistance to the "same" in same-sex that I want to locate what seems to me the most dramatic epistemistic challenge that sapphic subjects pose for early modernity: no less than an overturning of the hierarchical order of things that is nicely figured in what later seventeenth-century writers will figure ribaldly as "the game of flats." That a stratified order governs premodern Europe is a commonplace; as the historian Anthony Upton puts it, the "ordered hierarchy of authority, often called the 'great chain of being,' . . . rested on divine right" and extended "to the patriarchal head of a household of family and servants, which was the basic building block of society." In this supposedly orderly system, everyone's duty is "to render unquestioning obedience to their divinely ordained superiors and impose it on those entrusted to their charge . . . Without this seamless system of subordination and discipline, no man would be able to travel the roads unrobbed, nobody could sleep secure in their beds at night" (16–17).

It is just this system that modernity challenges with a new horizontal view, a view we can find in claims that priests are not needed to intercede for the faithful; that governments should be legislative bodies formed through consent; that persons are equal by nature and should not be enslaved; that enterprising commoners have the right to seek wealth and power. It is around 1600 that we see the first uses of "level" as a figurative verb regarding human relationships, used to mean "to put on a level, equality, or par with," a concept that will soon turn political where "levelers" attempt to wrest control of governments. The extent to which gender grounds this system of "differences of position" is evident in the widespread figuration of leveling through images of sex-role reversal, so that leveling is actually reimagined as an "upside-down" world in which a wife rules over her husband. At a time when the horizontal is both frightening and attractive, sapphic subjects may carry the power to represent a particularly vivid inscription of leveling. In taking men out of a structure of relationships, they remove women from their place as well; evading the universal order of male rule, they operate from the bottom layer of the human chain; in sapphic systems, men are not there to rule and so there *is* no logic of rulership.

I want to press on the aptness of the sapphic to the horizontal—the "game of flats"—by naming the new way of thinking figured by female homoeroticism as nothing less than a *sapphic episteme*, which is to suggest that the boundaries of thought in early modernity meet their limit point in a world in which the logic of woman + woman might operate. Preoccupations with the horizontal and vertical may not be unrelated to the prevalence within sapphic discourse of images of rising, falling, and flattening, as well as with the ways in which class is implicated in sapphic representations (Lanser, "Befriending" and "Sapphic"). In a world in which human relations are "leveled," sapphic representations become substitutional acts that allow women to appropriate the subject positions heretofore designated masculine. Erauso can put on clothing that "makes" her a colonial middleman rather than a convent girl; Joosten can leave her place as wife and mother to woo another woman; Teodora can service and then outsmart her mistress; women can write poems of desire to other women. If women can displace or replace men, on what grounds can the hierarchical relationship between the sexes rest? This is surely a "crisis of category" with respect not only to gender but also to world order.

In this way, the plenitude and variety of sapphic representations suggests precisely what the individual examples usually attempt to dissolve or diminish: that the era when a transgressive woman can be written off as an exception is beginning to pass, in cultural imagination if not in historical practice. Moreover, the sapphic also reveals a cultural anxiety less about change itself than about change that shows a fissure between what seemed then and what is now. It is small wonder, then, that "tribade lust," to repeat Johnson's terms, might become a signifier of modernity, a site for all sorts of horizontal explorations: for imagining the implications of human differences in a colonial world or perhaps even for imagining full equality between men, as Janel Mueller suggests Donne might have been doing in "Sapho to Philaenis." Certainly the poem imagines the highest perfection of human harmony in sapphic symmetry, in a love born of "likeness" that is explicitly "brest to brest" and "thigh to thigh."

This "flat" image may indeed have been the most disturbing among all the disturbing possibilities that sapphic subjects raise. Since the association of the sapphic with the politically horizontal is more overt in some later representations, I leap a century here to two specific—respectively eutopic and dystopic—versions of this scenario. Nicholas Rowe's poem of 1701, "Song," titled "The Game at Flats" by 1715, vividly renders the sense of sapphism as leveling through recursion. Explicitly evoking (the Donnean?) Sappho and Philenis in a "harmonious," indeed celestial arrangement in which each partner embodies "the Joys of either Sex in Love" so that "Alternately the happy Pair / All grant, and All receive," Rowe represents the sapphic partnership as sufficient unto itself. Able to provide "to themselves alone . . . What all Mankind can give," they also mirror the order of nature as Rowe sees it, in which stars "set by Turns, and rise" to create a "happier Fate" of "kinder Care." Here the relationship of women lovers enacts the natural working of the universe at its most harmonious, as each woman is able to be both "fierce Youth" and "yielding Maid." Like "Sapho to Philaenis," Rowe's poem implies a mutuality that, to his ardently Whiggish soul, figures the sapphic as a kind of utopian "turn-taking."[4] It seems, then, that for Rowe the sapphic couple stands in for a new order of shared governance.

A less sanguine representation of leveling appears in the Jacobite Jane Barker's 1723 "The Unaccountable Wife" as part of her *Patch-Work Screen for the Ladies.* This more equivocal and ultimately dystopic narrative likewise shows how sapphic subjects work as fitting figures for a modern, horizontalized worldview. In Barker's tale, an unattractive "gentlewoman of distinction" marries a handsome gentleman who then takes the family's maidservant into his bed, begetting children by her every year. Wife, husband, and servant share the bed, but it is the wife who gets up each morning to light the fire and make the meals. Eventually the servant's fecundity alarms the husband, who wants to evict her, but he cannot persuade the wife to part with her. Meanwhile, the wife washes and scours while the servant sits about in her "handsome Velvet Chair, dress'd up in very good lac'd Linnen, having clean Gloves on her Hands" (99). Such an arrangement, sanctioned by the wife, "offended God, disgrac'd her Family, scandaliz'd her Neighbours, and was a Shame to Womankind" (100). But the wife insists that her servant is "the only Friend she had in the World" (101) and that if the servant is sent away she will follow.

Convinced that he can call her bluff, the husband dismisses the servant, and indeed the wife goes, too. The women end up in court as vagrants until a relative recognizes the wife and takes her in. Yet again the wife insists that she must remain with her "truest Friend." The husband dies, and relatives beg the widow to "leave that Creature" and return to a state "suitable to her Birth and Education." But "all in vain; she absolutely adher'd to this Woman and her Children," though she was reduced to begging in the streets (104). At last, word gets to the Queen of England, who says that she herself will take care of the wife if she abandons the servant. But this "infatuated Creature" goes so far as to refuse the Queen and remains a beggar for the rest of her days. The people insist that only some "Spell or Inchantment" could lead a gentlewoman to "oppose her Husband, and all her nearest Friends, and even her Sovereign" (105) to follow such "unaccountable" desires. Here, too, in other words, the recourse to the miraculous—the "Spell or Inchantment"—becomes the only feasible (if here more ironized) explanation.

This insistently recursive cleaving of one woman to another threatens to topple the entire social order, rendering ineffective the authority of *all* "divinely ordained superiors" from the mistress to the husband to the queen, as a woman's desire gives sovereignty to the female servant near the bottom of the human chain. It seems plausible that Barker would be both attracted to and repelled by the possibility of such leveling: she championed a woman's right to remain single and remained so herself but was also an ardent Jacobite who supported the deposed Stuart monarch. We see here the tensions between different sorts of leveling, tensions similarly evident when Barker's contemporary Mary Astell challenges a husband's right to rule his wife but defends as beyond question a queen's superiority to a footman.

Sapphic subjects are also clearly a potent site for inscribing the dilemmas of desire and order that preoccupied early modernity. At their extreme, sapphic representations posit the radical autonomy of Europe's largest subordinated castein a way that imagines that caste not only free from dependence and dominance but also able to stand in place of the dominant. Perhaps for this reason, the sapphic subject poses not only the threat of modernity but also a threat to modernity as it is being configured in the period: Dror Wahrman argues that it is gender rather than rank that anchors the new modern society, and thus gender differences and the notion of an identity that is performed through one's anatomical sex begins to be a crucial component of modern subjectivity. The sapphic disturbs and even deconstructs this underpinning to the extent that the sapphic in early modernity is a dismantling of what femininity has signified and sometimes a questioning of the female body as well. Sapphic subjects thus operate on both sides of modernity, threatening to deconstruct not only old systems but also the new ones that are in some measure a way of containing them. It is this double valence that, I suggest, gives sapphic representation its particularly resonant potential.

I have been arguing for a broad eruption of sapphic representations in Europe around and beyond 1600, but it is time to take a closer look at my own geography as a way to understand more deeply how and why the sapphic imaginary functions as it does. Not every country is producing sapphic discourse of any sort, let alone of the same sort, and a more distinctive mapping tempers the universalizing tendency of my argument to recognize the specific aspects of individual nation-states, linguistic cultures, cities, or regions. First, it is not simply in Western but in western*most* Europe that we find the overwhelming majority of sapphic representations. All the locations have some investment in what we might call intellectual modernity and in the issues of authority, nature, and power that will characterize Reformation and Enlightenment debates. But not all sites invested in modernity engage in sapphic representation; despite the central role of German thinkers in both Reformation and Enlightenment dialogues, for example, there is almost no published writing about female homoeroticism of German origin before the nineteenth century.

The countries where sapphic representations are concentrated share at least four other commonalities: a coastal geography that gives ready access to major European trade and communication routes extending from cosmopolitan centers; a heavy investment in colonial conquest; a recent history of strong women rulers; and visible participation in vernacular print culture. The reverse is also true: except for Scandinavia, virtually all of Western Europe's coastal countries—England, France, Portugal, Holland, Spain, and Italy—show some preoccupation with sapphic subjects around 1600, while almost no inland countries do.

Fernand Braudel has suggested that the urban is "an example of deep-seated disequilibrium, asymmetrical growth, and irrational and unproductive investment on a nation-wide scale," and thus the site of a kind of leveling (556). I speculate that sapphic representation is not separate from the ways in which early modern cities function as both powerful and dangerous crossroads of identity, places characterized by cultural differences, leveling views and, relative to rural settings, rapid change. Those cities on or near waterways were also able, of course, to participate in a multinational cultural as well as economic network for the simple reason that travel by water was faster and extended farther than travel on roads; we might recall that even in 1789, news of the stormed Bastille came to London faster than it reached the French provinces.

Cultural differences were most evident in the early modern world, of course, in the context of European exploration and conquest, and I believe it no accident that every country producing sapphic discourse in early modernity is also involved in colonial enterprise that reached a tipping point around 1600. Germany and Scandinavia, by contrast, had little involvement in colonialism except as handmaidens or auxiliaries to the major imperial powers. I suspect that sapphic subjects become a place for working out the possibilities—both dreaded and welcomed—that difference might be not just "out there" but "in here." From this perspective, sapphic subjects may erupt into print when societies are on the verge of certain kinds of change, and the vast change that colonialism represents finds an at-home correlative in the notion of unfamiliar bodies, desires, and practices and that, moreover, some of these "others" might rise up to claim not only autonomy but also rulership.

That sapphic subjects erupt in cosmopolitan, urban, colonialist, power-invested, turbulent, and potentially democratic settings suggests that they are serving complex functions not limited to sex-related ones. But it is also plausible that sapphic writings are responding to a dramatic movement of women around 1600 into positions of power both as rulers—thus embodying a "world upside down"—and as writers, thus as purveyors of the new leveling wrought by print culture itself. As both early modern observers and later scholars have noted, Europe saw an unprecedented number of women as queens regnant, powerful regents, or consorts during the decades before and around 1600: Mary I and, more importantly, Elizabeth I of England; Catherine de Medicis as the powerful wife and mother of French kings; Spain's Juana of Castile after the even-more-powerful Isabella; Mary Queen of Scots and her mother, Marie de Guise; several influential royal figures of smaller Spanish, Italian, and French principalities; and a few decades later, of course, the transgressive, cross-dressing, and probably sapphic Christina of Sweden What St. Amand says of France is true more widely of Europe: "At no epoch . . . have women played a greater part . . . Their influence pervaded politics, letters, and the arts. They direct public affairs, make and break treaties, share in every intrigue, hazard, and danger of the civil wars" (cited in Cottrell, 103). Not surprising, then, that there is an intense renewal of speculation around 1600 that in the ninth century a woman might even have been pope, tripping up even the divinely inspired College of Cardinals and thus subordinating Christendom to female rule. As the historian Chilton Latham Powell observed long ago, most of the focus "of both serious and frivolous writing against woman was directed towards preserving her subserviency and condemning her attempts at sovereignty" (167). Certainly some of the examples I have given from around 1600 directly implicate particular courts—that of Catherine de Medicis and Elizabeth I most notably.

But there is another form of power that also may be propelling these representations, one that Ben Jonson's linkage of the tribadic to the poetic underscores. Sapphic discourses share their location with the strikingly new presence of women writers and intellectuals in the emerging culture of print. I want to emphasize the horizontality that print itself introduces; in Jacques Barzun's words, "From being more or less a duel, [intellectual life] becomes a free-for-all. The scrimmage makes for a blur of ideas, now accepted as a constant and fondly believed to be, like the free market, the ideal method for sifting truth" (61). In a world where a speaker's identity can separate itself so readily and publicly from his or her words, print becomes the very embodiment of modernity's potential for leveling. The literacy among women, strongly enabled by the Protestant value on personal access to Scriptures, allowed more women to share cultural authority especially if they published anonymously as most writers did in this period. While access to print remained class inflected if not class determined, the new system did allow Protestant women, for example, to "abuse" "noble churchmen" as "godless men" or a servant to use the Bible against her master, reversing hierarchies of class and sex. Still, such acts were readily deemed monstrous: as Natalie Zemon Davis reminds us, neither Catholicism nor Calvinism challenged "*the con*cept of social hierarchy" as such (93). Thus also between 1570 and 1600 emerges the first spate of books of instruction aimed solely at women—as if to reposition them into a gendered order from which print threatened to release them (see Hull)—but the period also saw the emergence of writings by women in the realms both of belles-lettres and of pamphlets on a range of topics, including the topic of women themselves. That France, Spain, and England lead in producing sapphic discourse might speak to the fact that they are three of the four great colonial superpowers, that all three have powerful women rulers, and that in all three, as in the fourth superpower, the United Provinces, women are becoming prominent as writers. By the eighteenth century, for reasons that lie beyond this chapter, sapphic representations will have fallen off in Spain but increased in the United Provinces, while continuing to flourish in England and France.

Braudel has argued that "whenever splits and chasms begin to open up in a society, it is the ever-present culture which fills them in, or covers them up, holding us to our tasks" (565). But sapphic subjects show us that the "ever-present culture" may even create the splits and chasms that it is also trying to fill in. Particularly in their modes of narrative resolution, sapphic subjects both reveal and attempt to conceal the fissures in societies confronting change. Varied and contradictory, blending moral opprobrium with erotic play, these representations form an equivocal tapestry of fascination and anxiety. Few of these writings could readily be construed to encourage respectable women to form publicly visible erotic attachments with members of their own sex. Yet in the seventeenth century, homoerotic attachment will become a major trope of women's own writings as Italian, English, French, Spanish, and Dutch writers seek to constitute women as political and social subjects (Lanser, "Political"). In the process, modernity itself moves toward the constitution not only of sapphic subjects but also of sapphic subjectivities.

NOTES

1. The French passage reads as follows:

> Qu'en vain j'avois pensé que le temps advenir
> Nous devroit pour miracle en longs siecles tenir :
> Et que d'un seul exemple, en la françoise histoire
> Nostre Amour serviroit d'eternelle memoire,
> Pour prouver que l'Amour de femme à femme épris
> Sur les masles Amours emporteroit le pris.

   Clearly, I differ with Terry Castle's reading of this poem's attitude as one of "disgust" and "catastrophe" (*Literature* 72). For a different view, see Griffiths.
2. See especially Andreadis; Bonnet; Donoghue; Lupo; Martín; Robinson; Sanfeliú; Canadé Sautman and Sheingorn; Shannon; Traub.
3. In the last decades of the sixteenth century, several European countries formalized injunctions against sex between women, distinguishing the continent from England, whose antibuggery law of 1533 was interpreted as applying only to men. Prosecutions of women for same-sex transgressions are recorded for 1405, 1444, 1477, 1482–1483, 1536, 1553, 1555, 1560, 1568, 1580, the 1620s, 1670, and several others after 1700.
4. A footnote to some posthumous editions (by 1733) claims that Rowe had a direct target for the poem: "These *Stanzas* were made on Mrs. B———*le*, and a Lady her Companion, whom she calls *Captain*."

WORKS CITED

Andreadis, Harriette. *Sappho in Early Modern England: Female Same-Sex Literary Erotics 1550–1714*. Chicago: U of Chicago P, 2001.

Aquinas, Thomas. *The Summa Theologica of Saint Thomas Aquinas*. Trans. by the fathers of the English Dominican Province. London: Burns, Oates, and Washbourne, 1920.

Astell, Mary. *Some Reflections upon Marriage*. London: Nutt, 1700.

Barker, Jane. *A Patch-Work Screen for the Ladies*. London: Curll and Payne, 1723.

Barzun, Jacques. *From Dawn to Decadence: 500 Years of Western Cultural Life 1500 to the Present*. New York: HarperCollins, 2000.

Bonnet, Marie-Jo. *Les relations amoureuses entre les femmes du XVIe au XXe siècle*. Paris: Jacob, 1995.

Brantôme, Pierre de Bourdeille, seigneur de. *Recueil des dames, poésies et tombeaux*. Paris: Gallimard, 1991.

Braudel, Fernand. *The Wheels of Commerce*. Trans. Sian Reynolds. 1979.

Brooten, Bernadette. *Love between Women: Early Christian Responses to Female Homoeroticism*. Chicago: U of Chicago P, 1996.

Canadé Sautman, Francesca, and Pamela Sheingorn, eds. *Same Sex Love and Desire among Women in the Middle Ages*. London: Palgrave, 2001.

Castle, Terry. *The Literature of Lesbianism: A Historical Anthology from Ariosto to Stonewall*. New York: Columbia UP, 2003.

Chester, Robert. *Love's Martyr, or Rosalins Complaint*. London: E. B., 1601.

Cottrell, Robert D. *Brantôme: The Writer as Portraitist of His Age*. Geneva: Droz, 1970.

Crompton, Louis. "The Myth of Lesbian Impunity: Capital Laws from 1270 to 1791." *Journal of Homosexuality* 11 (1980): 11–25.

Davis, Natalie Zemon. *Society and Culture in Early Modern France: Eight Essays*. Stanford: Stanford UP, 1975.

Dekker, Rudolf M., and Lotte C. van de Pol. *The Tradition of Female Transvestism in Early Modern Europe*. New York: St. Martin's, 1989.

Donne, John. *The Variorum Edition of the Poetry of John Donne*. Ed. Gary Stringer. Bloomington: Indiana UP, 1995.

Donoghue, Emma. *Passions between Women: British Lesbian Culture 1668–1801*. London: Scarlet, 1993.

Estienne, Henri. *L'introduction au traité de la conformité des merveilles anciennes avec les modernes; ou, Traité préparatif à l'apologie pour Hérodote*. Geneva: Estienne, 1566.

Farnsworth, Jane. "Voicing Female Desire in Poem XLIX." *Studies in English Literature* 36.1 (1996): 57–72.

Griffiths, Richard. "'Les Trois sortes d'aimer': Impersonation and Sexual Fantasy in French Renaissance Love Poetry." *Journal of the Institute of Romance Studies* 3 (1994/1995): 111–27.

Hull, Suzanne W. *Chaste Silent & Obedient: English Books for Women 1475–1640*. San Marino: Huntington, 1982.

Laurens, André du. *Toutes les oeuvres de Me André du Laurens*. Paris, 1621.

Lanser, Susan. "Befriending the Body: Female Intimacies as Class Acts." *Eighteenth Century Studies* 32.2 (1998): 179–98.

——. "The Political Economy of Same-Sex Desire." *Structures and Subjectivities: Attending to Early Modern Women V*. Ed. Joan Hartman and Adele Seeff. Newark, Delaware: U of Delaware P, 2007. 157–75.

——. "Sapphic Picaresque, Sexual Difference, and the Challenges of Homoadventuring." *Textual Practice* 15.2 (2001): 1–18.

Leo Africanus, Joannes. *A Geographical Historie of Africa: Written in Arabicke and Italian by John Leo a More . . . Translated and Collected by John Pory*. London: Bishop, 1600.

L'Estoile, Pierre de. *Registre-Journal du règne de Henri III*. Ed. Madeleine Lazard and Gilbert Schrenck. Geneva: Droz, 1997.

Lupo, Paola. *Lo specchio incrinato: Storia e immagine dell'omosessualità femminile.* Venice: Marsilio, 1998.

MacCulloch, Diarmaid. *The Reformation.* New York: Viking Penguin, 2003.

Martín, Adrienne L. "The Mediation of Lesbian Eros in Golden Age Verse." *Lesbianism and Homosexuality in Early Modern Spain.* Ed. María-José Delgado and Alain Saint-Saëns. New Orleans: UP of the South, 2000. 343–62.

Mueller, Janel. "Lesbian Erotics: The Utopian Trope of Donne's 'Sapho to Philaenis.'" *Homosexuality in Renaissance and Enlightenment England: Literary Representations in Historical Context.* Ed. Claude J. Summers. New York: Haworth, 1992. 103–34.

Niccholes, Alexander. *A Discourse of Marriage and Wiving and of the Greatest Mystery Therein Contained: How to Choose a Good Wife from a Bad.* London: Okes, 1615.

Pancrazio, James J. "Transvested Autobiography: Apocrypha and the *Monja Alférez.*" *Bulletin of Hispanic Studies* 78 (2001): 455–73.

Powell, Chilton Latham. *English Domestic Relations, 1487–1653.* New York: Columbia UP, 1917.

Robinson, David M. *Closeted Writing and Lesbian and Gay Literature: Classical, Early Modern, Eighteenth-Century.* Aldershot, Hampshire: Ashgate, 2006.

Robson, Ruthann. "Lesbianism in Anglo-European Legal History." *Wisconsin Women's Law Journal* 5 (1990): 1–42.

Rowe, Nicholas. *Poems on Several Occasions.* London: Curll, 1714.

Sanfeliú, Luz. *Juego de damas: Aproximación histórica al homoerotismo femenino.* Málaga: U de Málaga, 1996.

Serna, Melchor de la. "El sueño de la viuda." *Cancioneras de poesías varias: Manuscrito 2803 de la Biblioteca Real de Madrid.* Ed. José J. Labrador and Ralph A. DiFranco. Madrid: Patrimonio Nacional, 1989. 206–21.

Shannon, Laurie. *Sovereign Amity: Figures of Friendship in Shakespearean Contexts.* Chicago: U of Chicago P, 2002.

Swetnam, Joseph. *The Araignment of Lewd, Idle, Froward, and Unconstant Women.* London: Purslowe, 1615.

Traub, Valerie. *The Renaissance of Lesbianism in Early Modern England.* Cambridge: Cambridge UP, 2002.

Tyard, Pontus de. *Œuvres poétiques.* Paris: Galiot du Pré, 1573.

Upton, Anthony F. *Europe 1600–1789.* London: Arnold, 2001.

Wahrman, Dror. *The Making of the Modern Self: Identity and Culture in Eighteenth-Century England.* New Haven: Yale UP, 2004.

Wanley, Nathaniel. *The Wonders of the Little World, or, a General History of Man in Six Books.* London: Basset, 1673.

CHAPTER 4

"FAIR IS NOT FAIR"

QUEER POSSIBILITY AND FAIRGROUND PERFORMERS IN WESTERN EUROPE AND THE UNITED STATES, 1870–1935

FRANCESCA CANADÉ SAUTMAN

WHEN BARBETTE FLIES IN THE AIR, HE IS THE eternal androgyne who escapes the downgrading of time, as opposed to the woman acrobat, deformed by work, suggested French journalist Maurice Verne in 1930 (218), praising androgynous male beauty over female degradation. Barbette's performance, in effect, combined feminine and masculine gestures. That "mix" of attributes was not his alone. A 1914 issue of *L'intermédiaire forain* attributed the *forain* Andreys's popularity to his "feminine physiognomy," "dazzling costumes," "[costume] changes," and imitation of a "pretty feminine voice" ("Nos artistes").[1] Barbette first appeared as a woman, wearing makeup and shimmering gowns, and flew into the air, as a lightweight belle with a tiny waist, landing next to startled spectators. Then he would transform himself back into a man, one article of clothing at the time, staging his own body as the locus of gender ambiguities that unraveled right before the spectators' eyes, eliciting disquieting bodily proximity with them around their fears of the differenced body. Did the excluding norms of his society make him a "freak," or "queer"? Was the woman whose changing body aged disgracefully, losing all aesthetic purchase in her society, then "freakier" or "queerer" than him? Such questions reflect the variations of the "comparatively queer," situated in perimeters of inclusion and exclusion and in the sexing of objects of desire. In the performances of music-hall, midway, and sideshow artists, an endless concatenation of "queer possibility" arises, located in a space of constant motion, reconfiguration, and multiple border crossings.

Comparatively then, Barbette's queer potential fluctuated: very queer indeed, if "queer" unsettles both aesthetics and gender in relation to staid citizens with a well-heralded binary sex; less queer, if "queer" denotes the appearance of women whose loss of good looks signals time's merciless touch and the whims of "body-time." The androgyne, a carefully crafted construction built from the male body outward, conquered time; but the woman whose athletic performance inflected her to the masculine crumbled back onto an imperfect feminine. The former was, albeit transgressive, immortal, the stuff of myth, and of an unreal that art made into a higher reality. The woman acrobat temporarily challenged the limits of femaleness and femininity but remained trapped in the mishaps of the body. Thus, the beguiling notion of the "comparatively queer" is at once grounded in the distinctive function of gender and fueled with the power of "crossings"—as hybridizations (crossed identities, cross-dressing), as transfer of attributes and features, as disassembling and reassembling of parts into new wholes, as transgression (crossing someone or something) and trespass (illicitly crossing borders and property lines), and as permanently marked by the fate of ominous difference (as in star crossed).

This chapter focuses on the worlds of the carnival midway and fair sideshows before the Second World War, viewed through a "comparatively queer" made of many forms of blurring and crossing: across national cultures, borders, language barriers, genders, and across a range of performances and ascriptions to "art." "Queer" moves in relation not only to societal norms but also according to a sliding ruler of marginalization underlined by gender and social class and between the places where extremes outside the norm are performed. Thus the "queer" is always in process, shifting, and redeployed in contact with other instances or moments of queer potential, and "queer possibility" overshadows any one easily recognizable category of "queer." "Queer possibility" is suggested in this historical context by Amy Lowell's reference to "a queer lot" in her famous 1925 poem "The Sisters" (lines 1–3). This was "queerness" well before queer-affirming identity (Galvin 25–26), at once undefined yet resonant enough to evoke something like the "time that will be" and that "could have been," which Margaret Ferguson linked to "feminism in time." Perhaps it already translated a look inward at a difference too deep to be concealed and even thrust back at the norm, challenging the complacent majority occupation of the norm as terrain. While there is no term "queer" in the romance languages, my chapter considers precisely that type of "possibility" and its limits within sideshows, particularly in France.

From the nineteenth century to roughly the middle of the twentieth, throughout Europe and North America, sideshow performers, marked by birth or through trained acquisition with nonnormative physical traits (such as having no legs, or more than two) or physical capabilities (eating fire or swallowing swords), often succeeded in turning around social disapproval and erasure by manipulating shock value and public fascination. Far from remaining mere curiosities, outcasts, or objects of entrepreneurial exchange, several made small fortunes out of the entertainment business, at least in the United States, such as Chang and Eng Bunker (Nickell 122–24, Hartzman 23–25); Che-Mah, the "Chinese Dwarf" (Hartzman 27–28); Captain George Constentenus, the tattooed "Greek prince" (Hartzman 31–33); or the Hilton sisters (Pingree). Many molded their difference into popular performances that etched their existence into the cultural fabric of their time. Yet one can ignore neither the ethical issues that arise when others exhibit to the curiosity of the public persons suffering from serious challenges to the integrity of their body nor even the problems posed by their own consent to such exhibitions (Gerber). At the same time, their explicit and forceful efforts at exercising various forms of agency (Hartzman passim; Rosenberg) must not be denied. They could perfect a creative public performance of their own differenced bodies notwithstanding the power of the entrepreneurs who exhibited (and sometimes even "bought") them. Thus, the histories of racism and of the sideshow flagrantly merge in the life of Mille-Christine, the two-headed nightingale, or conjoined twins, born into slavery in 1851, and sold several times (Hartzman 65–66). Historically referred to as Barnum's "human curiosities" or "living wonders," freaks, human anomalies, oddities, *phénomènes vivants* (in French), or (in Italian) *tipi insoliti* (Trevisan) or *fenomeni* (Angiolini) sideshow performers were not always merely passive objects of the gaze. The considerable documentation of individual life stories points to constant tensions between the desire of the exhibited to be the true agents of the exhibit and of their own lives and the desire of the bankers, adventurers, and show entrepreneurs to control them. Sideshow performers could also participate in social control and exploitation themselves, such as when the enriched Bunker Siamese twins became slave owners in North Carolina (Hartzman 24). Yet many looked back, or "wrote back," by regaling the public with false ethnicities, fanciful biographies, and faked attributes that they scripted into the lore surrounding them.

Sideshows were included in dedicated fairgrounds, traveling carnivals performing in the circus midway, and in music halls, where the contained performances lost much of their edge. The Paris Moulin Rouge presented such a program, when, on 5 October 1889, it replaced the Reine Blanche music hall. Its garden could hold 6,000 people, with donkey rides, Spanish palaces for Moorish dances, shooting galleries, and an elephant statue bequeathed by the Exposition Universelle, in whose bowels clowns, acrobats, belly dancers, ventriloquists, and *pétomanes* (musical farters) performed (Oberthür 75). The circus was an ambiguous space. In France, small circuses were fair attractions sold to entrepreneurs (*Guide forain*), while the circus in the United States was a complete outdoor spectacle with a carnival often operating on a midway leading to the "big top" (Nickell 19–20). In the culture of the big top, Circus Day was a time of potential fragmentation that could encourage illicit and violently disruptive acts by the local folk (Davis 29–30). The circus carefully handled gender improprieties, for instance at once flaunting and controlling female nudity (Davis 82–116).

Bodily difference, especially when it queered sex and gender, was thus publicly reshuffled in various performance venues—but none attained the same level of strangeness, of disturbing power, and of potential queerness as the fair. The space of the fair itself was marked by such an accumulation of the sensorial, the transgressive, and the shocking that it was always destabilizing. Yet because it was a popular amusement that circulated all year round across the country and at different sites in large cities, the fair made the oddness of body transgression oddly familiar and its erratic production of fear and abjection a passionately desired cultural experience.

Sideshow performers also worked in traveling dime museums and museums of anomalies, such as the famous Barnum's in North America, and in France, the "Musée Dupuytren" prototype. These museums displaced the exhibited individual into an allegedly neutral space sanctified by scientific pretense, while relying on hype and sensationalism in order to draw crowds. The French "Musée Dupuytren" was located inside the fair or midway. It could include vast mazes with concealed exits in which visitors were led from one display to the next, eliciting an excess of impressions, emotion, and finally, fear. These museums could include various frightening "realist" reconstitutions such as jails and were exited via the *rigolarium* (or laughing space) to disconnect viewers from sadness and depression (Garnier 30–31). The body parts and bodies mummified or suspended in formaldehyde kept in cases and jars of the *musée anatomique* were to shock as much as educate, while fragmenting a worrisome "other" into a diminutive, helpless form. This commercial manipulation of the differenced body is dramatically underscored by the story of bearded-woman Julia Pastrana, whose manager Theodore Lent became her husband and, when she and their child died, proceeded to embalm the bodies to exhibit them as mummies on tour in London and the United States (Hartzman 81–83). The poet Pierre MacOrlan's evocations of fairs in the 1920s denounced the Musée Dupuytren type as a "hell" where Venus was made repulsive through displays of grotesquely deformed wax female organs covered with the marks of syphilis and other diseases (MacOrlan 139). A contemporary dubbed it "the realm of terrors. Where one speaks in a low voice, with tight throat and tense nerves . . . [and] one turns pale" (Mourey 21–24). Yet the "living wonders" such as bearded ladies or giants demanded other venues that, like the midway or traveling sideshow, were not sanctioned by the scientific hoopla of the museum and offered the performer more personal agency in the performance of the queer and the unsettling. Fair sideshows exhibiting forms of the anomalous—in the flesh, or as remains, or as wax molds—were secreted away behind heavy curtains or darkened booths (Malato 231–32). Once the viewers opened themselves to the shock of the visual, they beheld the eerie and the allegedly impossible that could generate a delectable free fall into terror while rattling public perceptions of sexual and body norms.

Performance acts of body or gender difference did not attain their maximum queer potential alone. Different levels of strangeness operated in separate contexts and thus triggered different connections to queer possibility, including the spatial and monetary position of the public, who could become part of the performance (as in the wrestling or boxing shows) or roam freely as in the street or fairground. When confined to a specific seat, that public became scripted as a passive recipient of the "tyranny of the visual," characteristic of such performances. The oscillation between illicit and queer potential also hinged on the official authorization of the performance: its inclusion in a commercially stable and controlled venue, as on the music-hall stage, or its demotion to a no man's land of marginalization, danger, and bare survival. The fair's economic fragility, on the brink of starvation and indigence, was brought home by many participants (e.g., in the memoirs of the nineteenth-century French animal-tamer Bidel, and well into the twentieth century by a "carny" memoir such as Howard Bone's).

Even normative observers record the undercurrent of disturbing spectability that emanates from the very dryness of lists of attractions that conjure a world of slipping norms and terrible potential. Mourey's 1927 impressions of the fair are generally hostile, combining horror, disdain, and disgust at sexual ambiguity in particular. The effect is also elicited, in a different tone, by nostalgic descriptions. The conventional author Jeanne Ramel-Cals wrote of her childhood visits to the fair at Villefranche in the 1900s, where she saw "the six-legged calf, the convicts of the Ile maudite, the unbeatable Robur, the birth of Venus, the true mermaid of the Adriatic seas . . . The latter, a hideous, enormous, sturgeon smelling of dried herring, was a fish from top to bottom. At the Palace of Illusion, the torso-lady was nestled in her pink-lined jewel box" (34–36). A description of the fair in the northern Italian town of Alessandria, from the late nineteenth century to the 1940s, lists *fenomeni viventi* along with the labyrinths, enchanted palaces, wax museums, shooting galleries, and lotteries (Angiolini 29).

The "queerness" of the fair as a performance and exhibit space was unique, with its own ideological and social codes and its multiple transgressions of normative systems, in and outside of gender. Always somewhere on the fringe, it also attracted the mainstay of society, and there was a frequent class-based tug-of-war over its operations and its content (Le Roux 18–21, 30). While the fringe is far from being necessarily queer, the fair thus remains on the outskirts of the fully normative. It sustained serious attacks for harboring a raw, illegal, underground, and sleazy sexuality and allowing actual sex traffic. Life stories were invoked to denounce its queer associations. Thus, the criminologist Emile Laurent wrote in 1890 of a young passive homosexual, handsome, beardless, and effeminate, who signed up as a clown in a troop of entertainers and was eventually sentenced to jail for stealing and getting into fights (122). Mourey's descriptions belabor the objectionable "queer" gender and sexual identities of performers, "that fantastic menagerie of two-legged beings whose accoutrements leave one to doubt their respective sex": "females with short hair, and males wearing it long" (81); those female athletes with the thighs of male wrestlers; the contortionists of "both sexes, or even, the third," who wrap and distend their body parts every which way, thereby "executing a thousand phenomenal and obscene poses" (132); "exquisite and fearsome girlies" in tutus, who hide ambiguous shapes under transparent gauze; and "mannish women, animal tamers and wrestlers with enormous thighs" (10–11). Thus, regardless of how fair and midway performers viewed themselves, their queerness, real or alleged, was largely a matter of public perception.

Even without questioning the sex/gender order, sideshow performers, whether showing their own body or training it to do astonishing, impossible things, mercilessly questioned the power and truths of "nature" and its conventions. While some did transgress and transform sex and gender, the mere existence and display of "human wonders"—who against all normative odds fulfilled their sexual and erotic lives, often made into narratives for the public's benefit—contributed to the edginess of gender identities, even as they attempted to reassert the norm through marriage and offspring. Such "comparatively queer" performances of gender were found in the "half-and-half" shows impersonating hermaphrodites, like Albert-Alberta, the man-woman (1899–1963) who, actually a man, maintained the claim to his dual sex—and to being a native of France—until his death (Hartzman 109–10), while the Great Omi the Zebra man (1892–1969), married to a woman who emulated his zebra tattooing, eventually donned lipstick and nail polish himself (163–64). Albert-Alberta's fake female breast was filled with bird seed, but he had modeled his body to fulfill a promise—making visible two sexes and two genders in one body—so that performed self and "actual" self merged completely.

In the fair, these already-troubling performances were heightened by their proliferation, by their accumulation, and by their seriatim presentation, which created a compelling, disturbing counternorm: a poetics of difference that embraced all its manifestations from beauty to horror. Comparatively, the queer potential of the fair sideshow outdid by far its potential for normativity: the sheer numbers of anomalous beings marked by stark bodily difference in one concentrated space created a brutal relativizing of "norms" suddenly shorn of the power conferred by majority status and the purchase of viewing. Further, fairs of the past built on the ambiguous eroticization of fear. Under the predictable gimmicks and the boasts of mountebanks lurked the unexpected, the unfathomable, and ultimately, the taboo, and this increased the sideshows' appeal. Sideshows played on people's expectations of gaining access to the forbidden, by paying a few cents more to view a "private salon" in a wax museum or the annex of a ten-in-one show (Mourey 23–24, Nickell 52–79, Stencell xix–xxi), only to discover that it held nothing remarkable or prohibited (Lazareff 22 Apr. 1926; Ostman).

In this period, the fair's associations with loose sexual mores and active sexual predators were consistent and contributed to its "queer possibility." Even the innocence of the ride on the carrousel's wooden horses was impugned by male observers as favoring the lewd self-display of loud factory and street women (Montorgueil 197–98). Language reflected this bad reputation, for instance, in the French southwest, as in a Gascon proverb recorded circa 1915, that warns against taking one's daughter to every fair, lest one end up with a whore (Thomas 321n53). It was also implied in the Tarn-et-Garonne expression for an unmarried pregnant girl, said to have "anada a la fièra" [gone to the fair], and in an instance in 1839 in Roquetaillade, where boys were arrested for singing an obscene song at a village girl, saying, inter alia, that "she went to the fair" (321–22 and n55). In France, as in Germany (Otterman), the morally righteous periodically led political campaigns against the depravity of the fairs and their crowds, noise, and infractions against cleanliness. In 1893, the mayor of Neuilly attempted to prohibit a wide range of activities, from selling confetti and paper spirals, to "exhibits having an immoral or repugnant character . . . and the sale of all objects that are indecent or of a nature to disturb public order" (Rearick 113–14). In 1929, the pornography of the fair exhibits was condemned in the same breath as its noise and interference with orderly daily life. The fairs were berated for being *écoles d'immondicité*, a collection of sexual vices including, precisely, its openly queer elements: "[ephebes] tarted up and showing off their depravity"; its shows "forbidden to children," such as "the Well of the Parisienne"; "plastic tableaux" (based on nudity); "the deformed woman"; "the mystery of woman"; and so on. The writer concluded that the show people [*forains*] should be moved outside city limits, where they would bother no one and become truly outsiders [*forain*] (Plessis). Some erotic fair booths, like the "Temple de l'Amour," the "Salon de la Belle Amande," and the "Palais de Phryné," were suspected of favoring prostitution, a charge bolstered by the suggestive photographs and reflectors and enlarging lenses that adorned them, allowing spectators to see the reproduction of tableaux from the salons, as well as by their adjoining "cabinets particuliers," reputed to draw pimps and hoodlums (Gallici-Rancy 104–5). Pierre Lazareff complained in the 1920s that these erotic acts were "poisonous mushrooms," producing "repulsive spectacles that deface and dishonor the fair"—to wit, "l'Ile de volupté," a lesbian and sadomasochistic tableau vivant; the "Eden Casino" sporting "naked and falsely perverse old ladies"; and "Scenes of Montmartre Life" (8 Apr. 1926). In the United States, Montmartre life generated a whole industry of attractions, such as Bostock's in the early twentieth century, when Parisian themes sufficed to provide erotic enticement essential to the girl-show genres of the carnival midway.

The fair both thrived and suffered from the reputed presence of sex, eroticism, violent images and emotions, and the social marginality of many of its employees—the fleecing of "towners" and "rubes" by carnies was a standard feature of its economic structure (Nickell 34–40; Ostman 123–26, 132–33). Municipal rules attempted to curb or even eradicate the spectacles of the fair, defining it as a liminal space, all at once tolerated, desired, and menaced. Even in capital cities, fair people at all levels were subject to vexations and discriminations (Bidel 190–91), sometimes life threatening. Accused of promoting immorality and disturbing the peace, fairground people were denied health care by the local police and officials and when gravely ill could die after being repeatedly turned away even from public hospitals (Bruché). Their nomadic habitat lumped them in the eyes of public sanitation officials with the dregs of society. A late nineteenth-century report on the thirteenth arrondissement in Paris thus argued for their removal from city streets (Seine), and similar concerns were detailed in the twenties (Juillerat 75–78). As a result, they organized—first in a mutuality fund, then in a union—basing themselves on an 1884 law governing associations (Gallici-Rancy 126–28), the animal-tamer Bidel founding his Union Mutuelle on 20 June 1887 (Bidel 98–99).

Yet competing descriptions of the *forains'* daily life stressed normalcy. Their spokespersons, usually big showmen, stressed marriage, family, and bourgeois entrepreneurial status; Bidel's depictions normalized the sideshow performers into innocuous white-collar employees (Bidel 183). This tension between a well-established ill-repute, the mingled emotions of fear and fascination they elicited, and efforts by performers' advocates to overcome marginalization is an enduring aspect of the life of the fair. It underscores its queer potential because queerness did not merely exist in contrast to the world outside—it also had to negotiate and maintain itself within its own professional space vis-à-vis the compelling pull of normative socialization.

Sideshows and games themselves could be fiercely politically norma- tive, participating in the building of empire through the vilification or caricature of colonized people, people outside the ethnic mainstream, and national adversaries of the moment. The fairground exhibits of the exotic, the colonized, and the monstrous merged with a deeply racist colonial perspective. While no Native Americans lived in France, for instance, a French turn-of-the-century industry staged them through the grotesque savagery of the geek show, like eating a live rabbit (Ruelle 133–34). The bodies of "others" were appropriated or offered up for mock violence in knock-down games, as in the 1900s Neuilly fair (Ruelle 44–45) or in the 1890s in Alessandria where puppets had African-sounding names (Angio- lini 30). Colonial "others" were displayed with fastidious detail, reproduc- ing the empire's "will to know," with the displacement of entire Hindu or African villages. Thus a 1903 guide for fair entrepreneurs sells a "black village with 120 persons," along with animal-taming shows, merry-go- rounds, a wax-figure museum with celebrities and famous criminals, theatres, circuses, and a Moorish palace. It reproduced an entire "Senega- lese village," with families, mosque, wrestling gym, dances, artisan work- shops, and an indigenous school. Its creator advertised a specialization in "colonial ethnographic exhibits" (*Guide forain*). This aspect of sideshows and fairs, their complicity in colonial wars and existing racial hierarchies based on the construction of racialized others (Adams; Cook; Lindfors; Vaughan), could be denounced even then (Mourey 54–61).

The pull toward the normative could result in an antagonistic relation to the outside and the foreign. In the traditionalist world of late-nineteenth-century rural fairs in the French southwest, geared to the sale of livestock, permeability to the uncontrollable generated virulent fear of outsiders and a backlash of discrimination against nomadic people, Gypsies, and also Spaniards (Thomas 269). Sudden cattle panics were blamed on Gypsies, suspected of masquerading as cattle merchants and provoking the panic in order to steal from the sellers, and thus they were summarily pushed out of town. During the great fair during Carnival in Pamiers in February 1903, local authorities stopped and expelled families of Gypsies and Spaniards merely for their reputation (Thomas 269–70). Other cattle panic incidents drew testimonies that people spotted outsiders or led to the arrest of a vagabond simply because he had neither work nor stable address (270). In 1884, the Gers Prefect had the fairgrounds watched before the transactions began to spot persons "not fully known in the area" (272). Panics and stampedes were also blamed on the discordant noise of the fair: "the loud voices during haggling, the whistles, musical instruments, the racket of the players and the animal fights" (271). Indeed, baiting of bears, dogs, and donkeys remained common amusements in nineteenth-century France, especially in improvised street fairs at the city barriers or on fairgrounds, gradually curtailed toward the end of the century (Holt 126–31), although they remained permissible rather late in provincial fairs (Le Roux 22). Human epidemics added to the danger, thus, a doctor writing in 1888 blamed the 1854 cholera epidemic around Ax-les-Thermes on the great fair of 14 September and its filth, claiming the disease was imported by merchants and heightened by the fair environment (Thomas 279). There was also a typically nineteenth-century concern that subversive ideas were spread through live theaters, mechanical theaters, wax museums, and the raw violence of organized animal fights (Thomas 323–25).

Nevertheless, the fairground mapped open, transnational borders, crossed by uncertain and borrowed identities and unstable notions of home and place. The business itself was international, and sideshow performers' origins and citizenship were often mysterious or frankly hidden. In France, they transgressed national borders with the unassuming ease of a daily marginal existence to which a wide range of normative codes did not apply. Performers sometimes changed their names to create for themselves an exotic, Orientalist persona but also retained foreign names and did not hide their foreign origin. Across France they hailed, among other places, from England, Germany, Italy, Hungary, Russia, and the United States. The famous Jo-Jo the Dog-Faced Man was reputedly born in Russia in 1868 Fedor Jeftichew (Hartzman 51–52) and died in 1903 in Turkey. The same individual was reported in the French press as Theodore Petrof, found in the Russian forests in a wild state, performing in France under Barnum's tent, and dying in Saloniki where Russian Church authorities prevented the autopsy. The obituary adds that his hands, "incomparably white and fine," were rather those of a woman ("La mort"). Orientalist strategies created a palimpsest of blurred subaltern origins—as with the tattooed women dubbed "Oriental beauties," and the "Belle Fatmah," "Belle Zohra," and other belly dancers—these "Oriental," veiled "Arab" dancers were often in fact Sephardic Jewish women or ordinary French women, and the imposture reflected a popularization of Orientalist political ideologies in the arena of entertainment (Çelik and Kinney).

The vast gender-transgressive and queer potential of women in the sideshows could not be contained by the normative limits of the sex/gender order. They ranged from the display of tattooed women as exotic pictures—like Salomé "the famous Oriental beauty tattooed in seven colors," seen at Luna Park in 1912 (ATP, Fonds Soury, vol. 19, 149 top and bottom), a deeply erotic, nonnormative performance—to the virile displays of the female animal tamer's courage, to the gender-inappropriate but familiar woman wrestler, and to the "monsters" such as mule women or lobster women. Indisputably nonnormative seemed the "bearded woman's" face-value transgression of the sex/gender order.

In a longstanding Western tradition, virility is linked to the beard, and facial pilosity in women, either to the laudably strong woman, or to the feared and disreputable virago. Late-nineteenth-century sexologists' hatred of sexual border-poaching promised to ostracize the bearded woman as abject. Yet, as a performer of her own difference, the bearded woman could control that position and substantially inflect it. The "freak" of the sideshow could become, in contexts of self-presentation that respected the boundaries of community and gender propriety, an almost perfectly integrated member of her community. Bearded women, inherently "queer," could redirect "queerness" exhibited outside of the ambiguously licit social space of the fair, leaving the questions of queer possibility unanswered. Yet, when limited to the fair and similar venues (midways, street shows, traveling museums, and circuses), the bearded woman risked losing her claim to dignity and agency. In the Victorian United States, her queerness was corrected through stressing a highly feminine manner of dress, female needle skills, and marriage and motherhood, as was the case for Annie Jones (Nickell 151–52), Jane Barnell [Lady Olga] (Hartzman 115–17), Madame Devere (Hartzman 35–36), and Baroness de Barcsy (Hartzman 34–35). Queerness, thus, is neither essential nor given once and for all, but its level increases when the burdens placed on the female body combine with the sleazy aura of the fair. Two biographies of European bearded women illustrate these contradictions.

An 1854 biography of the Swiss-born Josephine, "Madame Fortune Clofullia the bearded lady," produced by Barnum, traces her family history over several generations, suggesting heredity as a normativizing factor. Her maternal grandfather was described as small but "Herculean," with strong masculine features and a face and body covered with hair (Barnum 4). Her mother was mild and sweet, with delicate features, while her father "had *little beard*" (5). Yet she was born with a slight down over body and face. The down kept growing to hair and, when she was eight, was two inches long. The parents were advised by the Geneva medical faculty not to shave it lest it grow longer, which according to the biographer, may explain "the softness and silkiness of Josephine's beard"—in other words, its relative "femininity." Her two sisters were unremarkable, but her brother was "of a weak constitution, feminine appearance, resembles greatly his mother, and now, in his eighteenth year, shows no appearance of beard" (6). At boarding school, Josephine "excelled particularly in those works adapted to her sex, such as embroideries, lace, network, and all kinds of needle-work" (6). Indeed, such coding of gender appropriateness by tastes and occupations over mere physical appearance is a strong theme in bearded women's biographies.

At 14, Josephine lost her mother and had to tend to her siblings— another normative feminine activity. Her beard then reached about five inches, and she began to resemble her maternal grandfather. From her mother, she had "but the hair, which is long, silky, and of a dark brown; the breast full and finely developed," and over time, her neighbors ceased to pay attention "to this strange freak of nature" (7). Travelers recommended that she exhibit herself, engagements were proposed, and in 1849, she accepted the exceptionally good terms of a manager from Lyons. Josephine was properly accompanied on a year-long tour by her father, with a debut in Geneva and a stop in Lyons, both immensely successful. Much money was made, and when the contract expired, father and daughter elected to continue the exhibition tour on their own. In Troyes, Josephine met her future husband, a landscape artist from the Swiss Frisons (9). Father and newlyweds traveled to Paris, where the medical faculty as well as the Prince President wanted to see "this curious and most extraordinary phenomenon" (9). She then visited London for the Great Universal

Exposition in 1851 and was examined by a doctor from Charing Cross Hospital, receiving a crucial document for the rest of her career, an affidavit, that, while she had "beard and whiskers, large, profuse, and strictly masculine, on those parts of the face (the upper lip excepted) occupied by the beard and whiskers in men, and, although on her limbs and back, she has even more hair than is usually found on men, she is without malformation," and was strictly female by all other anatomical characteristics (10). The affidavit reflects a coherent discourse on gender: while upholding the truthfulness and naturalness of Josephine's transgendered body hair, it underscored every conceivably feminine aspect of her anatomy, occupations, skills, and inclinations, thus precluding that a true, biological, hermaphrodite could survive and function socially. Neither the biological implications for the production of sex nor the disturbing implications for sex-gender binaries thus had to be examined.

After nine months of marriage, Josephine gave birth to a daughter, with no symptoms of a beard, who died at 11 months; yet when this child was four months old, she became pregnant again (11). A boy was born in 1852 and soon showed symptoms of being like her, "and would turn out as decidedly a singularity and freak of nature as his mother" (12). In 1853, an American drew the family to the United States, where she met Barnum and was also examined by "eminent doctors" in New York. The boy appeared with her at the Barnum museum, his body thoroughly covered with hair. In conclusion, the booklet invited the incredulous to "call at the Museum, where the Bearded Lady will be most happy to see him"; indeed, *him*, the assumption being that only men were the arbiters of truth and gendered anomaly (13). Thus, in response to an incident in which a visitor claimed that the Bearded Lady was really a man and that she and Barnum were frauds and "humbugs" who should be arrested, Barnum adduced a certificate by three doctors referring back to a *Lancet* article about her and the initial British certificate. This was followed by her husband's sworn statement that she was mother to his children, plus a statement by her father that she was indeed his daughter, and finally, a deposition by Barnum himself to a Dr. Covil from the city prison that she was truly a woman (14–15).

This biography, albeit a Barnum publicity tract, provides interesting glimpses of the limits of the queer and of gender transgression. The complaint makes male impersonation a crime and disbelieves that a woman could naturally display such hairiness. Most importantly, however, the status of Josephine as a "freak," as a bearded woman whose womanly *essence* remained intact, had to be verified and confirmed by men, and by men who had legal control over her: father, husband, and sideshow entrepreneur. Thus it appears that Josephine was able to maintain respectability even in her bearded appearance with a carefully enhanced performance of feminine propriety—through manner of dress, motherhood (and desirability), female pursuits, and obedient social posture, perhaps at the price of personal agency. There is another enormously queer "unsaid" in this biography, as in that of some other bearded ladies who married, not once, but several times: it evokes a construction of heterosexual desire among males that is not normative. What is unspoken but strongly implied by the close pregnancies is the powerful sexual attraction that the bearded woman exercises for a husband, who, in such intimate terms, could hardly have remained oblivious to the flagrant ambiguity and to the echoing of characteristic male appearance in his wife and sexual partner. This latent homoeroticism in the apparently heterosexual incorporation of the bearded lady in the marriage norm could not be acknowledged in the Victorian area but was clearly spelled out by a performer like Stella MacGregor, born circa 1920, and who was said to have opted for a sex-reassignment operation (Hartzman 184–85).

The French Madame Delait's biography is startlingly similar in the way the troublesome gender disparity of the bearded woman was handled to maintain the normative fiction. Madame Delait's story was reconstituted through interviews with neighbors and family members in her hometown, including the mayor, the president of the Comité des fêtes, the hairdresser who regularly trimmed her beard, and her adopted daughter Fernande Leclerc who lived with her from adoption in 1919 at age five to her mother's death in 1939 (Nohain and Caradec 5). The work contains abundant photographs, lent by her daughter, besides the ones that were marked for sale. Indeed, Madame Delait posed in photographs in various male or female clothing and protected herself from imitators and alienating exhibitions by turning the exhibit into an enterprise, with her seal on all postcard representations, as a music-hall artist might have done (ATP, Fonds Tavaud, 79 ssq.; Fonds Soury, vol. 19, 114, 115). One family photograph shows her when she was still shaving: she is wearing a woman's dress and has pronounced breasts, but her face is puffy, with heavy jowls, a marked mustache, and it has a very ambiguous, masculine, appearance. In another, she poses in women's lacey clothes with elaborately coifed feminine hair and the large, parted beard.

She was born in 1865 and married Marie-Joseph Delait, baker at Thaon-les-Vosges, in 1885. In 1900, as the result of a public bet at her husband's café, following a visit to the Nancy fair and the dismal viewing of a bearded woman, she decided to stop shaving her beard. Originally, she went to the coiffeur every morning and only left the mustache quite visible. She was said to have been proud of it and of looking like a man, a useful trait when customers at the café she and Delait owned misbehaved (15). The beard's progress was carefully monitored, and it is reported that her husband, *ému* (moved or aroused), enjoyed caressing it. Rather than a defacement, she saw the beard as a new ornament to be cultivated and groomed (17), and she carefully cut and washed it every day (17). She became a local celebrity, and visitors came from Epinal, Chatel, and as far as Nancy. And in October 1900, she entered the cage of a lion tamer in Epinal and sat there with him, playing cards, as legend had it, scaring the lions (29).

In 1904, President Combes granted her official permission to wear masculine garb at her leisure—at a time when it was illegal for women to wear men's clothing unless they secured a dispensation from the prefect (7). A few days later, Doctor Berillon produced a medical report as important for her as her medical certificate had been for Madame Clofullia, making her a medically certified bearded lady, by affirming both the truthfulness of her hirsute condition and her untouched feminine essence.

This certificate is an elaborate disquisition on the construction of gender at work in her life story. It details her age of menarche (i.e., 12), the regularity of her periods until age 33, and her marriage and absence of children (22–24). It states that, regardless of masculine appearance, "her tastes were always feminine" and approvingly notes that she likes to sew but prefers more delicate needlework, such as fine embroidery, crochet, and so on. It praises her abilities and "wonderful taste" in this area, adding that she dresses elegantly without overlooking any aspect of her feminine apparel. Then it remarks, "She sometimes dresses as a man, but it is in order to engage with greater ease in bicycle riding, an exercise in which she excels." This, of course, is sheer nonsense. In turn-of-the-century France, women did begin to demand suitable attire to ride bicycles, but they wore bicycle pants, and the new sport did not—until it became a necessity during the German occupation—usher in wearing pants by women. The dangerous edge of Delait's transformation is thus rapidly disposed of with a corrective: "When she dresses as a man, the illusion is total. But those are only temporary whims, for Madame Delait is very proud of her sex" (24).

Had this not sufficed to explain not only the queerness of the beard but also Madame Delait's noteworthy departures from gender norms, details volunteered by her adoptive daughter reinforced a rhetoric of gender aimed at making the unseemly and disturbing just go away. She had, a small, arched foot (size 38) and a well-shaped leg, thus all the lower part of her body to the hips was "very feminine and enticing," while her bust was "vigorous, her stature athletic." Her strength was "Herculean," and beneath her kindness and sweetness, there always was a fighter ready to act, so "woe to the drunks who did not respect her or did not suspect her strength!" (27). Local men ended up in the gutter or the town fountain for misbehaving, and she once protected a bully against two more of his ilk, armed with knives. At 18, she returned home covered with the blood of the 20-pound pike she brought back after putting her arm in its mouth to drag it in (28).

Clementine Delait was thus not only accepted as a woman with an "unusual ornament" but also fully integrated in the life of her home town, where she exercised a great deal of unofficial influence over the men, something rather surprising in a morally and socially conservative region. For instance, in the 1934 municipal elections, many voted for her instead of for one of the legal candidates (the ballots were annulled). In spite of garb, coiffures, and jewelry, her photographs transmit a visual effect of fully assumed masculinity. When she wore masculine dress, the illusion was complete, accompanied by strikingly masculine body language, gendered according to the clearly defined body codes of the time. Yet, along with her strongly implied inclination to cross-dressing, if not transgenderism, all the time she maintained the fiction of perfect femininity. Like Clofullia and Grace Gilbert—raised on a farm, capable of performing "a man's work," she cultivated "ladylike refinement," in particular, lace-making (Nickell 154)—Madame Delait relied on gestures and activities that her society took as incontrovertible proof of feminine nature. Thus, she could sign photos in 1933 at the Luna-Park amusement park in Paris, while the Grand Prix of the Bearded Lady was created in Vichy, without endangering the norm she crafted. Normatively sanctioned by marriage and social position, Madame Delait created her own space of queer possibility by "surcharging" the "male" body language and postures in her photographs beyond the requirements of a stage performance or ludic disguise. Her "comparatively queer" performance of gender shifted between visible and invisible, so that queerness remained implied but denied, pressingly challenging a norm that still maintained face.

Bearded women were thus at the frontlines of multiple crossings, eliciting a redistricting of normative expectations and grids. Elusively queer was a bearded woman found mysteriously dead in 1876 in Leipzig, who turned out to be a Prussian spy during the 1870–1871 war and who claimed to have been a seer. Both queer anomaly and the familiar feminine are reflected in the performance of a celebrated star of the Neuilly fair in the 1920s, Madame Adrienne, who staged her beard along with elegant dresses by topflight couturier Paul Poiret (Nohain and Caradec 71).

But some bearded women had a miserable life. A 25-year old *foraine* examined in 1901 by the same Berillon as Madame Delait had a face covered by a beard and earned her living by exhibiting at the fair (Nohain and Caradec 71). She came from a middle-class family, married at 22, had no children, and also loved sewing, embroidery, and crochet. All she wanted was a domestic life with a husband, and she hated wearing the show trunks in front of men and displaying her legs. Her story evokes the difficulty for women of that time to overlook the expectations of gender and live a queer difference so fundamentally based on exhibition and departure from the sexual norm. Modesty, which appears in other female performers' stories, is not a constraint for males seeking to make a living out of self-exhibition. In the end, the "physically queer" may be forced to find refuge and revenue in the fair sideshow but can indeed see it as debasement and humiliation.

Conclusion

The contemporary terms "queer" and "queering" destabilize the assumption of an ironclad gender order and float between recognition of gender transgression and the space of the homoerotic. In the fair sideshow, gender ambiguity, transgendered bodies, and concealed identities could be crucial performance elements. I have thus proposed a multipronged definition of the "queer" that encompasses gender, nationality, social status, and body configuration all at once, in a comparison that is neither linear nor systematic, but unstable and in question. By multiplying and blurring origins, borders, and challenges to the naturalizing of bodies, the "comparatively queer" produces a complex definitional landscape of queerness. Counterposing instances of the distinctly local (Madame Delait) and the loosely transnational (the constant movement and indefinite national origins of sideshow performers), queer theory can at once inhabit the comparative and the historical.

Performers labeled "freaks" and "monsters" displaced many frontiers at once, straddling an ambiguous zone between secrecy and publicity, exploitation and power, abjectification and self-affirmation. When, by the late 1950s, public sentiment turned against exhibits of "human oddities" (Ostman 134), denounced as stripping the exhibited of all dignity and humanity, many of these individuals maintained their willingness to exhibit themselves, even if managed by others. Once society renounced the wonders of the sideshow, they were bereft of social meaning and recognition, more marginalized even than before—and unemployed. It was as if the rejection of the exhibition practices eventually led to a greater rejection even of the exhibited.

I have privileged the terms "performance," "performers," and "performance artists," rather than "freak show," "freak," or "freakery," although they are important in Anglo-American cultural studies, and theoretically informed, politically engaged discussions have reclaimed them (Adams 4–15). The terms "freak" and its cognates remained very negative in the period I have discussed, and regardless of Barnum's bombastic pirouetting around them, sideshow performers protested their use and, in 1903, organized into the Protective Order of Prodigies (Hartzman 22–23). Comparatively, the terms' past dimensions (accident of nature) and modern ones (losing boundaries, acting out, disrupting) create a richly dissonant semantic texture that is not readily translatable into French or Italian. Terms such as "phenomena" or "unusual types" (*tipi insoliti*) are far removed from the disruptive quality of "freak" and invoke instead the categorizations and classifications of early social psychologists.

For Elizabeth Grosz, the freak pulls out the mirror image in us and the fears it exudes, relativizing all our own bodily challenges. Yet the suffering and courage of those who are differentially bodily marked still precludes, in my view, mere appropriation of a term to which one has no right. When slurs and epithets, racial or homophobic, are reclaimed by marginalized groups, they still remain problematic, even when used by insiders; they are simply not acceptable when used by outsiders. I thus resist the facile glee of those who self-identify as "norms" (Hartzman) and brandish the term "freak." And I am antagonized by authors who, with a personal business stake in the matter, lambaste the "political correctness" of identifying some of the demeaning, racist, colonialist aspects of sideshow culture and practice (Stencell).

Comparison was ingrained in the daily experience of sideshow performers, with a norm that they could all at once twist, transgress, parody, revile, reject, and yearn for. It was intrinsic to the practice of arts that borrowed from other countries, nationalities, and language groups. They situated their personal and professional space within a perpetual crossing—across borders that delineate bodies, physical properties and capacities, sexual identification and gender scripts, as well as national and ethnic ones. The gender instability of sideshows became comparatively queerer—and disturbing—when inserted among a multiplicity of other "queerable" bodies whose difference, albeit not always linked to sex and gender, forcefully denaturalized nature. In the fair sideshow, the proximity and interference of all differenced performing bodies with the queer bodies of gender disobedience allowed the meanings of the sexually queer to expand and disseminate.

We cannot gauge today the emotions injected by the raw violence of certain shows into the fabric of the earlier fair or by the occasional indifference to human life—in two incidents in the 1880s, a dwarf forced to act as animal tamer to large feral cats is mauled to death (Le Roux 51), and a wrestler murders a soldier in an improvised bout (Le Roux 56–58). Yet intrinsic to the disturbing atmosphere of the fair remains a fear factor exacerbated through noise. Indeed, a relentless din contributed to that destabilizing effect; it was underscored by direct observers and condemned by social elites and the authorities as a source of social unrest. Cacophonic noise covered voices and dealings, allowing the unseemly or illegal to take place, isolating the individual in the crowd. The visitor was soon numbed by the racket, solicited on all sides by conflicting impressions, and seeking fun and marvel, could be suddenly drawn into the fair's space and time, inhabited by the weird, even the terrifying. In a world of illusion and potential danger, the "norm" was now the outsider, the one limited in body and physical possibilities—comparatively made queer by the queer.

One short story by the decadent writer and flamboyant homosexual Jean Lorrain illustrates that shock value of queer possibility. The narrator glimpses a carnival couple dancing: one woman, light, delicate, with beautiful hair and eyes, fine hands, feet and ankles, elegant clothes, waving a large fan in front of her face, dances passionately with another—heavy set, in an ill-fitting silk leotard, coarse of features and limbs. Then she closes her fan and shows her face: she is a bearded lady, with a long beard down to her breasts, and the crude one is in fact a man made up and in women's clothing. They disappear behind a door, and the narrator concludes, "We had . . . the feeling of a fall into an abyss, into the absurd, into the impossible" (Lorrain 100–101).

Together, multiple levels of queerness thus forged a poetics of sacred terror that could deflect and reject normative terror. Through the confrontational poetics of the fair, the broader culture could not ignore a social and visual fabric belonging to a marginalized world, an insidious and inexorable crossover, filled with the queer possible. And as art, queer possibility unfurled across a spectrum of performances that did not merely exploit difference but rejected, by all means, including travesty and falsification, the univocal constraints of an unconstructed real, or of what purported to be real.

Note

1. Translations in this chapter are mine.

WORKS CITED

Adams, Rachel. *Sideshow U.S.A.: Freaks and the American Cultural Imagination.* Chicago: U of Chicago P, 2001.

Angiolini, Piero. *Vecchia Alessandria: Fiere, mercati, baracconi.* Alessandria: Ferrari-Occella, 1949.

Arsenal, Bibliothèque de l'. Fonds Rondel, recueils factices. RO 16516 «Foire du Trône»; RO 16589 «Fêtes foraines et pornographie»; RO 17844 «Parcs d'attractions».

Arts et Traditions Populaires (ATP), Musée des. Paris, France. Fonds Soury, Fonds Taveau [photographic albums].

Barnum Museum. *Biography of Madame Fortune Clofullia the Bearded Lady (Josephine Boisdechene Clofullia Ghio).* New York: Baker, Godwin, 1854.

Bidel, Jean Baptiste. *Les mémoires d'un dompteur.* Paris: Librairie de l'Art, 1888.

Bone, Howard. *Side Show: My Life with Geeks, Freaks, and Vagabonds in the Carny Trade.* Northville: Sun Dog, 2001.

Bostock, Frank C. *A Treatise on Street Fairs.* Baltimore: Washburn, 1900.

Bruché, Ate. "Navrante histoire." L'intermédiaire forain 1–15 May 1914: 120.

Çelik, Zeinep, and Leila Kinney. "Ethnography and Exhibitionism at the Expositions Universelles." *Assemblage* 13 (1990): 34–59.

Cook, James W., Jr. "Of Men, Missing Links, and Nondescripts: The Strange Career of P. T. Barnum's 'What Is It?' Exhibition." Thomson 139–57.

Davis, Janet M. *The Circus Age: Culture and Society under the American Big Top.* Chapel Hill: U of North Carolina P, 2002.

Ferguson, Margaret. "Feminism in Time." *Modern Language Quarterly* 65.1 (2004): 7–27.

Gallici-Rancy, Henri. *Les forains peints par eux-mêmes.* Bordeaux: Gounouilhou, [1903?].

Galvin, Mary E. *Queer Poetics: Five Modernist Women Writers.* Westport: Praeger, 1999.

Garnier, Jacques. *Forains d'hier et d'aujourd'hui: Un siècle d'histoire des forains, des fêtes, et de la vie foraine.* Orleans: chez l'auteur, 1968.

Gerber, David A. "The 'Careers' of People Exhibited in Freak Shows: The Problem of Volition and Valorization." Thomson 38–54.

Grosz, Elizabeth. "Intolerable Ambiguity: Freaks as/at the Limit." Thomson 55–66.

Guide forain. Bordeaux: Agence Stephen, 1903.

Hartzman, Marc. *American Sideshow.* New York: Tarcher/Penguin, 2005.

Holt, Richard. *Sport and Society in Modern France.* London: Macmillan, 1981.

Juillerat, Paul. *L'hygiène urbaine.* Paris: Leroux, 1921.

Laurent, Emile. *Les habitués des prisons.* Paris: Storck, 1890.

Lazareff, Pierre. "Fin de la foire." *Soir* 8 Apr. 1926 and 22 Apr. 1926. Arsenal RO 16516.

Le Roux, Hughes. *Les jeux du cirque et la vie foraine.* Paris: Plon et Nourrit, 1889.

Lindfors, Bernth. "Ethnological Show Business: Footlighting the Dark Continent." Thomsom 207–18.

Lorrain, Jean. "Trio de masques." *Histoires de masques*. Paris: Ollendorf, 1900. 91–103.

Lowell, Amy. "The Sisters." *Complete Poetic Works of Amy Lowell*. Ed. Louis Untermeyer. Boston: Houghton Mifflin, 1955. 459–61.

MacOrlan, Pierre. "Fêtes foraines." *Œuvres poétiques complètes*. Paris: Le Capitole, 1929.

Malato, Charles. *Les forains*. Paris: Doin, 1925.

Montorgueil, Georges. *Paris au hasard*. Paris: Béraldi, 1895.

"La mort de l'homme-chien, Theodore Petrof." *L'illustration* 13 Feb. 1904: 110.

Mourey, Gabriel. *Fêtes foraines*. Paris: Delpeuch, 1927.

Nickell, Joe. *Secrets of the Sideshows*. Lexington: UP of Kentucky, 2005.

Nohain, Jean, and François Caradec. *La vie exemplaire de la femme à barbe: Clémentine Delait 1865–1939*. Paris: La Jeune Parque, 1969.

"Nos artistes: Andreys." *L'intermédiaire forain* 1–15 Feb. 1914: 114.

Oberthür, Mariel. *Montmartre en liesse: 1880–1900*. Paris: Musée Carnavalet, 1994.

Ostman, Ronald E. "Photography and Persuasion: Farm Security Administration Photographs of Circus and Carnival Sideshows, 1935–1942." Thomsom 121–36.

Otterman, Stephan. "On Display: Tattooed Entertainers in America and Germany." *Written on the Body: The Tattoo in European and American History*. Ed. Jane Caplan. Princeton: Princeton UP, 2000. 193–211.

Pingree, Allison. "The 'Exceptions That Prove the Rule': Daisy and Violet Hilton, the 'New Woman,' and the Bonds of Marriage." Thomsom 173–84.

Plessis, Yves. "Fêtes foraines et pornographie." *Petit bleu* 1929. Arsenal RO 16589.

Ramel-Cals, Jeanne. *Vacances à Villefranche: Un chapitre de ma vie*. Paris: E. Hazan, 1927.

Rearick, Charles. *Pleasures of the Belle Epoque: Entertainment and Festivity in Turn-of-the-Century France*. New Haven: Yale UP, 1985.

Rosenberg, Brian. "Teaching Freaks." Thomsom 302–11.

Ruelle, A. *La fête de Neuilly: Silhouettes foraines*. Paris: Vanier, 1908.

Seine (France). Conseil d'Hygiène Publique et de Salubrité du département de la Seine. Bunel, M. H. Rapporteur. *Rapport sur l'insalubrité résultant du cantonnement de forains et nomades sur des terrains du XIIIe arrondissement*. Paris: Chaix, 1892.

Stencell, A. W. *Seeing Is Believing: America's Sideshows*. Toronto: ECW, 2002.

Thomas, Jack. *Le temps des foires: Foires et marchés dans le Midi toulousain de la fin de l'Ancien Régime à 1914*. Toulouse: PU du Mirail, 1993.

Thomsom, Rosemarie Garland, ed. *Freakery: Cultural Spectacles of the Extraordinary Body*. New York: New York UP, 1996.

Trevisan, Albano. "Dal 'casotto' al Luna Park: Conflitti e adesioni popolari alle attrazioni forane a Venezia." *La piazza: Ambulanti, vagabondi, malviventi, fieranti: Studi sulla marginalità storica in memoria di Alberto Menarini* . . . Ed. Glauco Sanga. Brescia: Grafo, 1989. 77–86.

Vaughan, Christopher A. "Ogling Igorots: The Politics and Commerce of Exhibiting Cultural Otherness, 1898–1913." Thomsom 219–33.

Verne, Maurice. "Mr ou Miss Barbette ou l'androgyne du trapèze." *Musées de volupté: Le secret des nuits électriques.* Paris: Editions des portiques, 1930. 218–26.

CHAPTER 5

TIME'S CORPUS

ON SEXUALITY, HISTORIOGRAPHY, AND THE INDIAN PENAL CODE

ANJALI ARONDEKAR

AT STAKE HERE IS A DIALOGUE BETWEEN TWO MINORITIZED historiographies—one in South Asian studies and the other in queer-sexuality studies—and their shared preoccupation with the responsibility of historical emergence and recognition. To attempt such a dialogue, this chapter moves away from the conventional (and often reactionary) segregation of the two field formations as oppositional or discrete. Central to the argument is an understanding of area studies as constitutive of the histories of sexuality and vice versa.[1] My goal is not merely to narrate the analytical convergences between the two field formations; rather I am interested more in what I will call the "comparative imaginaries" that animate such a conversation. By "comparative imaginaries," I mean to gesture to the incursions of temporality, to the "politics of time" that emerge in our desire for knowledge and in our ethical stances toward otherness.[2]

In many ways, the recent focus on transnationalism has made a conversation between area studies and sexuality studies, in all its historical variants, not only more pressing but also more difficult than ever before. Let me begin then with some provisional and situating generalizations. The current fetishization of all matters "transnational"—understood both as the rearrangement of geopolitical formations and the scholarly analysis of that shift—appears to be under considerable conceptual strain. On the one hand, there is still much to be gained from its prominence as a theoretical rubric. Even as the turn to transnationalism can be generally attributed to the structural inequities created by a dominant post-Fordist global economy, and even as such a turn (despite its "trans" label) rarely eclipses the hegemony of the nation form, transnationalism has emerged as a heuristic modality with endless promise, creating connecting conversations across a diverse and previously segregated range of spatialities and temporalities. For many of its followers, the "transnational turn" instantiates a powerful political metaphorics, a vigorous corrective to the hegemony of national and temporal boundaries, particularly in an era of increased surveillance and U.S. imperialism.[3]

On the other hand, this enthusiastic embrace of transnational talk, as it were, has equally occasioned serious debate on the precise value of such an emphasis and on the false rapprochement between a progressive politics and the politics of the transnational. The critical question for many scholars is whether a transnational approach can indeed articulate an innovative perspective that foregrounds ignored and underrepresented knowledge formations and publics within the more-flattening discourses of globalization.[4] In the case of area studies, for example, the transnational turn has certainly strengthened the critique of a spatially bound area-studies model by underscoring the contested geographies that undergird national and international borders. Yet, for the most part, such critiques have focused largely on contemporary configurations of empire (specifically, U.S. empire) and rarely provide analysis that places earlier anticolonial thought alongside new forms of critique that take on the ideological circuits of contemporary neoimperialism. For sexuality studies, the emphasis on transnational approaches has provided more of a cautionary tale, a haunting reminder of the colonial genealogies that found the very languages of its articulations. Thus, while we may now agree upon the need for a more-situated (and wonderfully diverse) understanding of the entanglements of sexuality and geopolitics, racialized and uncritically appropriative consumption of sites of alterity continues to abound. I want to be careful here and add that this is not a facile reduction (or dismissal) of the languages of transnationalism; rather, the struggle here is to carve out theoretical spaces that supplement the complex graphings of empire.

One such theoretical space of supplementarity, I want to suggest, is the renewed interest in what one could call "comparative imaginaries." The term "comparative"—often falsely used interchangeably with terms such as "global," "international," and even "transnational"—has had an overdetermined and often problematic disciplinary history. Largely mobilized to explicate and stabilize entrenched geopolitical relationalities, the term was previously consigned to the disciplines of anthropology (as a rubric for approaching cross-cultural work), history (as a method of accessing multiple temporalities), political theory (as a concept for assessing capital development), and literature (as a mode of reading and constituting "worlds" of literary texts). Rather than rehearsing the different genealogies of comparative frameworks in each of these disciplinary formations (a task that lies beyond the limited scope of this chapter), it would suffice to say that these early appropriations of the comparative model relied primarily on axes of similarity and difference and rarely interrogated the Eurocentricity of the normative categories that founded the very grounds of comparison.[5]

More recently, however, such flattening and hierarchical habits of comparative analysis have largely been jettisoned, making way potentially for what Ann Stoler has termed as a more sustained "politics of comparison" (23–70). For Stoler, the project of comparative analysis must not just move beyond the national framework but also attend to what objects of study constitute the terms of comparison and what is at stake for us to continue to do so. Stoler's call for a more self-reflexive language of comparison thickens the turn to transnational analysis by rendering locations of the metropole and the colony not as discrete units to be rapidly traversed or linked but more as a singular analytical field. Such a shift to thinking of locations of difference (west vs. east, north vs. south, metropole vs. colony) as conceptually commensurate is made possible through Stoler's commitment to histories of intimacy, histories that exemplify the "tense and tender ties" (Anderson 2) binding the project of colonial expansion. What is of most interest here is that such practices of comparison are not just resonant with current historiographical methods but rather echo comparative frameworks mobilized by colonial governments themselves.[6]

In light of recent debates in the field of comparative literature, scholars such as Rey Chow have further pushed for a revitalization of the comparative modality against and beyond its older formulation as "Europe and Its Others." The "and" here does not refer to a mere matter of "taxonomic addition or inclusion," but rather gestures to "a relation of temporality" that produces Europe as a "cluster of lingering ideological and emotional effects whose force takes the form of a lived historical violation, a violation that preconditions linguistic and cultural consciousness" (89).[7] Working against similar facile understandings of the comparative as merely the multilingual (the piling up of linguistic alterities under the sign of comparative expertise), Chow proposes an alternative paradigm of comparison. For Chow, comparison becomes a Foucauldian archaeological project, whose historical remnants "interpret cultural narratives symptomatically, as fragments that bear clues—often indirect, perverse, and prejudiced—to a history of ideological coercions and exclusions" (89).

Chow's invocation of metaphors of violence ("violation, coercion") situates new and old comparative practices squarely within a landscape of spatial and temporal incommensurability. It is this insistence on epistemic and material violence that most animates Gayatri Chakravorty Spivak's contributions to the comparative debate. While Spivak's text *Death of a Discipline* (2003) predates Chow's work, in many ways it offers a supplementary reading to many of the questions Chow raises. Comparative literature's Eurocentric romance with national literary cultures, Spivak argues, is as epistemologically dangerous (and irrelevant) as area studies' geopolitical ambitions. More specifically, area studies lacks the imaginative potentialities of comparative literature (an attentiveness to figuration and close reading), while the latter flattens the worlds outside of (Western) Europe and (Northern) America. For Spivak, the "politics of friendship," needed to conjoin the estranged fields of area studies and comparative literature, thus depends not just on the acquisition of non-metropolitan languages or self-reflexive models of cross-cultural analysis (not that those languages or models are not necessary) but also on more ethical forms of comparative imaginaries. The Spivakian text exhorts its reader to approach the "ungraspable other" (32) through the imaginative process of "teleopoiesis," a movement into emergence, into futurity, that copies rather than cuts, pastes rather than erases, a movement that is both singular and unverifiable.[8] "Teleopoiesis" (a term Spivak borrows from Derrida) becomes a reading practice that gives in to subaltern learning without the guarantee of prediction: "This is imagining yourself, really letting yourself be imagined (experience the impossibility) without guarantees, by and in another culture, perhaps. Teleopoiesis" (52).

In what follows I attempt to carve out a space for such comparative imaginaries within the conjoined field formations of South Asian studies and queer-sexuality studies. Spivak's insistence that we transform the site of cross-cultural (for lack of a better word) knowledge into an open field of new self-other relations is of particular significance to sexuality studies. That is, even as we ask what can sexuality studies learn from sites of alterity, we might equally conclude that our most challenging task is not just to acknowledge the "other" as producer of knowledge but rather to question our very responsibility as scholars within such a process. To consider such questions, I examine contemporary legal struggles around the eradication of Section 377 of the Indian Penal Code in India alongside the historiography of a failed sodomy case in late colonial India. Overall, this chapter has a rather modest end: to understand how the languages of contemporary legal reform are constantly deflected by, if not into, a revisionist comparative framework produced and institutionalized by certain forms of nationalist and queer historiography.

NOT HERE, NOT NOW

"Time" is a word to which we give flesh in various ways.
—Gayatri Chakravorty Spivak, *A Critique of Postcolonial Reason*

Whoever voluntarily has carnal intercourse against the order of nature with any man, woman or animal shall be punished with imprisonment for life, or with imprisonment of either description for a term which may extend to ten years, and shall also be liable to fine.
Explanation: Penetration is sufficient to constitute the carnal intercourse necessary to the offence described in this section. The offence made punishable under this section requires that penetration, however little, should be proved strictly. Thus an attempt to commit this offence should be an attempt to thrust the male organ into the anus of the passive agent. Some activity on the part of the accused in that particular direction ought to be proved strictly. A mere preparation for the operation should not necessarily be construed as an attempt. Emission is not necessary.
—*Of Unnatural Offences*, Section 377, Indian Penal Code

In 2001, Naz Foundation, a Delhi-based HIV/AIDS prevention nongovernmental organization, with the assistance of a progressive legal-reform group, the Lawyers Collective, filed a petition against the Union Government seeking to declare Section 377, the antisodomy statute of the Indian Penal Code (IPC) as violative of the right to equality (Article 14), the right to freedom (Article 19), and the right to life and liberty (Article 21) of the Indian Constitution. The petition cautiously and strategically staged its arguments through careful references to the mushrooming global discourse of gay civil rights, alongside a more aggressive attentiveness to local instantiations within the context of postcolonial India. More significantly, the petition relied not on questions of gay identity, but more on the relationality between sexual acts and civil rights, developing its defense of a citizen-subject's privacy as the organizing constitutional right for the repealing of Section 377.[9] Hence, for example, the petition carefully mobilized the term MSM (men having sex with men) and not "gay" men, as the placeholder for community actions adversely affected by the continued enforcement of the law. That is, the enforcement of Section 377 was read as a major obstacle to HIV/AIDS prevention and outreach work within the MSM community, as it arguably drove high-risk behavior underground and beyond the reach of safe-sex interventions. This, of course, is in marked contrast to the shift in the United States, where gay civil-rights legal activism has shifted from a focus on privacy issues to speaking more in the language of discrimination—that is, a shift from the protection of acts, to a protection of identity, which often leads to the legal paradox of states that have both antisodomy statutes and extensive domestic partnership laws.[10]

Despite such carefully staged shifts in legal strategy, the central challenge for the petition lay in breaking the stranglehold of the Westernization narrative, the familiar argument, not unique to India in many ways, that "unnatural acts" (more specifically, sodomy) and homosexuality were not part of an Indian past and were mimetic byproducts, remaindered through the onslaught of an aberrant and contaminating Western temporality and spatiality. To break such a stranglehold meant providing the state with convincing evidence of sodomy's indigeneity within the Indian context—an indigeneity that needed to narrate a history of presence, markedly distinguishable from colonial figurations of ontological perversity. To accomplish such a goal, the petition returns over and over again to a diffuse language of "history" as a site of recovery and legitimacy to sanction its argument, where the historical turn is mandated through a language of temporal breaks, with the late colonial period marking the space of critical transformation in the shift from sodomy as "something we did" to sodomy as "something we were criminalized for."

To bolster such a claim, sodomy is recovered amid a stretch of archival evidence, threaded together by claims to diverse temporalities and spatialities that make it constitutively Indian and not an extension of Western influence or behavior. Same-sex texts, subjects, and themes are discovered amid a wide array of archival materials, ranging from literature, anthropology, sociology, art history, and even medical evidence; thus, the process of "queering" Indian history is executed through corrective reformulations of "suppressed" and misread colonial materials (see Vanita 1–14). Such formulations carefully reiterate an ironic reversal of the Indian state's accusations of Westernization: within the logic of historicity that the petition attempts to stage, to criminalize sodomy is to embrace a judicial Westernization (the constitution of the IPC by the British, drafted, as the petition reminds us, within a Judeo-Christian frame of temporality and morality that condemned not only "unnatural acts" but also a range of other native sexual and social behaviors). Thus, even as the geopolitical ubiquity of same-sex behavior is acknowledged by the petition's references to evidence from around the world, the emphasis remains on its prevalence and acceptance within a landscape and archive that is wholly Indian. For example, the petition pointedly cites excerpts from texts understood as conventionally Hindu: the *Upanishads*, the *Bhagwad Gita*, the *Kama Sutra*, and so on. By referring to citations from a Hindu canon of texts, the petition refuses the Hindu-right's repeated coupling of sodomy with Islamic bodies and texts (see Kapur 51–94; Menon).

Throughout the petition, the turn to the historical is deliberately used to narrate a different version of coeval temporalities whereby we learn that to outlaw sodomy is to represent an "outmoded" Christian colonial state, making decriminalization of sodomy a decisively "modern" intervention. Within such critical oscillations, India is both in time, and out of time, folded into a peculiar time-lag of modernity. Its embrace of sodomy in the historical past marks India's modernity, its "in-time-ness," just as its denial of sodomy in the present marks its "out-modedness" with the "West" (a geopolitical marker that shifts from including England to including England and the United States). The Eastern past thus now becomes the Western present. Yet, such hermeneutical mutations work with varied effect as they often reproduce the very temporal orders they hope to exceed. To claim "sodomy" and "same-sex acts" as traditional, as a "historical value," and as part of who we essentially are as Indians is to merely invert the language of historical ontology (if one understands, historical ontology, as Ian Hacking does, as concerned with objects or their effects that do not exist in any recognizable form until they are objects of study) and to engage in a "dynamic nominalism" that fixes even as it tries to shift meaning (1–27). Thus, one set of assumptions pathologizes the ontological connection, while the other affirms it.

On 2 September 2004, after two years of delays and postponements, the Delhi High Court brought up the petition, only to dismiss it summarily. The grounds for the dismissal were clear and unambiguous: There can be no petition, the court's judgment stated, if there are no alleged victims. Any public interest litigation, the court added, must be filed on the behalf of persons. Hypothetical and academic archival inquiries into the potential violation of constitutional rights enabled by a continued enforcement of Section 377 were not sufficient grounds for a repeal of Section 377. Without victims, without literal bodies seeking redress, the petition had no legal standing—it was merely an academic exercise, seeking redress for an imagined community of victims it had, as yet, not managed to produce. Moreover, while the petition may have marshaled interdisciplinary evidence to "naturalize" same-sex behavior, the state argued that they provided no "convincing reports" that homosexuality or other offences were acceptable in Indian society.[11]

The dismissal of this petition understandably came as an enormous blow to the Naz Foundation and members of the Lawyers' Collective, who are currently in the process of appealing the court's judgment. Collective outrage from various quarters of the Indian intelligentsia has also been on display on multiple fronts, from public protests to signed collaborative statements of support. While such efforts are clearly important and worth sustaining, some gestures of outrage bear particular scrutiny. In his widely circulated statement of support on the need to do away with Section 377 of the Indian Penal Code, Amartya Sen begins by stating that "even though I do not as a general rule, sign joint letters, I would like, in this case to join my voice." He goes on to add that the "criminalization of gay behavior goes not only against fundamental human rights, but it also works against the enhancement of human freedoms in terms of which the progress of human civilization can be judged." Sen then concludes his brief statement by noting that the Civil War in the United States began the same year as the establishment of 377 (1861) and that while the United States had managed to abolish slavery as a result of the war, the Indian state had, as yet, not stepped up to its promise as a modern democracy by refusing to abolish Section 377 (Sen). While I am one of the many individuals who signed and supported the statement, what interests me about Sen's tentative support of the petition is his mobilization of the "gay case" as the limit case for India's entry into modes of civilizational progress. As such, he cannot but support the petition to abolish 377. His pat comparison of the abolition of 377 to the abolition of slavery notwithstanding, what is worth noting is Sen's absorption of the colonial into a standardized paradigm of the modern without any sense of historical irony.

While much has been written about the flawed recourse to legal reform and the perils of the gay rights debate in sites such as India, I want to leave those questions aside for a moment and assume that the conceptual agon of the Spivakian invocation of "we cannot not want rights" necessarily founds our political struggle.[12] What I want to do instead is to speculate on the ideologies of historicity and causality that animate both the petition and the language of its dismissal by the state and to focus, in particular, on the referent of the "colonial record" within such formulations. Such speculations cannot, of course, be attempted without an attentiveness to the larger shifts in historiography that animate the political and intellectual landscape of contemporary India. To make some space-clearing generalizations here, two forms of recuperative historicizing appear to dominate: the first, a largely progressive and expansive enterprise, has rigorously extended the categories that define the historical, and the second, a more conservative project, has contracted the historical form onto itself by returning to categories of static identity and exclusion. The expansion model (exemplified in the work of the Subaltern Studies Group, as well as feminist and queer historians) recruits the language of a success-in-failure model to accentuate the coming of Indian history into its own, whereby divergent historical temporalities and spatialities exist within a model of a differentiated politics. On the other hand, the contracted model (exemplified in the recent textbook rewritings by the right-wing Hindu Sangh Parivar) celebrates a past that stabilizes homogeneity and externalizes difference, as opposed to staging it as constitutive of Indian history.

The critical challenge here, for me, lies in thinking about such models of historicity and causality within a historiography of sexuality of colonial India that is attentive to the political exigencies and pitfalls of revisionist history, even as it maintains the radical indeterminancy of sex. Some questions to consider here include the following: If revisionist history, to cite Radha Radhakrishnan here, is always in some ways tautological, in "a hermeneutical time-lag, where one returns to take a second look at what already was," how do we produce records of sexuality such that their repetition is both a return to and a rupture of their founding indeterminacy? How does the crime of sodomy provide us with forms that do not emerge purely out of teleological necessity? What categories remain fixed in a landscape of such historical rewritings? Can the "colonial record" be both the marker and the erasure of possible (radical) histories? Let me turn to one such possible interpretation.[13]

THE PAST PRESENT

On 13 August 1946, a criminal appeal was filed in the Allahabad High Court by Mirro, a resident of Agra. The archival materials available on the case place us in medias res, with Mirro, the accused, appealing his sentencing to "rigorous imprisonment for seven years" under Section 377 for having "committed unnatural offence upon a boy named Ram Dayal" (Mirro v. Emperor). The details of the appeal as provided in the summary judgment are sketchy and follow a tangled temporal and spatial narrative: Ram Dayal, a young Chamar boy, goes to the shop of a man named Sakoor, a blacksmith, where he is accosted by Mirro, who attempts to take him away. A series of strange altercations are described where Mirro is slapped around by Sakoor and yet somehow manages to forcibly whisk Ram Dayal to the house of his brother-in-law, Ajmeri, where the offence is then allegedly committed. Even as the offence is being committed, at peak public-activity hours, between 4:30 and 5 pm, Sakoor runs off to inform the members of Ram Dayal's family and the larger Chamar community. A motley crew of Ram Dayal's supporters is gathered (Sia Ram, Ghasi, Girander Singh, Ram Chand) who then proceed to Ajmeri's house and ostensibly "caught the accused red-handed" (Mirro v. Emperor) and beat him severely with lathis. The assistant sessions judge who first heard the case in 1945 found Mirro to be guilty of the crime, despite the "unanimous opinion of the assessors" who all found Mirro not guilty.

In his appeal of the sessions judge's decision, Mirro's advocate argued that the charge of "unnatural offence" was trumped up by the Chamar community, of which Ram Dayal was a member, to punish Mirro for the "enemity" [*sic*] that existed between the Chamars and the Muslim community. His defense addressed the conflicting and contradictory nature of the evidence submitted, all of which was equally available the first time the case was brought before the court to bolster the appeal. For instance, the medical evidence, the deciding factor of the colonial legal process in such matters, produced no conclusive forensic traces of the crime—no subtended anus in Ram Dayal and inconclusive marks of semen on Mirro's dhoti. To a large extent, medical jurisprudence became the most reliable truth technology of a colonial legal system ravaged by disputes over witness unreliability, codification, and orders of evidence. As legal medicine crystallized as a discipline, it emerged as a powerful form of colonial knowledge, allowing a distinctly ethnographic understanding of native ontologies to acquire truth value in court.[14] The medical evidence in this case, we are told, did not provide us with a truth narrative and "does leave a gap in the story" (Mirro v. Emperor), a gap that is barely filled by the other evidence provided. Other confusing and absurd details also emerge: Ram Dayal claimed the offence took five minutes, while the eyewitnesses to the account claim the offence took 15 to 20 minutes. Yet we are told that the learned assistant sessions judge at the time disregarded these evidentiary incoherencies and concluded that Mirro must have indeed committed the crime solely on the basis that "the station officer, Imdad Husain, was a Musalman and it was impossible that he should have brought a false case against an innocent Musalman" (Mirro v. Emperor). When addressing Mirro's appeal and reviewing the evidence, the appeals judge overturned the earlier judgment and concluded that while he wished no ill will against his predecessor, "there was no warrant for introducing this communal tinge in the case. Sakoor, the principal prosecution witness, is a Musalman. All the assessors who found the accused not guilty, are Hindus" (Mirro v. Emperor). In his final assessment, the judge added that "a careful examination of the entire evidence does leave an impression that the accused is an undesirable person who has made many enemies and the case is an outcome of that enemity" (Mirro v. Emperor).

Several significant historical details emerge in this dizzying account of a case filed under Section 377 in the 1940s. Indeed, its appearance a mere year or two before the 1947 brutal partition of India and its complex

narration of communal relations all make it a case worthy of careful exploration. As many historians of colonial India have previously noted, Agra
(and the larger region of what is now known as Uttar Pradesh) functioned
as a critical testing ground for both the emergence of Indian nationalism
as well as that of Indian communalism. The rise of the Indian National
Congress, the Muslim League, the Hindu Mahasaba made the region a
veritable hotbed of Indian politics, where the differences between Hindus
and Muslims became the representational playing field for nationalists
and colonial officials alike. Yet as scholars such as Salil Misra have carefully argued, the overdetermined focus on communalism was a cover story
needed for eliding unified caste and class mass movements. Others such
as Sanjay Joshi, Sandria Freitag, and C. A. Bayly have similarly noted that
that Uttar Pradesh's key role in the early stages of self-governance (produced through the famous Morley-Minto enfranchisement reforms and
the Government of India Act of 1935) made it impossible to disarticulate
mythologies of communalism from structures of electoral politics (see
also Brass; Pandey). As the Mirro case demonstrates, communal differentiation, more than communal violence, appears attached to the crime
of sodomy. Chamars, while Hindu, were and are a lower-caste dominant
majority in the region and not easily folded into the language of Hindu
hegemony and Muslim minoritization. In fact, the period between 1930
and 1947 marked the rise of various mass Adi-Dharma movements, one
of the earliest organized casteless movements in British India, wherein
lower-caste Hindus, such as the Chamar community, came together to
found religious communities that openly opposed the dominance of
upper-caste Hindus (Rawat). In the Mirro case, then, the scene of sodomy is one of profound exaggeration and estrangement from the popular
mythology of communal discord.

Yet, despite such immense historical potential, no references to the
Mirro case appear either in the petition against Section 377 or in any
of the available critical materials on sodomy. It is a narrative in which
sodomy's presence and absence are both questioned and asserted. What
happens if we think of the case less as another instantiation of colonial
legal bungling than as a challenging (and potentially subversive) colonial
record? Located in its topography, we find figurations of scattered violence (e.g., dangerous slapstick communal humor, mob mentality) that
make the crime of sodomy more a crime of narrative corroboration than a
crime of action. For sodomy to emerge, it must be corroborated, its form
sedimented in a history of recall that, in this case, neither the witnesses
nor the evidence can sustain. We must know and not know the colonial
record, not once, but twice. Such a reading radicalizes our understanding

of the historical turn in recording the "cognitive failure" at the heart of both our past and present readerly attempts, making the distinction between success and failure indeterminate. The most successful historical record of sexuality becomes, as it were, a successful record of cognitive failure (see Spivak, "Subaltern").

CODA

To contemplate the kinds of comparative imaginaries I have been outlining here means acknowledging that the field of sexuality studies, like other field formations, too, has a sedimented politics of time. And that, for better or for worse, that politics often reproduces subjects, critical genealogies, and methodological habits that duplicate the very historiographies we seek to exceed. The shift I have in mind here has attempted to push against the stabilizing of time's corpus, toward a historiography of sexuality that settles into uncertainty as the very possibility of return.

POSTSCRIPT

Even as this collection goes into press, much has changed in the political landscape of lesbian, gay, bisexual, and transgender (LGBT) rights in India. In the two years since I wrote this chapter, the Naz foundation-led campaign against Section 377 has made significant headway. Most recently, on 2 July 2009, the Delhi High Court finally passed a decision repealing Section 377, even as it sternly added that such a repeal was in no way an indication of the court's "tolerance" of homosexuality in India (see Repeal). While there has clearly been much (understandable) euphoria over the court's decriminalization of consensual same-sex behavior, there has also been some sustained skepticism about the continued focus on Section 377 as a sign of LGBT liberation. To link the repeal of Section 377 to the idea of a stable community of (gay) subjects, as scholars such as Jason Fernandes have argued, prioritizes the interests of urban, English-speaking, middle-class leaders at the expense, or rather elision, of the very subalternity they claim to represent. That is, one of the primary arguments against Section 377 has been the fact that it is arbitrarily mobilized by corrupt policemen to intimidate and extort monies from sex workers soliciting MSM clients. The reading down of the law may thus now ostensibly allow for same-sex acts within private spaces, yet it ironically offers no protection for same-sex practices outside the normative parameters of home and domesticity. Solicitation continues to be outside the law, making it unlikely that policemen will cease their harassment and brutalization of sex workers (Fernandes). In searching for a moment through which to figure a more differentiated relationship to sexuality, we might thus do well to turn to the cautionary tale of Section 377 to meditate on what (post)colonial legal activists must often absent to produce a more timely "gay" corpus.

NOTES

1. I am of course not the first one to make this claim. Other scholars, such as Ara Wilson, have argued for a "queer regionalism" that more locally translates the relationship between Asian studies and queer studies. See also Boellstorff, Murray, and Robinson's introduction. My engagement, however, lies more with the broader historiographical questions undergirding such possible dialogues.
2. I borrow the expression "politics of time" from Prathama Banerjee's meditations on history writing and the time(s) of the primitive in a postcolonial world.
3. For example, see Grewal, Gupta, and Ong's introduction to a special issue on the subject. The authors argue for a "transnational mode of analysis" to complicate current area studies, comparative studies, and disciplinary understandings of locality.
4. Coopan provides an excellent analysis of the "split personality" of current globalization discourses.
5. A strident and, by now, well-known critique of the similarity-difference model of comparison in cross-cultural explorations comes from the anthropologist Johannes Fabian: "There would be no raison d'être for the comparative method if it was not the classification of entities or traits which first have to be separate and distinct before their similarities can be used to establish taxonomies and developmental sequences" (26–27). For a sustained discussion of the entanglements of normative categories and comparative analysis, see Cheah.
6. Stoler's project echoes and complicates some of the claims made by Benedict Anderson's canonical text *The Spectre of Comparisons*. Anderson challenges the falseness of regional assemblages and argues for a more nuanced comparative framework that understands (and is indeed haunted by) pre- and postcolonial arrangements of geopolitics and disciplinary formations. One must compare, he argues, from "simultaneously close up and from afar" (2).
7. Chow's focus on the epistemic violence of such Eurocentric time-space alignments echoes McClintock's earlier formulations on the intersections of empire and sexuality. For McClintock, the colonial site (specific but not restricted to questions of sexuality) remains fixed within the languages of what she terms as "anachronistic space" and "panoptical time" (1–35).
8. Worth noting here is that Spivak begins her theorizations on "teleopoiesis" through an invocation of what she calls the "originary queerness" of the subaltern trace. While Spivak steps back from extending her usage of the

term "queer" beyond signaling its potentiality as a reading practice, her "queer" turn, as it were, certainly bears further exploration.

9. I thank Sameera Khan and members of the Mumbai-based Lawyer's Collective for early access to these materials. See also Fernandez.

10. For a more extensive reading of this shift, see Katyal.

11. See the Counter Affidavit in *Naz Foundation v. Govnt. of Delhi*.

12. For specific critiques of legal scholarship in colonial and postcolonial South Asia, see Parker; Kolsky; see also Robertson.

13. I have elaborated more substantially on the project of archival hermeneutics and histories of sexuality elsewhere (see Arondekar).

14. A notable example of the tenets of medical jurisprudence is Chevers, *Manual*. See also Chevers, *Commentary*.

Works Cited

Anderson, Benedict. *The Spectre of Comparisons: Nationalism, Southeast Asia and the World*. London: Verso, 1998.

Arondekar, Anjali. "Without a Trace: Sexuality and the Colonial Archive." *Journal of the History of Sexuality* 14.1–2 (2005): 10–27.

Banerjee, Prathama. *Politics of Time: "Primitives" and History-Writing in Colonial Society*. New Delhi: Oxford UP, 2006.

Bayly, C. A. *The Local Roots of Indian Politics: Allahabad 1880–1920*. Oxford: Clarendon, 1975.

Boellstorff, Tom, David A. B. Murray, and Kathryn Robinson. "East Indies/West Indies: Comparative Archipelagoes." *Anthropological Forum* 16.3 (2006): 219–27.

Brass, Paul. *Language, Religion and Politics in North India*. New York: Cambridge UP, 1974.

Cheah, Pheng. "Grounds of Comparison." *Diacritics* 29.4 (1999): 3–18.

Chevers, Norman. *A Commentary on the Diseases of India*. London, 1886.

———. *A Manual of Medical Jurisprudence for India: Including the Outline of a History of Crime against the Person in India*. Calcutta, 1870.

Chow, Rey. *The Age of the World Target: Self-Referentiality in War, Theory, and Comparative Work*. Durham: Duke UP, 2006.

Coopan, Vilashini. "Ruins of Empire: The National and Global Politics of America's Return to Rome." *Postcolonial Studies and Beyond*. Ed. Ania Loomba, Suvir Kaul, Matti Bunzl, Antoinette Burton, and Jed Esty. Durham: Duke UP, 2005. 81–100.

Fabian, Johannes. *Time and the Other: How Anthropology Makes Its Object*. New York: New P, 1983.

Fernandes, Jason Keith. "The Dilemma after the Decision: Stray Thoughts after Gay Liberation." *Tehelka* 14 Aug. 2009. <http://www.tehelka.com/story _main42.asp?filename=Ws220809The_Dilemma.asp>. 1 June 2010.

Fernandez, Bina, ed. *Hum Jinsi: A Resource Book on Lesbian, Gay & Bisexual Rights in India*. Mumbai: India Centre for Human Rights and Law, 1999.

Freitag, Sandria B. *Collective Action and Community: Public Arenas and the Emergence of Communalism in North India.* Berkeley: U of California P, 1989.

Grewal, Inderpal, Akhil Gupta, and Aihwa Ong. "Introduction." *positions* 7.3 (1999): 653–66.

Hacking, Ian. *Historical Ontology.* Cambridge: Harvard UP, 2002.

Joshi, Sanjay. *Fractured Modernity: Making of a Middle Class in Colonial North India.* New Delhi: Oxford UP, 2001.

Kapur, Ratna. *Erotic Justice: Politics of Postcolonialism.* New Delhi: Permanent Black, 2005.

Katyal, Sonia. "Exporting Identity." *Yale Journal of Law and Feminism* 14 (2002): 97–176.

Kolsky, Elizabeth. "A Note on the Study of Indian Legal History." *Law and History Review* 23.2 (2006): 703–6.

McClintock, Anne. *Imperial Leather: Race, Gender and Sexuality in the Colonial Contest.* New York: Routledge, 1995.

Menon, Nivedita. *Recovering Subversion: Feminist Politics beyond the Law.* Urbana: U of Illinois P, 2004.

Mirro v. Emperor. *All India Reporter* 34 (1947): 97.

Misra, Salil. *A Narrative of Communal Politics: Uttar Pradesh, 1937–39.* New Delhi: Sage, 2001.

Naz Foundation v. Govnt. of Delhi, Police Commissioner of Delhi, Delhi State. AIDS Control Society, Union of India, Civil Writ Petition. 2001.

Pandey, Gyandendra. *The Ascendancy of the Congress in Uttar Pradesh 1926–34: A Study in Imperfect Mobilization.* Delhi: Oxford UP, 1978.

Parker, Kunal. "The Historiography of Difference." *Law and History Review* 23.2 (2006): 685–95.

Radhakrishnan, Radha. *History, the Human, and the World Between.* Durham: Duke UP, 2007.

Ranchhoddas, Ratanlal, and Dhirajlal Keshavlal Thakoree. *The Indian Penal Code.* 27th ed. Nagpur: Wadhwa, 1992.

Rawat, Ramnarayan S. "Making Claims for Power: A New Agenda in Dalit Politics of Uttar Pradesh, 1946–48." *Modern Asian Studies* 37.3 (2003): 585–612.

Repeal of Section 377. <http://lobis.nic.in/dhc/APS/judgement/02-07-2009/APS02072009CW74552001.pdf>. 1 Aug. 2009.

Robertson, Stephen. "What's Law Got to Do with It? Legal Records and Sexual Histories." *Journal of the History of Sexuality* 14.1–2 (2005): 161–85.

Sen, Amartya. "Amartya Sen's Statement on the Need to Do Away with Section 377 of the Indian Penal Code." *The Hindustan Times* 15 Sept. 2006. <http://www.sacw.net/SexualityMinorities/ASen_377sept2006.html>. 1 June 2010.

Spivak, Gayatri Chakravorty. *A Critique of Postcolonial Reason: Towards a History of the Vanishing Present.* Cambridge: Harvard UP, 1999.

———. *Death of a Discipline.* New York: Columbia UP, 2003.

Stoler, Ann Laura, ed. *Haunted by Empire: Geographies of Intimacy in North American History.* Durham: Duke UP, 2006.

Vanita, Ruth, ed. *Queering India: Same-Sex Love and Eroticism in Indian Culture and Society.* New York: Routledge, 2002.
Wilson, Ara. "Queering Asia." *Intersections: Gender, History and Culture in the Asian Context* 14 (2006). <http://wwwsshe.murdoch.edu.au/intersections/issue14/wilson.html>.

CHAPTER 6

DOUBLE TROUBLE

DOING GENDER IN HONG KONG

MARIE-PAULE HA

IN *GENDER TROUBLE*, JUDITH BUTLER EXPLAINS HER CHOICE OF the term "trouble" in the title of her book as follows:

> Contemporary feminist debates over the meanings of gender lead time and again to a certain sense of trouble, as if the indeterminacy of gender might eventually culminate in the failure of feminism. Perhaps trouble need not carry such a negative valence. To make trouble was, within the reigning discourse of my childhood, something one should never do precisely because that would get one *in* trouble. The rebellion and its reprimand seemed to be caught up in the same terms, a phenomenon that gave rise to my first critical insight into the subtle ruse of power: The prevailing law threatened one with trouble, even put one in trouble, all to keep one out of trouble. Hence, I concluded that trouble is inevitable and the task, how best to make it, what best way to be in it. (vii)

Within a short time of its publication (1990), Butler's book had indeed stirred up quite a bit of trouble in the field of gender studies through her questioning of the epistemic-ontological regime of presumptive heterosexuality that has hitherto framed gender studies in Western or Western-informed institutions. Her analysis exposes the "assumed" ontological status of gender categories, which she argues are "the *effects* of institutions, practices, discourses with multiple and diffuse points of origin" (ix) rather than natural givens. In her deconstructive undertaking, Butler targets exclusively the modern sexual regime of Western societies, which she presents as operating under a monohegemonic sociocultural order. In this chapter, I would take Butler's critique a step further by investigating what additional trouble would befall gender studies when the discourses and practices that produce gender identities partake of two cultural, albeit unequal, sites as is, I would argue, the case of Hong Kong. By bringing Butler into comparison with gender studies in the Hong Kong context, I hope to trouble the waters of queer theory; indeed, I will argue, comparison can be deployed to make theoretical trouble as a way of further queering Western queer theory by bringing it into contact with its Hong Kong other and therefore by doubling the trouble, so to speak.

Besides Butler's work, my sense of trouble in doing gender in Hong Kong has another source that is linked to the wider issue of the deployment of Western theories in non-Western texts and contexts. The initial framework in which I was first led to rethink gender work in Hong Kong could be described as "pedagogical." Here I use the term "pedagogical" in Pierre Bourdieu and Jean-Claude Passeron's sense, according to which "all pedagogic action is, objectively, symbolic violence insofar as it is the imposition of a cultural arbitrary by an arbitrary power" (5). In the gender courses I teach at the University of Hong Kong, I make rather ample use of critical and theoretical works developed by "Western" and "Western-trained" scholars.[1] Whenever I introduce a "Western" theoretical text, invariably I would ask students to reflect on whether the text's arguments are applicable to the Hong Kong situation. At one level, my question is informed by Bourdieu's concern over the role of the school as an ideological state apparatus to legitimize the culture of the dominant class at the expense of that of the disenfranchised groups. In his work, which deals mainly with the power dynamic in contemporary French society, Bourdieu was critiquing primarily the hegemony of the bourgeois class. But in postcolonial Hong Kong, the power relations that shape the politics of academic institutions straddle both class and cultural arenas. By interrogating the relationship between "Western" theories and the indigenous situation, the objective was to bring out the contingent character of the former so as to question their universalizing stand.

Yet, at another level, my question could be criticized for assuming the much-contested division of academic qua intellectual labor between disciplines and area studies that characterizes the institutional structure of many a North American university and their look-alikes elsewhere. In this labor division, critics say, the disciplines are entrusted with the task of theory building while the area studies find themselves relegated to the role of provider of raw empirical data. This disciplines-area studies divide, Pheng Cheah contends, rests on other more fundamental epistemological oppositions such as the contrast "between pure and applied knowledges," which is in turn based on the dichotomy between the universal and the particular: the particular being tied to the immediacy of experience while universality is the mark of discursive knowledge, which supposedly carries universal validity through the mediation of abstract and universally communicable concepts (44). Given that the standards of knowledge derived from the disciplines emerge from Western sociocultural contexts, the implication is that, Cheah further argues, "there is an unspoken . . . isomorphism between the universal structures of reason and the social structures of the West" (45). In other words, the theories elaborated by the disciplines in Western institutions would take on the role of a universal conceptual matrix through which non-Western cultures are to be apprehended, thereby creating what Naoki Sakai describes as "a centrifugal flow of information" that would "render intelligible the details and trivia coming from particular peripheral sites to a 'Western audience'" (75). Within the terms of this debate, my question of the applicability of Western gender theories to the Chinese or Hong Kong context could be construed as yet another instance of using indigenous data to, in the words of Dipesh Chakrabarty, "flesh out a theoretical skeleton that is substantially 'Europe'" (29). Hence, rather than calling them into crisis, my questions may bring about the renewal of Western theories.

But in the Hong Kong context, would we have the option of doing gender work without using Western theories? For a number of practical and ideological reasons, the answer is "no." For if the "we" in the question refers to the academics currently employed by the tertiary institutions in Hong Kong, most of us (including both ethnic Chinese and non-Chinese) either have received a Western training or were actually trained in the West. In fact, it is such training that qualifies us for the jobs in the first place. The expectation, if not requirement, that her academics be conversant with Western knowledge is of course not peculiar to Hong Kong. For, as Chakrabarty argues, since the end of the nineteenth century the hegemonic status of Western knowledge in non-Western tertiary and research institutions has generated a situation he describes as one of "asymmetric ignorance." That is, while European scholars could produce their work in relative ignorance of non-Western knowledge and languages, "we cannot . . . afford an equality or symmetry of ignorance at this level without taking the risk of appearing 'old-fashioned' or 'outdated'" (28). Indeed, in today's tertiary institutions, most exchanges are mediated by Western disciplinary discourses that structure the very way we articulate our research problems and define what count as legitimate topics of inquiry and meaningful explanations. Within the institutional frame of the academia those objects or questions that fall outside the discursive boundaries of Western disciplines would be considered as beyond the intellectual pale and therefore unfit for research, let alone publication in the so-called international venues. Hence, the challenge (and it is a tall one) is to see whether our Western apprenticeship would necessarily mean that our self-understanding and self-determination could be achieved, to quote Cheah again, "only by being . . . possessed by the specter of the West" (48).[2]

In this chapter I start with a review of the debate that centers on the issues of appropriateness and adequacy of Western theories in the investigation of gender issues in the Chinese-Hong Kong context. I then proceed to scrutinize some of the premises of the debate, in particular the assumption of the ontological status of Chinese gender configurations that are presumed to exist prior to a given conceptual framework. In part three, I discuss some of the insights Chakrabarty develops in his critique of the use of Western historiography in Indian historical writing and that, I believe, help to shed new light in our gender research. In the fourth section of the chapter, I elaborate the view that gender identities among Hong Kong Chinese are the effects of both the Chinese cosmological and Western biomedical body schemas, each of which envisions sexual differences in completely dissimilar ways. In the conclusion, I suggest that while we need to retain the Western conceptual matrix in doing gender we should also articulate a research framework that would allow us to stay with our heterogeneities by positioning ourselves at the juncture where, to paraphrase Chakrabarty, we forsake neither Butler nor "difference."

The deployment of Western theoretical languages to account for non-Western texts and contexts has long been a contentious issue among critics of every ideological stripe involved in cross-cultural researches (see Said). For the purpose of this chapter, I limit my observations to the debate in the area of gender studies. In "Under Western Eyes: Feminist Scholarship and Colonial Discourses" (1988) Chandra Talpade Mohanty discusses a number of works on "Third World women" by Western feminists in the Zed Press series. In her analysis she points out that "assumptions of privilege and ethnocentric universality on the one hand, and inadequate self-consciousness about the effect of Western scholarship on the 'third world' in the context of a world system dominated by the West on the other, characterize a sizable extent of Western feminist work on women in the third world" (197–98). One consequence of such an attitude is that in these Western feminist studies, the material and historical heterogeneities of the lives of Third-World women were subsumed under a composite singular image of "the Third-World woman." A similar point was later made by Gayatri Chakravorty Spivak, who in "The Politics of Translation," criticizes the "monolingual" Western feminists for promoting cross-cultural and universal feminist solidarity but only in their terms: "There are countless languages in which women all over the world have grown up and been female or feminist, and yet the languages we keep on learning by rote are the powerful European ones" (192).

The same debates have also been taken up in Chinese studies within Western or Western theory-informed academic settings. A case in point is Rey Chow's response to the view held by certain sinologists that Chinese texts should be studied with "Chinese" rather than Western methodologies so as to avoid "misreading" of Chinese materials. Chow finds such a position quite untenable within the modern Chinese historical context, which was profoundly marked by the event of Western imperialism: "What is missing from the preoccupation with tradition and authentic originariness as such is the experience of modern Chinese people who have had to live their lives with the knowledge that it is precisely the notion of a still-intact tradition to which they cannot cling—the experience of being impure, 'Westernized' Chinese" (28). More recently these questions have been raised in the field of Chinese gender research, in particular among critics working on Chinese masculinities. In "Chinese Masculinity: Theorizing *Wen* and *Wu*" Kam Louie and Louise Edwards express strong resistance to the application of a Western gender paradigm to Chinese gender studies as it would, they argue, "only serve to prove that Chinese men are 'not quite real men'" (138). Instead, the Chinese paradigm should be used to study Chinese masculinity. The Chinese paradigm they propose is the *wen wu* model. The *wen* refers to those "genteel, refined qualities that were associated with the literary and artistic pursuits of classical scholars" (141), while the *wu* consists of attributes of physical strength and military prowess (142).[3] The *wen* and *wu* constitute the two types of Chinese masculinity embodied respectively by the scholar and the soldier even though there are also instances of men possessing both *wen* and *wu* qualities.[4]

One often-cited example of the problematic application of Western theories to the study of Chinese gender is Sun Longji's *The "Deep Structure" of Chinese Culture*, which was discussed at length by Xueping Zhong in her *Masculinity Besieged?*[5] Using the Oedipus complex model to interpret May Fourth literature and the data collected by American sociological researchers in Taiwan between the 1950s and 1970s, Sun argues that Chinese men suffer from the problem of "Wombnization," that is, the "failure" to cut the umbilical cord, a "failure" that he attributes to the "flawed" Chinese familial structure that prevents the "proper" separation of the son from the mother. According to Sun's analysis, which is premised on the conflation of modernization and Westernization, the only possible way for Chinese men to achieve "real" manhood and for China to progress is to become Westernized, for in Sun's view, Zhong writes, "a Western model for male acculturation is 'naturally' better than the Chinese one" (31). While challenging (and rightly so) Sun's undue privileging of the Oedipus model in assessing Chinese gender formation, interestingly enough Zhong herself also draws extensively on psychoanalytical theory in her subsequent discussions of Chinese masculinity. Hence, it is not clear whether Zhong is critiquing the use of Western theories in Chinese materials or rather the misuse of them.

The uneasiness toward the use of Western theories likewise characterizes much of the work on gender studies in Hong Kong. To date, many of the Hong Kong academic gender researches are undertaken by scholars in the fields of social sciences and (more recently) cultural studies. From the disciplinary backgrounds of the researchers, one could safely infer that the works are most likely informed by Western theoretical frameworks. As an illustration of some of gender work currently done by Hong Kong academics, I will briefly refer to a recent bilingual gender work titled *Gendering Hong Kong*, edited by Anita Kit-wa Chan and Wong Wai-ling. This is a hefty 770-page reader that offers an extensive coverage of local gender research issues. In their general introduction, the editors preface their explanation of the analytical framework of the reader with a statement on their relationship to Western theories: "In the following, we shall first briefly introduce our analytical framework, a gendering perspective, by reviewing the theoretical development of the concept of gender in the Western literature. This does not mean that we consider a simple transplantation of Western theories can *adequately* explain the local context. Instead, we believe the discussion necessary as it provides readers with a more systematic guide to understanding our selection of the articles and the overall structure of this collection" (xvii; emphasis added). This statement seems to register the editors' sense of ambivalence vis-à-vis the deployment of Western theories in local context, yet a few sections later in their introduction, when commenting on the state of local gender research, the editors write, "When one closely examines the ways gender is used in this emerging research field, one soon realizes there are two popular approaches. The first one is to treat it merely as an independent variable . . . whereas the second one is to conceptualize gender as role differences. We regard both approaches as less than satisfactory, as they have under-utilized the conceptual insights generated by the concept of gender and the theoretical and political rigour of feminist knowledge." A footnote informs the readers that "our assessment is mainly based on our theoretical understanding of the concept of gender, which is outlined in Part 1" (xxvii–xxviii). The theoretical understanding of the concept of gender outlined in the first part refers precisely to those Western theories that the editors deem as not quite "adequate" to the local context.

My foregrounding of the editors' dilemma is meant not to be a critique but rather an illustration of the "trouble" of doing gender in Hong Kong. At one level, many of us do share the editors' awareness that the concepts of sex and gender we are using today were developed in Western societies and were quite alien to traditional Chinese understanding of sexual differences. In fact, it has been pointed out by many critics that the Chinese terms *xing* (sex) and *xing pie* (gender) made their appearance in the Chinese language only at the beginning of the twentieth century.[6] In *Sex, Culture and Modernity in China*, Frank Dikötter argues that it was not until the late nineteenth century that the former neo-Confucian-based Chinese gender-hierarchy scheme was replaced by the Western biomedical discourse of sexual differences in the writings of new bourgeois intellectual elite. Before the twentieth century, a person's gender identity in China was defined in terms not of her physiology, but of her relation to the family kinship system as mother or father, daughter or son, wife or husband, which was in turn linked to the cosmological yin-yang pair.[7] One of my arguments in the chapter is that while it may be the case that at the institutional level the traditional Chinese gender framework has been displaced by Western biomedical discourse, the former still maintains a strong hold in a large number of our everyday practices.

From the foregoing discussion on the different views surrounding the use of Western theories and disciplinary knowledge in non-Western texts and contexts I think it would be fair to say that thus far the debate tends to be framed in the either-or form: Is it appropriate to apply Western theories to analyze Chinese gender issues? Could Western theories adequately account for our local context? In other words, while disagreeing over the question of appropriateness, both camps in fact share the common assumption that the contexts, or "data," to be analyzed have a prior existence that is separate from and independent of the conceptual matrix, the latter being seen as an analytical tool to study the former. Instead of continuing the debate in these terms, I propose to shift our attention to examine the assumption itself. My contention is that the assumption underlying the debate in its current form is grounded on, to use an expression popularized by Butler, "the metaphysics of substance" (*Gender Trouble* 10). In the humanist conception of the subject, Butler argues, the person is presumed to possess a pregendered substance or core that serves as the bearer of essential and nonessential attributes, with gender being one of the essential attributes. In other words, the metaphysics of substance fosters the illusion of the prior ontological reality of substance and attribute. The same fallacy, I believe, underlies the current debate on how Chinese gender issues could best be studied. That is, our questions presume that Chinese gender categories preexist the theoretical framework we use and that the former are independent of and prior to the latter. The debate is viewed as a matter of deciding which theoretical approach or paradigm (Western or non-Western) could best account for Chinese gender configurations. But what if, as Butler contends, the conceptual matrix is in fact *prior* to the emergence of gender categories and relations? Could we then say, to paraphrase Butler, that conceptualization produces as an *effect* of its own procedures the very gender configuration that it nevertheless and simultaneously claims to discover as that which precedes its own action (*Bodies* 30)? In *Translingual Practice*, Lydia Liu makes a similar argument in her study of the cultural and ideological interactions between China, Japan, and the West. Liu states, "When I say that May Fourth literature puts itself at the service of a humane knowledge that specializes in probing the psychological depths of the mind, I mean precisely what the words themselves suggest. The mind becomes analyzable when terms like *xinli* (psychology) and *yuwang* (desire) become translatable and when translingual models of narration begin to reconfigure what is real and what is unreal about the human mind" (132).

From this perspective, interrogating the appropriateness or adequacy of Western theories for Chinese gender issues would not take us very far, since the conceptualization and articulation of the issues is intricately linked with a particular episteme. Given the hegemonic status of Western knowledge, it would be very unlikely that researchers could operate outside the Western conceptual matrix, but the need to do so does not mean that we could not resist the universalizing impulse of Western theories.

In my rethinking of gender work, I find many of the issues Chakrabarty raises in his critical discussion of history as an institutional discourse quite pertinent to the problems I am struggling with. One of the starting points Chakrabarty makes in his book *Provincializing Europe* is the recognition of the role of European thought as a "silent referent" in the enquiry of the political modernity of non-Western nations. The core of the dilemma for a historian writing non-Western history within the disciplinary discourse of history is tied to the very nature of history as a discipline. For within the modern Western academic setting, history is foremost understood as a secular subject working within a godless, continuous, empty, and homogeneous temporality. This "disenchanted" character of modern historical consciousness, Chakrabarty argues, makes no allowances for practices that involve the interventions of gods, spirits, and supernatural beings, practices that are still being observed in many non-Western societies. For historians such as Chakrabarty and his colleagues in the subaltern studies group whose research interest lies with the histories of Indian workers and peasants, their challenge is how to write about these histories without having to translate their life-worlds into universal sociological categories such as "labor" or "capital." But within the institutional context of the academy, such translation is, in Chakrabarty's view, both "unavoidable and inevitable," since historians like him write not for the peasants but for their colleagues in the profession. Hence the challenge for cross-cultural historians is how to conduct "these translations in such a manner as to make visible all the problems of translating diverse and enchanted worlds into the universal and disenchanted language of sociology" (89).

The solution Chakrabarty proposes is not to jettison Western historicity but to bring about what he calls "subaltern" or "minor/minority" histories of which the central strategy in writing subaltern pasts is "to stay with heterogeneities without seeking to reduce them to any overarching principle that speaks for an already given whole" (107). Such an overarching principle in modern historiography is the deployment of a homogenous and secular calendar time taken as "a naturally existing, continuous flow of historical time," which is used to frame all historical explanations and to which one could assign peoples, events, and objects irrespective of a given culture's understanding of temporality (73). In Chakrabarty's project, subaltern histories are characterized by "a split running through them": that is, on the one hand they do not situate themselves outside the master code of secular history; on the other hand they would not "grant this master code its claim of being a mode of thought that comes to all human beings naturally" (93). In other words, in the weaving of modern historical narratives, "subaltern pasts are like stubborn knots that stand out and break up the otherwise evenly woven surface of the fabric" (106). The challenge of writing the subaltern pasts for modern historians is to resist the temptation to incorporate them within the mainstream hegemonic historical discourse.

The tensions between the general secular time of history and the singular times of gods and spirits evoked by Chakrabarty are not unique to Indian historiography, as these types of tensions are also present in other fields of practices, in particular those that straddle different life-worlds. A case in point is Hong Kong gender practices, which, I argue, partake simultaneously of two distinct cultural formations of the body—the Western biomedical one and the Chinese cosmological one—each of which sustains a separate conception of sexual differences. In the following I will review briefly the differences between the two body schemas and discuss a number of anthropological studies on contemporary Chinese's practice of medical pluralism that is linked to their multiple embodiment.

Until the introduction of biomedical discourse to China in the late nineteenth century, Chinese gender configurations were patterned in accordance to a conceptual body scheme that is intricately tied to the Chinese cosmological outlook.[8] The *Huang ti nei ching* (translated as *The Inner Canon of the Yellow Emperor* and hereafter as *The Inner Canon*),[9] the locus classicus most frequently referred to by medical anthropologists and cultural historians in their discussions of the Chinese body, conceives of the human body as a microcosm that "correspond(s) part to part and function to function" to the cosmos (Sivin, *Traditional Medicine* 54). Like the cosmos, the human body is made of the primordial stuff known as the *qi* (ch'i), which is regulated by the two opposite yet complementary yin-yang forces,[10] yin being associated with cold, moisture, darkness, passivity, the moon, and the feminine and yang symbolizing brightness, heat, the sun, activity, and the masculine. These two forces serve as the organizing principles of all bodies and states, human as well as cosmic. The way to achieve well-being at both the macrocosmic and microcosmic levels is to maintain a fine yin-yang balance.

Within the Chinese cosmological framework, the gender markers of the Chinese body, or to use a phrase coined by Charlotte Furth, "the Yellow Emperor's body" (19), differ radically from those of its European biomedical counterpart. The human body as constructed by biomedical science is made up of discrete parts constituted as organs, muscles, bones, and sinews. It was such an anatomical conception of the body that made it possible for the eighteenth-century scientists in Europe to use body parts to construct what Thomas Laqueur describes as "an anatomy and physiology of incommensurability" of the sexes ("Orgasm" 2). Within this anatomical body schema, sexual differences were not only said to reside in genitalia and the so-called reproductive organs but also ascribed to every single body part from the skull to the pelvis.[11]

Rather than an ensemble of discrete parts, the body in *The Inner Canon* is conceived of as "a congeries of vital processes" (Sivin, *Traditional Medicine* 4). The internal organs that biomedicine visualizes as entities with well-delineated spatial contours do not enter into the scheme of the Yellow Emperor's body. Their Chinese correlates, Sivin notes, would be more appropriately thought of as visceral systems of functions closely interconnected with each other via the *ching-lo*, or circulation tract system (213). Such a nonanatomical view of the body not surprisingly envisages sexual differences in ways entirely dissimilar to those of biomedicine. To begin with, the infamous definition of woman that Simone de Beauvoir quotes in the introduction of *The Second Sex*—"*Tota mulier in utero*" (woman is a womb)—would have no place in *The Inner Canon* in which, Furth points out, "female difference based on the womb as anatomy was reduced to an irrelevancy" (44). For within the Chinese body schema, the categories of "male" and "female" were explained in terms not of biological differences but of relative predominance of yin and yang. The Yellow Emperor's body, Furth further contends, is truly androgynous in that unlike the Galenic "one-sex" model, which defined the female body as the inferior version of the male one, the classical Chinese body has no morphological sex. It is a site in which the yin and yang could figure in multiple combinations that might vary not only from person to person but also within the same individual according to time and circumstances. An example Furth provides is *The Inner Canon*'s account of the sexual development of boys and girls who are portrayed as "the work of a single human body of dynamically interpenetrating yin yang vitalities" (45). Far from being fixed essences, yin and yang maintain in the body highly fluid relationships with each other. Therefore, it would have been misleading to associate men with yang and women with yin for, as Sivin explains, an old man may position himself as yang in relation to a woman, but he would be yin with respect to a young man. In other words, sexual differences here are to be understood as moving along "a continuum of probability" (Bray 235).

The Chinese cosmological paradigm as a whole faced its most serious challenge during the early decades of the twentieth century, when many Western-oriented Chinese intellectuals expressed strong doubts as to the viability of traditional methods to cope with the numerous domestic problems and imperialistic aggressions that plagued the nation.[12] One branch of knowledge that was particularly hard-hit was Chinese medicine (*chung i*), which was faulted for its cosmological underpinning. The call to replace Chinese knowledge with Western science was launched by Ch'en Tu-hsiu (Chen Duxiu), one of the most influential May Fourth intellectuals, in his 1915 essay "Call to Youth," in which he stated that "our physicians know no science; not only are they not acquainted with human anatomy, but contagious diseases, they have never heard of them. They only parrot the talk about the five elements . . . heat and cold, *yin* and *yang*, and prescribe medicine according to the old formulae . . . The height of their marvelous imaginations is the theory of *ch'i* (primal force) . . . All these nonsensical ideas and reasonless beliefs can be cured at the root only by science" (245).[13] Ch'en's plea for the adoption of Western sciences had apparently been heeded by the intelligentsia of his time, as evidenced by the numerous childbirth manuals and medical treatises that journalists, social reformers, university professors, and sex educators put out in the 1920s and 1930s to initiate the Chinese public to the biomedical body language. Dikötter, who conducted an extensive study of these publications, notes that in these texts "physical bodies were no longer thought to be linked to the cosmological foundations of the universe: bodies were said to be produced by biological mechanisms inherent in 'nature'" (14).

Yet, despite the relentless May Fourth iconoclastic attacks and the concerted efforts on the part of the Kuomingtang government to replace it with biomedicine, *chung i* still managed to survive as the most widespread source of medical care for the majority of people in China from the preliberation years to the present.[14] Its enduring appeal is due to, among other factors,[15] its being rooted in Chinese cosmological framework, which continues to inform the sociocultural habitus of contemporary Chinese alongside the Western scientific episteme. As documented by a large body of researches by medical anthropologists and historians, one important characteristics of contemporary Chinese's health care management is their practice of "medical pluralism."[16] Within this pluralist scheme different strategies are devised to decide on the most appropriate medical system for the patient's needs at a particular time. Generally it is believed that biomedicine is good at bringing about fast relief to illness symptoms while *chung i* is more effective in treating the "roots" of the problem.[17]

Given the fundamental differences between the paradigms underlying the two medical systems, one implication of medical pluralism is that many Chinese in fact function within a plurality of body schemas. This multiple embodiment is best illustrated by the fieldwork conducted by Furth and Ch'en in 1985 on Taiwanese women's experience of menstruation. Their study shows that their interviewees' view of menstruation is informed by three frameworks: biomedicine, traditional Chinese medicine, and popular Buddhist teachings. In their narratives the women simultaneously draw on the biomedical lexicon of "contamination," "infection," "germs," the Buddhist view of "unclean menstrual blood," as well as the *chung i* idiom of "dampness," "fire," and "taking nutritional 'supports'" to bring about the yin-yang balance.

A second case study that illustrates a similar medical pluralism of body management was conducted by Diana Martin on contemporary Hong Kong women's observance of food restrictions in pregnancy. The interest of Martin's anthropological study for my own interrogation is twofold: first, it provides powerful examples of the culturally heterogeneous character of Hong Kong gender practices, and second, it shows the limitations of Western scientific framework to account for such heterogeneity. The question that propels Martin's research is not so much the observance of food restrictions per se as the fact that they "are observed in a place which is in so many ways 'modern,' urban and sophisticated" (100). In other words, it would not have been odd if these "indigenous non-scientific beliefs and practices" (100) were adopted by rural or lower-class uneducated Chinese women who had never been exposed to Western modern knowledge.[18] But the fact that they are observed by urban Western-educated women, who at the same time also seek biomedical care in the form of regular hospital prenatal check-ups and attendance of mothercraft classes, seems most puzzling to Martin. The challenge then is to explain these "contradictions" in the behavior of modern Hong Kong women who, Martin believes, may not be even aware of their own inconsistencies: "It is clear when talking to Chinese women in Hong Kong about matters to do with pregnancy that two unrelated world views affect their thoughts and behaviour, and yet these seem to occupy separate spheres and not to conflict on a day-to-day practical level" (100).

Martin's presentation of Hong Kong women's observance of food and activities restrictions during pregnancy as an "issue" that "needs," yet resists, "logical" explanation, shows the constraints of a Western knowledge scheme. Within this framework, whatever fails the causality test is deemed "non-scientific": "By non-scientific," Martin explains, "I mean that the link between cause and effect cannot, *at present*, be demonstrated . . . This does not, of course, mean that there are no scientific or medical grounds for observing the restrictions, merely that these have *not yet* been shown" (100; emphases added). In other words, within the Western scientific model, as long as Chinese practices do not pass the "scientific" test, they are bound to represent, like the Indian nationalist narratives, "a sad figure of lack and failure" (Chakrabarty 40).

One possibility Martin has not considered in her investigation is that many of us in Hong Kong operate within two systems of knowledge, which, it is true, are of unequal footing, in particular within academic and professional institutions.[19] In the absence of a "proper place" as its power base, Chinese knowledge in the form of practices has to insinuate itself as "tactics" into the terrain organized by the law of a foreign power.[20] In fact, in her study, Martin has provided a most telling example of how Hong Kong Chinese use food practices as tactics to remain other within the

Western paradigm that they assimilated and that assimilated them. The example is the story of banana restriction for pregnant women: bananas, being a type of "cold" food, could cause poor health in the future baby or even miscarriages, and pregnant women are advised not to eat bananas. The so-called food-restrictions practice that Martin labels "folk beliefs" in fact derives from the yin-yang scheme.[21] In her article, after explaining to the readers the banana restriction, Martin follows up with a little vignette: "At the end of an earlier discussion at a government hospital with a group of midwives who were for the most part skeptical about the restrictions, the head midwife took my helper aside (a Cantonese-speaking English woman obstetrician well-known to the midwives) and emphasized to her 'A pregnant woman really mustn't eat bananas'" (107). This temporary professional "lapse" of the Western-trained head midwife must have caused quite a bit of frustration to Martin, who ends the story with the remark that, "as with all other restrictions, however, the causal connection between the food and the outcome is not known" (107). Maybe more than the "mystery" around the link between eating bananas and miscarriage (which may one day be explained scientifically), what truly eludes the logical mind of Martin is the greater riddle surrounding the relation (or the lack of it) between the head midwife's scientific training and her "unscientific" belief in the danger of bananas to pregnant women. Yet the persistently (and resistantly) "unscientific" character of these practices is precisely their way of retaining their otherness within the dominant system. These practices, like Chakrabarty's subaltern stories, function as stubborn knots that would disrupt the otherwise seamlessly homogeneous surface of the hegemonic Western worldview that dominates in particular academic and professional institutions.

If the numerous case studies by anthropologists and historians have established the coexistence of the biomedical and Chinese cosmological body schemas among contemporary Chinese, very few works, if any, have studied the possible implications this double embodiment could have in our research in Chinese gender issues. Thus far, most of the current researches on Hong Kong gender are informed by Western theories. We have noted earlier that the criteria the editors of *Gendering Hong Kong* use in their selection of articles are based on the conceptual insights of "feminist knowledge," which is grounded almost exclusively in Western feminist theories as evidenced by the works cited in their reference list. Yet, as Elizabeth Grosz argues in *Volatile Bodies*, many Western feminists uncritically adopt Western philosophical assumptions regarding the role of the body in social, political, cultural, psychical, and sexual life. One such problematic central assumption is the body-mind dualism, which is tied to other binary pairs such as nature-culture and emotion-reason. And it is in relation to these binaries that Western feminist scholars elaborate their research issues and define their positions, even if negatively. Yet, as Sivin points out, the body mind dichotomy is in fact quite "exotic" to East Asians. For in Chinese cosmology, the terms for body, *shen* and *t'i*, denote not only a physical entity but also the whole person as seen in the expression *shen fen* (identity). Likewise, the Western concept of nature acquires its significations in opposition to something else: society, arts and sciences, law, culture and civilization,[22] whereas in China, Sivin contends, there was no equivalent to nature in the Western sense before the late nineteenth century ("State"). The expression *tzu-jan*, meaning spontaneous state or "what is so of itself," was used to translate the word *nature*. In other words, the binaries that are so fundamental to the Western construction of sexual differences have little relevance to Chinese cosmological body schema.

If it is indeed the case that, like the Taiwanese women interviewed by Furth and Ch'en, we see our bodies not as natural organisms endowed with fixed attributes but sites that are simultaneously inscribed by both Chinese and Western sociocultural texts, our challenge is to reconfigure our research framework in such a way as to accommodate the heterogeneity of our embodiment without having to translate Chinese cosmological body practices in the universalistic scientific and sociological language. One possible way to proceed is to consider cultural identities not as given but as, to paraphrase Butler, "performatively produced and compelled by the regulatory practices of cultural coherence" (*Gender* 24). In fact, there is a long-established practice among scholars in the field of Chinese overseas studies to treat identities in performative terms well before Butler's work. In his study of Chinese identities in Southeast Asia (1983), Peter Gosling describes a whole spectrum of performative tactics ranging from adaptation through accommodation, acculturation, to assimilation. Gosling also draws our attention to a group of people he refers to as "intermediate Chinese." What characterizes the intermediate Chinese is their practice of "situational ethnicities." By mixing Chinese and indigenous cultural practices, the intermediate Chinese put on different intermediate identities in accordance with the demands of the situations and the delicate power balance between them as a group and the social and political climate of their host societies (2). An example of intermediate Chinese is the Baba (Malay Chinese) in Melaka. Tan Chee-beng shows that in her interaction with others, a Baba can emphasize or deemphasize her Chinese, Baba, and Malay cultural traits as a way to show or withhold solidarity with a given group.[23]

As postcolonial Chinese, we find ourselves in the same "intermediate" position as the Chinese overseas. Like them, we also have to engage in multicultural social practices, including gendered ones, which vary in accordance to the contexts we find ourselves in. For example, within the pedagogical setting in which only science could claim the status of "real" knowledge, most of us both learn and teach the biomedical discourse of the body and sexual differences.[24] But in our daily lives, as the studies of Furth and Ch'en and Martin show, we are exposed to both the Chinese and Western gender narratives and we often have to negotiate between them in performing our culturally heterogeneous genders. In our rethinking of gender work, we no doubt need to retain the Western conceptual matrix, which produces one set of gender configurations we live by, but we also need to articulate a research framework that would enable us to stay with our own heterogeneities and resist the universalizing impulse of Western theories. In other words, rather than devising an overarching metanarrative that would homogenize our different body schemas, our research efforts should aim to bring out the many tensions, the shiftiness, and the instabilities of our double embodiment that would incessantly trouble the monohegemonic gender discourse of Western science.

NOTES

1. In the Hong Kong academic context "Western" refers mainly to Euro-American.
2. Similar critiques of Western sciences from the gender perspective have been made by feminist scholars. See Haraway; Harding, *Whose Science?* and *Is Science Multicultural?*
3. For a discussion of the construction of the *wen* type of masculinity in premodern China, see Song.
4. For examples of using Asian gender paradigms to study contemporary Asian masculinities, see Louie; Louie and Low.
5. Besides Zhong, Louie and Edwards have also criticized Sun's work.
6. For a discussion of the meanings of *xing* and *xing bie* in modern Chinese society, see Chou.
7. For a discussion of the changes in the Chinese terms for "woman," see Barlow.
8. The Chinese cosmological outlook should not be taken to refer to a monolithic structure as it draws on multiple philosophical and religious systems.
9. For useful discussions of the *Inner Canon* in English language, see Porkert; Unschuld; Sivin, *Traditional Medicine*; Farquhar, *Knowing Practice*; Furth.
10. For a detailed discussion of *ch'i*, see Sivin, *Traditional Medicine*.
11. See also Laqueur, *Making Sex*; and the excellent work of Schiebinger, her "Skeleton in the Closet" and *Nature's Body*.

12. For a discussion of the historical and political development of scientism in early twentieth-century China, see Kwok; Wang.

13. Besides Ch'en, the other highly outspoken critic of Chinese medicine was Lu Hsun (Lu Xun), who was himself a Western-trained medical doctor. For a discussion of Lu's criticisms of Chinese medicine, see Croizier, chap. 4, "Medicine and Cultural Iconoclasm in the May 4th Era."

14. For a history of the introduction of Western medicine to China during the late nineteenth and early twentieth centuries and the struggle between Western and Chinese medicines, see Croizier; Unschuld. For studies of the practice of Chinese medicine in contemporary China, Taiwan, and Hong Kong, see Sivin, *Traditional Medicine*; Farquhar, *Knowing Practice*, "Objects," and "Technologies"; Topley; Furth and Ch'en.

15. For a discussion of the political and economic factors for the survival of Chinese medicine, see Croizier.

16. Medical pluralism is, in fact, a quite common practice among peoples who had been subjected to Western colonialism, which used Western medicine as one way of establishing Europe's hegemonic presence. For a history of the deployment of biomedicine in the colonies and the subsequent development of medical pluralism, see Vaughan; Arnold; Kumar; Lal; Bashford.

17. According to Furth and Ch'en, Chinese would find the slow and gentle action of Chinese medicine most suited for chronic conditions such as those generated by menstrual and gynecological problems. See also Farquhar, *Knowing Practice*.

18. In her article, Martin cites the works of Marjorie Topley and Margery Wolf, who conducted similar researches among illiterate and poor Hong Kong women in the late 1960s and Taiwanese village women, respectively.

19. The professional and academic status of Chinese medicine has improved in Hong Kong, as some local universities started offering training in Chinese medicine and some government hospitals have introduced to patients the option of *chung i* service, while in the past biomedicine was the only legally recognized healthcare provider. Recently there are also discussions to get workplaces, schools, and insurance companies to accept medical certificates issued by Chinese medicine practitioners to apply for medical leave and reimbursement.

20. I here borrow the term "tactics" from de Certeau, who makes a distinction between strategy and tactic. In contrast to strategy, which, as a manipulation of power relationships by a subject of power (such as a business or a scientific institution), operates from a "place" delimited as its own from which it manages its relations with an exteriority (which could be customers or objects of research), a tactic has no spatial or institutional localization of its own. As such, it has to "insinuate itself into the other's place" (xix). According to de Certeau, many everyday practices (such as talking, reading, moving about, cooking) are tactical in character. The way a tactic functions is that in the absence of a "proper place" serving as its power base, it "must play on and with a terrain imposed on it and organized by the law

of a foreign power" (37), yet it always manages to remain "other within the system which [it] assimilated and which assimilated [it] externally" (32).

21. There exists in China, Hong Kong, and Taiwan a huge body of publications on food therapy. As with all elements in Chinese cosmology, every kind of edible is grouped in relation to the yin-yang pair. Food therapy is widely and routinely practiced by contemporary Chinese in their daily diet. Even restaurants use the therapeutic values of food to advertise their seasonal specialties. For an anthropological study of medicinal meals among mainland Chinese, see Farquhar, *Appetites.*

22. For a discussion of the multiple meanings of the term "nature" in Europe, see Bloch and Bloch.

23. For studies of Southeast Asian Chinese's identity management tactics, see Gosling; Tan; Ha.

24. For a discussion of sex education provided in Hong Kong schools that all adopt the biomedical view, see Ho and Tsang.

WORKS CITED

Arnold, David. *Colonizing the Body: State Medicine and Epidemic Disease in Nineteenth-Century India.* Berkeley: U of California P, 1993.

Barlow, Tani E. "Theorizing Woman: *Funü, Guojia, Jiating*" [Chinese Woman, Chinese State, Chinese Family]. *Body, Subject, and Power in China.* Ed. Angela Zito and Tani E. Barlow. Chicago: U of Chicago P, 1994. 253–89.

Bashford, Alison. "Medicine, Gender, and Empire." *Gender and Empire.* Ed. Philippa Levine. Oxford: Oxford UP, 2004. 112–34.

Bloch, Maurice, and Jean Bloch. "Women and the Dialectics of Nature in Eighteenth-Century French Thought." *Nature, Culture, and Gender.* Ed. Carol MacCormack and Marilyn Strathern. Cambridge UP, 1980. 24–41.

Bourdieu, Pierre, and Jean-Claude Passeron. *Reproduction in Education, Society and Culture.* London: Sage, 1977.

Bray, Francesca. "A Deadly Disorder: Understanding Women's Health in Late Imperial China." *Knowledge and the Scholarly Medical Traditions.* Ed. Don Bates. Cambridge: Cambridge UP, 1995. 235–50.

Butler, Judith. *Bodies That Matter: On the Discursive Limits of "Sex."* New York: Routledge, 1993.

———. *Gender Trouble: Feminism and the Subversion of Identity.* New York: Routledge, 1990.

Chakrabarty, Dipesh. *Provincializing Europe: Postcolonial Thought and Historical Difference.* Princeton: Princeton UP, 2000.

Chan, Anita Kit-wa, and Wong Wai-ling, eds. *Gendering Hong Kong.* Hong Kong: Oxford UP, 2004.

Cheah, Pheng. "Universal Areas: Asian Studies in a World in Motion." *Traces: A Multilingual Journal of Cultural Theory and Translation* 1 (2001): 37–70.

Ch'en, Tu-hsiu. "Call to Youth." *China's Response to the West: A Documentary Survey, 1839–1923*. Ed. Ssu-yü Teng and John K. Fairbank. Harvard UP, 1982. 240–45.

Chou, Wah-shan. *Tongzhi Politics of Same-Sex Eroticism in Chinese Societies*. New York: Haworth, 2000.

Chow, Rey. *Women and Chinese Modernity: The Politics of Reading between East and West*. Minneapolis: U of Minnesota P, 1991.

Croizier, Ralph C. *Traditional Medicine in Modern China: Science, Nationalism, and the Tensions of Cultural Change*. Cambridge: Harvard UP, 1968.

De Certeau, Michel. *The Practice of Everyday Life*. Trans. Steven Randall. Berkeley: U of California P, 1984.

Dikötter, Frank. *Sex, Culture and Modernity in China: Medical Science and the Construction of Sexual Identities in the Early Republican Period*. Hong Kong: Hong Kong UP, 1995.

Farquhar, Judith. *Appetites: Food and Sex in Postsocialist China*. Durham: Duke UP, 2002.

———. *Knowing Practice: The Clinical Encounter of Chinese Medicine*. Boulder: Westview, 1994.

———. "Objects, Processes, and Female Infertility in Chinese Medicine." *Medical Anthropology Quarterly* 5.4 (1991): 370–99.

———. "Technologies of Everyday Life: The Economy of Impotence in Reform China." *Cultural Anthropology* 14.2 (1999): 155–79.

Furth, Charlotte. *A Flourishing Yin: Gender in China's Medical History, 960–1665*. Berkeley: U of California P, 1999.

Furth, Charlotte, and Ch'en Shu-yueh. "Chinese Medicine and the Anthropology of Menstruation in Contemporary Taiwan." *Medical Anthropological Quarterly* 6.1 (1992): 27–48.

Gallagher, Catherine, and Thomas Laqueur, eds. *The Making of the Modern Body: Sexuality and Society in the Nineteenth Century*. Berkeley: U of California P, 1987.

Gosling, Peter. "Changing Chinese Identities in South East Asia: An Introductory Review." Gosling and Lim 1–14.

Gosling, Peter, and Linda Y. C. Lim, eds. *Identity, Culture and Politics*. Vol. 2. Singapore: Maruzen Asia, 1983.

Grosz, Elizabeth. *Volatile Bodies: Towards a Corporeal Feminism*. Bloomington: Indiana UP, 1994.

Ha, Marie-Paule. "Cultural Identities in the Chinese Diaspora." *Mots pluriels* 7 (1998). <http://www.arts.uwa.edu.au/MotsPluriels/MP798mph.html>.

Haraway, Donna. *Simians, Cyborgs, and Women: The Reinvention of Nature*. London: Free Association, 1991.

Harding, Sandra. *Is Science Multicultural? Postcolonialisms, Feminisms, and Epistemologies*. Bloomington: Indiana UP, 1998.

———. *Whose Science? Whose Knowledge?* Ithaca: Cornell UP, 1991.

Ho, Sik-ying, and Tsang Ka-tat. "The Things Girls Shouldn't See: Relocating the Penis in Sex Education in Hong Kong." Chan and Wong 690–708.

Kumar, Deepak. "Unequal Contenders, Uneven Ground: Medical Encounters in British India, 1820–1920." *Western Medicine as Contested Knowledge*. Ed. Andrew Cunningham and Bridie Andrews. Manchester: Manchester UP, 1997. 172–90.

Kwok, D. W. Y. *Scientism in Chinese Thought 1900–1950*. New Haven: Yale UP, 1965.

Lal, Maneesha. "'The Ignorance of Women Is the House of Illness': Gender, Nationalism and Health Reform in Colonial North India." *Medicine and Colonial Identity*. Ed. Mary P. Sutphen and Bridie Andrews. London: Routledge, 2003. 14–40.

Laqueur, Thomas. *Making Sex: Body and Gender from the Greeks to Freud*. Cambridge: Harvard UP, 1990.

———. "Orgasm, Generation, and the Politics of Reproductive Biology." Gallagher and Laqueur 1–41.

Liu, Lydia He. *Translingual Practice: Literature, National Culture, and Translated Modernity—China 1900–1937*. Stanford: Stanford UP, 1995.

Louie, Kam. *Theorising Chinese Masculinity: Society and Gender in China*. Cambridge: Cambridge UP, 2002.

Louie, Kam, and Louise Edwards. "Chinese Masculinity: Theorizing *Wen* and *Wu*." *East Asian History* 8 (1994): 135–48.

Louie, Kam, and Morris Low, eds. *Asian Masculinities: The Meaning and Practice of Manhood in China and Japan*. London: Routledge, 2003.

Martin, Diana. "Food Restrictions in Pregnancy among Hong Kong Mothers." *Changing Chinese Foodways in Asia*. Ed. David Y. H. Wu and Tan Chee-beng. Hong Kong: Chinese UP, 2001. 97–122.

Mohanty, Chandra Talpade. "Under Western Eyes: Feminist Scholarship and Colonial Discourses." *Colonial Discourse and Post-colonial Theory: A Reader*. Ed. Patrick Williams and Laura Chrisman. New York: Columbia UP, 1988. 196–220.

Porkert, Manfred. *The Theoretical Foundations of Chinese Medicine: Systems of Correspondence*. Cambridge: MIT P, 1974.

Said, Edward W. "Traveling Theory Reconsidered." *Reflections on Exile and Other Essays*. Cambridge: Harvard UP, 2000. 436–52.

Sakai, Naoki. "Dislocation of the West and the Status of the Humanities." *Traces: A Multilingual Journal of Cultural Theory and Translation* 1 (2001): 71–94.

Schiebinger, Londa. *Nature's Body: Gender in the Making of Modern Science*. Boston: Beacon, 1993.

———. "Skeleton in the Closet: The First Illustrations of the Female Skeleton in Eighteenth-Century Anatomy." Gallagher and Laqueur 42–82.

Sivin, Nathan. "State, Cosmos, and Body in the Last Three Centuries B.C." *Harvard Journal of Asiatic Studies* 55.1 (1995): 5–37.

———. *Traditional Medicine in Contemporary China*. Ann Arbor: Center for Chinese Studies, U of Michigan, 1987.

Song, Geng. *The Fragile Scholar: Power and Masculinity in Chinese Culture*. Hong Kong: Hong Kong UP, 2004.

Spivak, Gayatri Chakravorty. "The Politics of Translation." *Outside in the Teaching Machine.* New York: Routledge, 1993. 179–200.

Sun Longji. *Zhongguo wenhua de "shen zeng jie gou"* [The "Deep Structure" of Chinese Culture]. Hong Kong: Yi shan chu ban she, 1983.

Tan, Chee-beng. "Acculturation and the Chinese in Melaka: The Expression of Baba Identity Today." Gosling and Lim 56–78.

Topley, Marjorie. "Chinese Traditional Etiology and Methods of Cure in Hong Kong." *Asian Medical Systems: A Comparative Study.* Ed. Charles Leslie. Berkeley: U of California P, 1976. 243–65.

Unschuld, Paul U. *Medicine in China: A History of Ideas.* Berkeley: U of California P, 1985.

Vaughan, Meghan. *Curing Their Ills: Colonial Power and African Illness.* Stanford: Stanford UP, 1991.

Wang, Hui. The Fate of 'Mr. Science' in China: The Concept of Science and Its Application in Modern Chinese Thought." *Formations of Colonial Modernity in China.* Ed. Tani Barlow. Durham: Duke UP, 1997. 21–82.

Zhong, Xueping. *Masculinity Besieged? Issues of Modernity and Male Subjectivity in Chinese Literature of the Late Twentieth Century.* Durham: Duke UP, 2000.

CHAPTER 7

UNIVERSAL PARTICULARITIES

CONCEPTIONS OF SEXUALITY, NATIONALITY, AND CULTURE IN FRANCE AND THE UNITED STATES

THOMAS J. D. ARMBRECHT

AS THE NUMEROUS ANTHOLOGIES DEVOTED TO ISSUES OF SEXUALITY and globalization attest, "queerness is now global" (Cruz-Malavé and Manalansan 1).[1] Self-identified lesbian, gay, bisexual, and transgender (LGBT) people can be found in all four corners of the globe because they either live or visit there. Just because there is same-sex sexuality all over the planet, however, and just because certain cultures have the financial or ideological wherewithal to export their version of queer sexuality does not necessarily mean that queerness has the same meanings or manifestations for everyone. As Arnaldo Cruz-Malvé and Martin Manalansan argue in their introduction to *Queer Globalizations*, "while globalization is seen to liberate and promote local sexual differences, the emergence, visibility and legibility of these differences are often predicated in globalizing discourses on a developmental narrative in which a premodern, prepolitical, non-Euro-American queerness must consciously assume the burdens of representing to itself and others as 'gay' in order to attain political consciousness, subjectivity, and global modernity" (5–6). As the "non-Euro-American" qualifier implies, the premise of this and similar volumes is that "legitimized" versions of gayness are essentially extensions of the dominant cultures (i.e., those that are "First World," white, Christian, etc.) from which they spring. Even though these anthologies consider distinct cultures and even individual queers, what unifies them is the positing of a Western European-American queer hegemony, against which, they convincingly demonstrate, many other forms of sexuality struggle for self-realization, even within Western Europe and the United States themselves.

Despite the historical, cultural, and economic similarities among these "Euro-American" cultures, things are not so simple as they seem. While countries like France and the United States share consumerist, postmodernist cultures (categories that are themselves produced by shared intellectual traditions and theoretical apparatuses), it is a mistake simply to lump these nations together. Although LGBT people in both countries enjoy many of the same types of social enfranchisement and legal rights, the arguments surrounding queer culture in each country are surprisingly different. Recent work on queer cultural studies has shown that it is impossible to isolate sexuality from questions of ethnicity, economic privilege, history, and relationships to other nations. Understanding various global manifestations of sexuality demands not only that sexuality itself be reconsidered but also that the idea of nationality be called into question. Reenvisioning sexuality as a hegemonic force calls into question Euro-America's self-assured practices, including the practice of cross-cultural comparison, which all too often depend on binaries and static generalizations rather than viewing cultures as permeable and dynamic. Qu(e)erying, but not polarizing, queerness in France and the United States can reveal a lot not only about these nations but also about theories of national and sexual identity in general.

Of course, any comparison of France and the United States necessitates generalizations about these countries and therefore falls into the very trap that anthologies about queer theory and cultural studies seek to avoid when "deconstructing universalizing ideas about sexuality . . . [and] catching the lilt of each local articulation of desire" (Patton and Sánchez-Eppler 2). This chapter therefore identifies various axes (particularly nationality) around which discussions of sexuality in France and the United States turn, with the intent of confusing and collapsing them. It does not aim to pass judgment but rather seeks to cast doubt on cultural and social differences that are often assumed self-evident (particularly in France) in "us-versus-them" discussions of homosexuality. This chapter also questions other cultural values (such as respect for women as beings who are distinct from men and for the individual as a member of society); although both countries might claim such beliefs, their conceptions of them are surprisingly different. A more nuanced consideration of French and American ways of thinking about sexuality and its intersection with values supposedly embodied by the nation clarifies debates surrounding issues like marriage and adoption, which are controversial topics in both countries. It also sheds light on questions of assimilation and cultural expression, matters related to homosexuality too often left unconsidered.

As a point of departure, this chapter compares the role of universalism and its binary opposite, communitarianism (sometimes called "particularism") as they relate to French and American conceptions of national, personal, and most specifically, sexual identity.[2] Although they have been used in various contexts during the past two centuries, these terms have come to represent two sides of what are simplistically seen as the opposing ways in which the French and Americans conceive of themselves. In its sociopolitical context, universalism proposes that certain ideas universally desirable and applicable to all members of a nation should be used to define a nation. Examples of such ideas are often reflected in nations' mottos, like "Liberty, Equality, Fraternity" for France or "In God We Trust" for the United States. Although in circulation since the French Revolution, the idea that shared ideology is more important than ethnicity, language, or religion was most poignantly articulated by French philosopher Ernest Renan in his celebrated lecture of 1882, "What Is a Nation?" in which he asked, "In what way does the principle of nationalities differ from that of race?" Renan's timely question captured the French public's attention because, as cultural critic Maxim Silverman suggests in *Deconstructing the Nation*, Renan "eliminate[d] 'race,' religion, language and geographical frontiers as suitable criteria for the foundation and legitimizing of nations; [he argued that] nations are formed, instead, through the association of individuals who voluntarily affirm their shared and common past and future" (20). This way of thinking not only respected postrevolutionary values but also stood in contrast with neighboring countries' understanding of alterity.

Although it is outside the scope of this chapter to trace the historical origins of Renan's ideas or the different conceptions of universalism, the centrality of such thought in French and American societies explains debates over sexuality within and between the countries. Renan's ideas have retained their cultural currency through the present time. (It should be noted, however, that Renan did not use the terms *universalisme, communitarisme,* or *particularisme.*) In debates about everything from sexuality to Francophone literature, universalism is still associated with his name. In an article about "the headscarf affair" (the debate about the right of Muslim school girls to express their religiousness by covering their heads in public schools), published in national newspaper *Le figaro* in

December 2004, Mustapha Benchenane observes, "The concept of secularity that has prevailed for the last century is that of Ernest Renan."[3] This is not to suggest that social questions in France have been consistently conceived of in the philosopher's terms. Renan's address to the Collège de France was essentially a response to the perceived threat of German romanticists, whose ideas about the German *Volk* were founded not upon social agreement but upon social origin (i.e., being born German) (Silverman 19). Although Germany's essentialist view of who is German and France's definition of what is French have remained issues for France since the time of Renan's lecture, the rise of identity politics in the 1970s renewed interest in his ideas. Universalism seemed like a way to hold an increasingly diverse society together and to resist a new cultural menace: American communitarianism.

First and foremost, the debate about French universalism versus American communitarianism was a reaction first to feminism and then to political correctness. As journalist Clarisse Fabre and sociologist Eric Fassin argue in *Liberté, égalité, sexualités*, "The gap between the mentalities of the two countries grew during the 1980s, when France was beginning to react against '1968 thinking'—at the same time when radical thought was taking hold on American campuses" (28). In other words, France became increasingly critical of American universities' adoption of 1970s-style French feminism, deconstruction, and other movements, which it had come to reject as untenable and divisive. Consequently, French intellectuals also dismissed what they viewed as the offspring of 1968-style thinking: political correctness. According to Fabre and Fassin, labels were coined and battle lines were drawn in France in 1991 during the hearings about Clarence Thomas's alleged sexual harassment of Anita Hill. Some in the French press represented the investigations as "a left-wing McCarthyism" (CIDEM) and "a witch hunt" (Badinter 50). They claimed that the United States' cultural prudishness was infringing upon individual citizens' personal liberties.

The French reaction to the idea that "the personal is political" was so strong that, by the early 1990s, being in favor of sexual privacy and being anti-American were practically synonymous. According to Fabre and Fassin, "at the beginning of the 1990s, what one might call the 'nationalization of sexual questions' [took place in France]: instead of a choice among different sexual politics, American-style politicization and French-style non-politicization were positioned as opposites and the only alternatives. Here in France, it was said that sex was a question of mores and not politics, that it was a private matter not for public debate" (26). The debate quickly framed questions surrounding homosexuality, perhaps because so many issues related to it in both the United States and France fell in neatly with this polarization. In 1993, for example, the "Don't ask, don't tell" policy was instituted by the American military, much to the amazement of the French, who could not believe that it was in the interest of the military to exclude homosexuals from its troops. Other "American exports," like gay pride parades, rainbow flags, and outing, were seen as part and parcel of this way of thinking (see Caron). Philosopher Alain Finkielkraut claimed, for example, that identity politics caused this sort of discrimination because they exacerbated the differences between people, thereby casting one side as the victim and the other as perpetrator: "As soon as a homosexual speaks from this subject position, he turns the person standing in front either into another homosexual (out or not), or into a heterosexual. This is a kind of reductionism that spares no one. Moreover, what I hate about communitarianism is the idea that above all one must maintain one's victimhood and deny any facts that seem to contradict it" (44). Perhaps somewhat ironically, one of the people most opposed to recognizing homosexuals as a group was Frédéric Martel, author of *The Pink and the Black: Homosexuals in France since 1968*. The epilogue to this book was little more than a reaction to what was perceived as "'the American nightmare' of . . . infinitely fragmented social realities" (Lionnet 121). Although his book was arguably the first real history of the French gay-rights movement, Martel wrote that he felt "obliged to express reservations about this self-pride, an exacerbation of otherness and an ostentatious form of the right to difference. In the same way, it is a short step from self-affirmation to exhibitionism" (356). Although some scholars and activists argued that, by writing such a book, the author fell into the very trap of particularism that he was condemning; Martel (a gay man himself) was not simply condemning homosexuality as type of sexual difference. He was asserting instead that capitalizing on *any* personal difference, whether religious, racial, or sexual, threatened "the very bonds of society in contemporary France" (354).

Martel's arguments were not unlike those concerning other issues of identity in France at the time. In 1996, President Jacques Chirac stressed the importance of social cohesion over the expression of religious identity in a speech to "The National Consultative Commission for the Rights of Man" about "the headscarf affair": "We will not allow . . . those who advocate for a form of segregation to infringe on the freedom of thought. We will not allow certain groups to constrain people's souls and to destroy the freedom of choice while protecting themselves behind the freedom of belief and of religion . . . Together we must find a balance in which the freedom and the dignity of every individual, and the principles of the founders of the Republic, are fully respected . . . We must maintain social cohesion." The conflict between religious expression and the French principle of public secularity has been an issue in France since at least 1989, when three girls were expelled from school for refusing to remove their headscarves, which were considered by the state to be ostentatious signs of religiosity. By 1994, the press was saying that between 2,000 and 10,000 female students risked suspension for this reason (Fabre and Fassin 239). With the 1992 Los Angeles riots a recent memory and antigay legislation in Colorado and other states still working its way through the American courts, the United States hardly seemed the model of social cohesion to which France aspired. When the United States' social failures were considered in tandem with its ever-increasing economic and cultural influence, resisting "the American way" seemed realist rather than nationalist. Although Frédéric Martel's *The Pink and the Black* was criticized for both its research and its reasoning, the book accurately expressed the Zeitgeist even if it did not represent the views of many LGBT people in France.

Some French and American intellectuals at the time questioned the political polarization, and took issue with the entire "universalism-versus-communitarianism" debate. The now-defunct gay magazine *Ex Æquo* consecrated a "dossier" to this issue in June 1997 and again in November 1998 that shifted the argument from a question of culture to a question of rights. In one interview, Arnaud Marty-Lavauzelle, the president of the advocacy group AIDES, perceptively asked, "How are we supposed to have rights if we are not even acknowledged as individuals?" (42). In another, Fouad Zeraoui, president of Kelma, an association for LGBT people of North African descent, pointed out the link between difference and discrimination: "As soon as you assert your identity, and it is even worse if you have more than one identity, you are lumped in with those savages who are assaulting the Republican Citadel. How is a *Beur* [a child of Arab immigrants in France] supposed to think that he is just like everybody else? Because he is beur, no one will hire him, and because he is gay, no one will rent him an apartment. In France, no one is doing anything since everyone is supposedly integrated in society" (49). It is remarkable not only the extent to which Zeraoui's words bring up issues raised in the volumes about queer globalization mentioned at the beginning of this chapter but also how they anticipated the explanations for the riots that took place in France in fall 2005, during which Arab and African immigrants and their children protested their cultural disenfranchisement in the face of official integration. In 1997, however, Zeraoui's comments were indicative of a growing focus on issues of legal disparity instead of cultural difference. Although *beurs*, immigrants, and queers continue to suffer from discrimination, the realization that some French citizens were not receiving the same rights as others has changed the entire universalism-versus-communitarianism paradigm and has given credence to France's focus on "equality."

The definitive shift took place in 1999, when laws about PaCS (short for *pacte civile de solidarité*) and *parité* were passed. Although these two pieces of legislation seemed to develop independently, their creation was actually symbiotic. PaCS "is a contract between two adults, of the same gender or of different genders, which provides a legal structure for [*pour organiser*] their life together" ("Article 515-1"). It is an agreement that is like marriage but that has elements determined by the participants (unlike marriage, all aspects of which are defined by the law). Despite any self-avowed similarity, PaCS is specifically not marriage, a social rite and legal right that is still only reserved for heterosexuals in France.

Parité is shorthand for constitutional legislation enacted in 1999 that, according to a French government Web site devoted to the issue, "is determined to make the place of women in society a virtue of French democracy, through equal political representation, through equal pay, and by fighting against violence against women" (Ministre délégué). One of the important effects of this policy was the creation of a law in June 2000 that stipulated that in political elections "the difference in the number of candidates of each sex cannot be greater than one. In each roster of candidates there must be an equal number of men and women" (Ministre de la parité). Enforced electoral parity is an example of what is known in France as *la discrimination positive*, and in the United States as affirmative action.

Other commentators have debated the problems attendant on a *parité* that applies only to women (see Fassin; Eribon; Scott); this chapter draws attention to the ideological shift that these laws represented. PaCS and *parité* effected a sea change in the status of identity politics in France in general and in the conception of (homo)sexuality in particular. The arguments behind the one facilitate those behind the other, since they both depend on conflicting, but universal, ideas about gender difference and legal sameness. Even many of the people who were for PaCS but still opposed homosexual marriage and adoption based their arguments on the supposed obviousness and immutability of sexual difference (as opposed to the privacy and flexibility of sexual behavior). As Fabre and Fassin have claimed, "Opposition to PaCS was first presented more as a defense of heterosexuality than as the rejection of homosexuality . . . It was more than anything a question of protecting important 'gender differences'" (82). According to this view, which counts among its champions Sylviane

Agacinski, the well-known philosopher and wife of then-Prime Minister Lionel Jospin, marriage is an institution designed to unify two people with an essential sexual difference, which she claimed in 2002 in *Le figaro* "is an irreducible fact" (see Schnapper). Sexual difference is, of course, necessary for procreation, the unspoken goal behind the legal establishment of families, which is why, the thinking goes, marriage should remain unavailable to homosexuals. Now that everyone in France has the same legal rights as married couples, disparity seems no longer an issue. Essentially, PaCS legislation implies that nonprocreative couples do not *need* to be married. Similar arguments are being used with increasing regularity in the United States to deny same-sex couples the right to marriage. The Supreme Court of the State of Washington, for example, wrote in its decision of 26 July 2006, "Limiting marriage to opposite-sex couples furthers procreation, essential to the survival of the human race, and furthers the well-being of children by encouraging families where children are reared in homes headed by the children's biological parents" (cited in Savage).

The flip side of this argument is, however, that if women and men are in fact *not* essentially the same, then women's underrepresentation in the government means that half of humanity itself is discriminated against. As Joan Wallach Scott has explained in *Parité*, her book on the eponymous subject, Agacinski and others argued that "to treat women as fully equal required asserting not that women were individuals (like men), but that individuals were women and men, that *anatomical duality was part of the definition of abstract individuals*" (*Politique* 109; emphasis added). This way of thinking means not only that sexuality is not an essential part of a person but also by extension that "the full equation of homosexual and heterosexual couples [denies] the foundational role of sexual difference in the constitution of individual psyches and social solidarity" (110). In other words, in the case of laws concerning *parité*, it is not identity but equality that is the question. Since homosexuality is not an essential biological difference (at least according to Agacinski and to many who supported *parité*, but not gay marriage or adoption), parity for homosexuals would be redundant, since homosexuals are already protected as either men or women. (It is important to note that this way of thinking does not consider intersexed people or people who have elected to change their gender, nor does it accept that gender may be more than a binary state of being.) PaCS, therefore, was conceived to protect nonmarried (i.e., nonprocreative, nonamorous) heterosexual couples just as much as it was to protect homosexual ones, who are (supposedly) nonprocreative by definition and whose amorous relationships are not of concern for the state, since they do not lead to or support procreation.

Ironically, both PaCS and *parité* aim to rectify disparities among French citizens, whether the unequal treatments are in spite of their similarities (as gays) or because of their difference (as women). As long as LGBT people were clamoring for recognition and rights as a group, the French government felt that to recognize them would be to accord them special and, therefore, unequal status. By liberating the question from one of identity or "special interests" to one of equal rights, however, all questions of identity and morality were sidestepped, since, by very definition, to be French was to believe that all citizens deserved the same treatment. Therefore, by essentially refusing to recognize LGBT people as a community, the government acknowledged some of the specificities (that it was being singled out and discriminated against) that this particular group was claiming. *Parité* depended upon the opposite reasoning; in order to rectify the fact that women were underrepresented in the government, they had to be seen as essentially (biologically) different from men but as constitutive of humanity itself. In other words, the government realized that it had to identify woman as different so that everyone could be treated the same, and it had to identify queers as the same, so that they would not be treated differently. The chiasmic structure of these inherently philosophical pieces of legislation is not a coincidence; the issues of PaCS helped clarify people's ideas about *parité*, and vice versa. The philosophy also supports the universal nature of "Frenchness" because it universalizes the idea of gender (albeit a narrow and stable one) and abstracts the idea of the individual, thereby making certain ideas applicable to everyone, regardless of their sexuality, religion, and so on.

Acknowledging the logic and benefits of this manner of reasoning also denaturalizes the American conceptions of gender. Current American feminist and queer thinking, which owes a lot to French theorists of the 1950s, 1960s, and 1970s, generally argues that sexual difference is socially constructed and its meaning socially determined; although PaCS and *parité* take the exact opposite tactic, together they have created rights for women and queers in France that are the envy of American feminists and LGBT activists. While the way in which the French government met the demands of these groups might seem almost backward to American eyes, which are perhaps still more accustomed to focusing on one particular aspect of a person's identity, it might even be argued that the French government essentially, if unwittingly, queered the elements of the debate by collapsing the homo-hetero binary by still maintaining the male-female one. This move, in turn, confused the universalism-communitarianism duality, since, as Pierre Bourdieu asked rhetorically in his book *La domination masculine*, "how is one to thwart hypocritical universalism without universalizing a particularism?" (167). Essentially, the French government was forced to acknowledge a particularity for the sake of a universal (and vice versa) by simultaneously claiming that queers are just like everyone else, and therefore they must be treated as such (a universalist's view), but that women are different from men, and therefore need special consideration to ensure their equality (a particularist's view). The conception and implementation of this idea suggested, however, that the arguments were not so much a reaction to American communitarianism as an attempt to sidestep its influence completely, since to give sufficient credence to the American way of thinking would inadvertently acknowledge the relativism (as opposed to the universalism) of the very ideas that the French were asserting. The chiasmus of PaCS and *parité* was, therefore, also a way of keeping the argument "French" and therefore tacitly supported the very positions supposedly under debate.

Ultimately, this legislation did make the "French-versus-American" debate moot because, as Fassin has noted, the supposed cultural specificity of their arguments disappeared: "From one day to the next, the debate about French universalism versus American communitarianism, which had seemed so very important, became completely uninteresting: today it is almost with a kind of nostalgia that one relates this debate, which is really only a few years old" (Fabre and Fassin 88). In reality, the opposition of the two countries and their ideologies always was nonsensical because, in point of fact, the United States always operated under the assumption that there were universal values (as spelled out in the U.S. Constitution, like the freedom of speech) when dealing with recognized minorities. A prime example is *Lawrence v. Texas*, in which the U.S. Supreme Court decided that gay people in particular have a constitutional right to privacy—just like anyone else—which was exactly what France had been saying the whole time.

Despite the decision to sidestep the American question by framing the debates in uniquely French terms, it still might be argued that France's progressive legislation suggests that the debate about communitarianism was as much about resisting a kind of "imported sexuality" as it was about homosexuality itself. It was perhaps a rejection of the perceived growing homophobia in the United States or a rallying around the specificity of a French or European cultural identity that may have pushed France to legalize domestic partnerships. Recent research on globalization suggests that France is not the only country to have felt this international "peer pressure" to conform to the United States' version of gay identity. Critics have pointed out that American queerness has become, for better or for worse, another type of cultural export. As Cindy Patton writes in her essay "Stealth Bombers of Desire," "as much as the global flow of information technology, the globalization of queerness, carried by bodies, . . . threatens the terms in which nations have, up to this point, envisioned themselves" (210). In her essay, Patton refers not to "American queerness" in particular so much as "Western queerness" in general, of which it can be assumed that France is also a producer. If PaCS and *parité* can be considered, at least in part, as a rejection of American conceptions of sexuality, then it is evidence that globalized queerness is "threatening" even to nations in the "First-World" club.

Although questions of LGBT rights are hardly settled in France, since queer people are still not allowed to marry or to adopt, the progress achieved through the quasi-exclusive focus on the nation-state's definition of gender and sexuality has all but done away with another side of the universalist-communitarian debate that deserves to be revisited. The question of "queer culture," that is, the notion that LGBT people can produce art that is both representative and typical of their common experience as homosexuals, is practically no longer discussed in France now that the law has provided French queers with most of the means of cultural assimilation. In keeping with the universalist approach, many French LGBT activists and intellectuals do not seem concerned by the existence of gay culture or its potential disappearance. As long as they are treated the same as everyone else, many LGBT people still agree with the notion that sexuality is an inherently private matter that does not determine the way that one relates to the world. In keeping with this thinking, Rommel Mendès-Leite's *Le sens de l'altérité: Penser les (homo)sexualités* argues against the notion of LGBT cultural production. He even notes the specific "Frenchness" of his arguments:

> French tradition demands that the sexuality of individuals remains a completely private affair and writers, scientists, or other public personalities who publicly declare their sexual identity are considered to have a "bad reputation" even if their proclivities or penchants are more or less already known by the public. This is the case for not only any politician, government minister, or actor, but also for public figures like Michel Tournier, Roland Barthes, or Michel Foucault. Which does not mean that certain celebrities (like these last three examples) refuse to hide their sexuality. This is not the question. Quite simply, in the French context, "one just simply does not talk about such things." Could one really say that Barthes or Foucault produced "homosexual books" or works that belonged specifically to gay and lesbian studies? Or, following the same train of thought, could Tournier be said to write "gay and lesbian literature?" Perhaps to the astonishment of our Anglo-Saxon colleagues, we state that no, he does not. Even better, we assert that in the French literary tradition, such a question makes absolutely no sense. (51)

The notion that gay literature "makes no sense" is not so much a rejection of the grouping as it is a rejection of the group (i.e., gay authors) itself. Mendès-Leite is not arguing, of course, that Barthes or Foucault did not write of homosexuality. He is, however, eschewing the notion that these authors' sexuality in some way produced their works or, more specifically, that their sexuality somehow defined them.

The fact that queer culture is either summarily rejected or not considered at all does not mean, however, that it does not exist or that comparing the post-PaCS-*parité* attitude of the French to that of Americans does not further reveal strategies of individual and collective determination. This is because there is a universal idea behind the claim that there is no queer culture, at least not one that is (overtly) culturally specific: the creative process can transcend a writer's identity. In other words, one is in no way bound to write (or paint, or sculpt, and so on) about what one is, or even about what one knows. In this way of thinking, saying that Tournier, for example, is a gay author who writes queer literature would be to reduce his importance by implying that it comes out of and is produced for a specific cultural context. As Martel writes in *The Pink and the Black*, the idea of queer literature is actually against the idea of art itself: "Gay art and culture [currently lack influence in French society]. Male and female homosexuals sometimes encouraged these forms of expression by privileging a specific body of literature or art. The intention was laudable: to supply widely scattered individuals with peers, to link them to a history, and bring them together in a 'destiny group.' This is not insignificant. At the same time, however, the desire to pile ghetto upon ghetto seems to be a hypermodern folly. Such a plan serves to negate the very purpose of art, which is to promote dialogue, openness, and freedom from isolation and confinement" (349). Mendès-Leite's and Martel's views are not limited to critics who are considering the gay community. Their views are echoed by politicians and intellectuals concerned with questions of culture in general. This was very evident during the press surrounding the 2006 Salon du Livre (Book Fair), whose theme was Francophone literature. In conjunction with this social and commercial event, *Le monde* solicited the opinions of Francophone writers about the viability of the term "Francophone." Several of the authors queried, including the 1993 Prix Goncourt winner Amin Maalouf, rejected the term as reductive and limiting: "Let's finish with that aberration [the opposition between 'French' and 'Francophone' writers]. Let's leave the words 'Francophone' and 'Francophonie' in the realm of diplomacy and geopolitics. Let's get in the habit of referring to 'authors who write in the French language,' instead. Let's consider previous slip ups an unhappy parenthesis, a regrettable misunderstanding, and make a fresh start." Maalouf argued that classifying literature under the Francophone rubric devalues it by distinguishing it from "French literature," an opposition that he calls "sterile." Politician Robert Grossmann and philosopher François Miclo make similar arguments about "gay literature" being an empty term in *La république minoritaire: Contre le communautarisme*: "Just as there is no such thing as heterosexual literature, there is no gay literature, either. That is to say, no literature can be described by an epithet. There is simply literature and nothing else" (158).

The idea that writing that deserves to be called literature does not depend on the identity of its author but upon the universality of its ideas calls to mind the motto of Saint Vincent of Lérins: "Quod ubique, quod semper, quod ab omnibus creditum est" [that which is believed by everyone, everywhere, at all times]. This idea, which is still associated with the "universality" of Catholicism, if not Christianity, was originally invoked to suggest that one could judge new and possibly heretical interpretations of the Scriptures by comparing them to the common and traditional understanding of the Catholic Church. Just as the Vincentian Canon asserts that the universal acceptance of this reading makes it the most valid, the claim that true literature conforms to accepted values and precedents is also a kind of cultural absolutism. It implies an unwavering faith in the worth of literature as it is defined by the very civilization that made it, as if the specific cultural tradition out of which it was produced were as universal as it were infallible.

This process of exclusion is the very same that Silverman has identified in Renan's logic as he wrote about the "insignificance" of race. As he explains in *Deconstructing the Nation*, a hierarchy of cultural values can also be used indirectly to devalue a group: "It is true that Renan's imagery is not that of a biologistic essentialism, but it often seems to verge on a cultural essentialism or absolutism . . . Cultural absolutism can also be grounds for racist exclusion . . . In the history of modern France, the tradition of biological racism has probably been less prominent than that of a national cultural racism (or perhaps, more appropriately, a cultural/racist nationalism)" (20). The shared history and experiences that form the common culture of a nation are really available only to a certain segment of the population (a segment of the population that is all too often determined, in part, by its race or its sexuality). In *AIDS in French Culture*, David Caron argues that denying groups of people the ability to identify themselves in the name of assimilation is in itself a form of exclusion: "The strict polarization [between race and culture] is . . . untenable . . . The contractual model of nationhood is already undermined by its own essentialization . . . In other words, the [French] Republic invents the very communities it condemns, and essentially in the same terms with which it invented itself" (153).

Even though current efforts in France focus on giving access to a particular version of French culture to everyone, the desirability (or even the possibility) of this is rarely questioned. A similar phenomenon is happening in the United States, as LGBT people try to acquire (or to defend) their right to marry or to form marriage-like partnerships. Most of this lobbying is done without really questioning the secondary effects that marriage would have on LGBT communities or even on individual identities. According to a 30 July 2006 *New York Times* article, for some gays in the United States, "the fight for gay marriage is the mirror image of the right-wing conservative Christian lobby for family values and feeds into the same drive for a homogeneous, orthodox American culture" (Hartocollis). Most LGBT people do not feel threatened by heterosexual marriage, even if gaining the same rights as straight people will potentially throw the meaning of their sexuality into question. The situation is similar in France; although most current opponents of gay cultural specificity would never argue against its existence on religious or moral grounds, the effect is a dogmatic faith in a particular expression of heterosexual culture. It is perhaps this assumption about the absolute value of that culture that needs to be called into question in France and in the United States, as the current desires for other types of assimilation in both countries show.

This brief history of sexual-identity politics in France and America records only the version of events that played out in political discourse and in the papers. It describes theories and participants that depend on the stability of the concept of the nation, which is itself increasingly problematic in an era of globalization. Even if "France" and "the United States" are still operative terms, can they really be compared without resorting to reductionism? What about the adjectival and noun forms of the "queer" (or "gay"? or "lesbian"?), which, both universalists and communitarians would argue (if from different perspectives), do not take into consideration issues of class, age, race, religion, or any of the other "coarse axes of categorization" (22), as Judith Butler has called them, that constitute a person's identity? Perhaps there is some merit in rejecting the "French" idea of a queer community as a useless or, more accurately, inherently ambiguous term in order to focus instead on the *active* meaning of the word, that is, "to queer" as a process of resistance or dissent. Particularly in the current climates of France and the United States, when many LGBT individuals are pulled between seemingly conflicting desires to assimilate and to assert their specificities, we can all agree on the universal value of queering both our surroundings and ourselves. Even if all the categories collapse, as binaries are wont to do, comparing the intersection of sexuality and nationality in France and the United States demonstrates that focusing on particularities does not preclude according universal rights (or vice versa). It also calls attention to what (or who) is excluded in such a debate and perhaps gives a glimpse of a future where, paradoxically, sexuality might lose its universal meaning, and queer will be a modus operandi instead of a modus vivendi.

NOTES

1. See also, for example, Luibhéid and Cantú; Patton and Sánchez-Eppler.
2. The word *universalisme* is not in the eighth edition of the *Dictionnaire de l'Académie Française* (the official source for French words) despite its frequent use in the French media. (It is, however, in *Le trésor de la langue française*.) In the *Oxford English Dictionary* (*OED*), the meaning of the word "universalism," as it is construed in this chapter, dates from 1939. The word *particularism(e)* appears in the *Trésor* and the *OED*; in both cases, it is Catholic in origin and conservative in meaning. While "communitarianism" is in the *OED*, its contemporary definition is actually closer to what the French would consider "universalism." The terms are perhaps more ambiguous (and less opposed) than first appears, and *universalism(e)* was invented after the fact, that is, as the opposite of an already existent idea: particularism (much like the term "heterosexual," as Foucault has demonstrated).
3. All translations are my own, unless an English version of the book is indicated in the bibliography.

WORKS CITED

"Article 515-1. Loi n⁰ 99-944 du 15 novembre 1999 art. 1 Journal Officiel du 16 novembre 1999." *Legifrance: Le service public de l'accès au droit.* <http://www.legifrance.gouv.fr/texteconsolide/AREBT.htm>. 17 May 2010.

Agacinski, Sylviane. *La politique des sexes.* Paris: Seuil, 1998.

———. "L'épouse de Lionel Jospin répond à Elisabeth Lévy: Philosophe, féministe et midinette?" *Le figaro* 26 Mar. 2002. <http://www.lefigaro.fr/archives/cgi-bin/ACHATS/acheter.cgi?offre=ARCHIVES&type_item=ART_ARCH_30J&objet_id=20020306>. 17 May 2010.

Badinter, Elizabeth. "La chasse aux sorciers." *Le nouvel observateur* 17–23 Oct. 1991: 50–51.

Benchenane, Mustapha. "Interdire le voile? La loi française et les signes religieux." *Le figaro* 12 Dec. 2004: 12.

Bourdieu, Pierre. *La domination masculine.* Paris: Seuil, 1998.

Butler, Judith. *Gender Trouble: Feminism and the Subversion of Identity*. New York: Routledge, 1990.

Caron, David. *AIDS in French Culture*. Madison: U of Wisconsin P, 2001.

Chirac, Jacques. "Allocution prononcée par M. Jacques Chirac, Président de la République, devant la Commission Nationale Consultative des Droits de l'Homme." *Palais de l'Elysée*. 10 Dec. 1996. <http://www.elysee.fr/elysee/ francais/interventions/discours_et_declarations/1996/decembre/allocution _prononcee_par_m_jacques_chirac_president_de_la_republique_devant_la _commission_nationale_consultative_des_droits_de_l_homme.2400.html>. 17 May 2010.

CIDEM (Civisme et Démocratie). "Lexique: Maccarthyisme de gauche." <http:// www.cidem.org/lexique.php?lettre=m>. 17 May 2010.

Cruz-Malavé, Arnaldo, and Martin F. Manalansan, IV, eds. *Queer Globalizations: Citizenship and the Afterlife of Colonialism*. New York: New York UP, 2002.

"Dominique Schnapper." *Sciences Po 2005: Projet collectif "Mariage homosexuel et homoparentalité.*" <http://sciencespo2005.free.fr/sociologie/dominique _schnapper.php>. 17 May 2010.

Eribon, Didier. *Papiers d'identité: Interventions sur la question gay*. Paris: Fayard, 2000.

Fabre, Clarisse, and Eric Fassin. *Liberté, égalité, sexualités*. 2nd ed. Paris: 10/18 Belfond, 2003.

Fassin, Eric. *L'inversion de la question homosexuelle*. Paris: Amsterdam, 2005.

Finkielkraut, Alain. "Le communautarisme est hideux." Interview with Olivier Razemon. *Ex Æquo* 8 (1997): 44.

Grossmann, Robert, and François Miclo. *La république minoritaire: Contre le communautarisme*. Paris: Michalon, 2002.

Hartocollis, Anemona. "For Some Gays, a Right They Can Forsake." *New York Times* 30 June 2006. <http://www.nytimes.com/2006/07/30/fashion/ sundaystyles/30MARRIAGE.html>. 17 May 2010.

"Lawrence et al. v. Texas." No. 02-102, 558, SUPREME COURT OF THE UNITED STATES, 539.

Lionnet, Françoise. "Performative Universalism and Cultural Diversity: French Thought and American Contexts." *Terror and Consensus: Vicissitudes of French Thought*. Ed. Jean-Joseph Goux and Philip R. Wood. Stanford: Stanford UP, 1998. 119–34.

Luibhéid, Eithne, and Lionel Cantú Jr. *Queer Migrations: Sexuality, U.S. Citizenship, and Border Crossings*. Minneapolis: U of Minnesota P, 2005.

Maalouf, Amin. "«Contre 'la littérature francophone'»; Prix Goncourt 1993, Amin Maalouf exhorte la France à se regarder dans 'le miroir du temps.'" *Le monde* 10 Mar. 2006. <http://www.lemonde .fr/cgi-bin/ACHATS/acheter.cgi?offre=ARCHIVES&type_item=ART _ARCH_30J&objet_id=936962>. 17 May 2010.

Martel, Frédéric. *The Pink and the Black: Homosexuals in France since 1968*. Stanford: Stanford UP, 1999.

Marty-Lavauzelle, Arnaud. "Le communautarisme." *Ex Æquo* 8 (1997): 45.

Mendès-Leite, Rommel. *Le sens de l'altérité: Penser les (homo)sexualités*. Paris: L'Harmattan, 2000.

Ministre délégué à la cohésion sociale et à la parité. "Parité." <http://www.femmes-egalite.gouv.fr/>. 17 May 2010.

Ministre de la parité et de l'égalité professionnelle. "Le bilan de la loi sur la parité." <http://www.femmes-egalite.gouv.fr/grands_dossiers/dossiers/vie_politique/vie_politique_bilan.htm>. 17 May 2010.

Patton, Cindy. "Stealth Bombers of Desire: The Globalization of 'Alterity' in Emerging Democracies." Cruz-Malavé and Manalansan 195–218.

Patton, Cindy, and Benigno Sánchez-Eppler. *Queer Diasporas*. Durham: Duke UP, 2000.

Renan, Ernest. "Qu'est-ce qu'une nation?" *La collection électronique de la Bibliothèque Municipale de Lisieux*. <http://www.bmlisieux.com/archives/nation04.htm>. 17 May 2010.

Savage, Dan. "Same-Sex Marriage Wins by Losing." *New York Times* 30 July 2006. <http://www.nytimes.com/2006/07/30/opinion/30savage.html>. 17 May 2010.

Schnapper, Dominique. "Entretien." <http://sciencespo2005.free.fr/sociologie/dominique_schnapper.php>.

Scott, Joan Wallach. *Parité!* Chicago: U of Chicago P, 2007.

Silverman, Maxim. *Deconstructing the Nation: Immigration, Racism and Citizenship in Modern France*. New York: Routledge, 1992.

Zeraoui, Fouad. "Une communauté beure?" *Ex Æquo* 8 (1997): 42.

CHAPTER 8

"WORDS CREATE WORLDS"

RETHINKING GENRE IN THE ANIMAL FABLES OF SUNITI NAMJOSHI AND VIKRAM SETH

BIANCA JACKSON

FROM THE CELEBRATION OF PEDERASTY IN THEOCRITUS'S "IDYLLS" TO descriptions of male-to-male love in Walt Whitman's "Calamus Poems," the pastoral tradition has often functioned effectively to construct positive representations of sexual dissidence.[1] By locating queer relationships and practices in bucolic settings, "homophile pastoralism" (Shuttleton 134), or what I term "ecoqueerness," reclassifies alternative sexualities (as well as peripheral societies) as "natural." Yet ecoqueerness is not limited to love affairs between shepherds or sexual liaisons that unfold in the forest. The depiction of animals, particularly in the form of the fable, has also been used to explore social anxiety about same-sex sexuality. According to Judith L. Goldstein, animals are useful tropes for problems of identity because of the essential difference between beasts and humans (24). In her discussion of "Bat Boy" in the tabloid papers, Goldstein claims that the division between humans and animals is so great that it obscures more "conventional" differences among human beings themselves, such as race, class, or sexual orientation (24).[2] Thus, the portrayal of animals in literature becomes a form of humanism, in which humans create an inclusive community that defines itself contra animals. Yet while Suniti Namjoshi and Vikram Seth employ the fable form to examine sexual alterity, both authors portray animals in order to align, rather than further separate, queers and beasts. Presenting the marginalization of (other) animals from the "human world" as analogous to the social ostracism of sexual dissidents, Namjoshi and Seth attempt to create communities of animals and humans that exist outside the nation-state.

Although scholars have generally interpreted their use of beasts as a metaphorical device, Namjoshi and Seth's animal fables do not offer an allegorical depiction of a queered, interspeciated community. Rather, they propose an actual society composed of sexual dissidents and animals. Identifying the dominant patriarchal and heteronormative order as merely one subjective reality, Namjoshi, in an act she attributes to her pantheistic Hindu background, asks her readers to consider the possibility of multiple, alternative realities. Similarly, Vikram Seth's bestial writings suggest that a posthumanist community is accessible to any human willing to acknowledge animals as her equals. In blurring the borders between animals and humans as well as reality and fantasy, both authors not only identify the sociopolitical marginalization of animals and sexual dissidents as homologous but also compare the "queering" of these boundaries to the "queering" of other supposedly impermeable borders, in particular the division between homosexuality and heterosexuality. The very act of comparison, therefore, becomes an implicitly queer process. However, Namjoshi and Seth maintain divergent views on the potentiality of these queer crossings. While Namjoshi posits this animal-queer coalition as a utopian sphere based on (queer) othering, Seth maintains that the dominant reality of heteropatriarchy will ultimately pervade all other spaces and realities, setting up (queerphobic) communities in its likeness. But though their respective outlook on the position of queerness in a posthumanist space may differ, both Namjoshi and Seth defy the genre of fable by deconstructing the boundaries not only between male and female, heterosexual and homosexual, human and animal, but also between reality and fantasy.

In an article on contemporary British fabulists, acclaimed author A. S. Byatt writes, "The fabulists look at life from a distance, through a telescope, and from very close, with a microscope. They study worms and stars. They describe discrete fragments and turn them into glittering patterns in a kaleidoscope. They are metaphysical makers of imaginary time and space and objects, who reflect on what they are doing" (6–8). With characters such as the Blue Donkey and the Brahmin Cow, this juxtaposition of "worms and stars," of the familiar and the foreign, lies at the heart of fabulist and storyteller Suniti Namjoshi's work and, indeed, of the writer's own life as a diasporic queer author. Born in Bombay in

1941, Namjoshi has generated a significant portfolio of poems, fables, novels, articles, and reviews, as well as an autobiography (*Goja: An Autobiographical Myth*, 2000) and a collaborative anthology (*Flesh and Paper*, 1986) with her partner, Australian poetess Gillian Hanscombe. Although she began her career as a published writer in 1967 while working as a civil servant in the Indian Administrative Service, Namjoshi's focus soon shifted entirely to the analysis and writing of English literature. In 1968, managing to get study leave from the government of India, she left her native country to earn a master's degree at the University of Missouri in the United States, followed by a doctorate from McGill University in Montreal, Canada, examining the metaphysics of Ezra Pound's "The Cantos." Although in North America Namjoshi suddenly found she was "Nobody from Nowhere," a foreigner whom the "natives" hoped to "civilize," in diaspora she was able to explore her sexuality outside the "be discreet" policy of India (*Because of India* 14). In her 1980 collection of poems titled *The Jackass and the Lady*, written on sabbatical at Cambridge University, Namjoshi "came out," the first Indian female author to openly declare herself a lesbian. As she writes in *Because of India: Selected Poems and Fables*, she came to feminism and a queer identity quite late: "In the early days at Scarborough College I had one colleague who was a strong feminist. She recommended Stein and Duras to me. Somehow, nothing much happened. Perhaps I wasn't ready. Perhaps it was because her primary literary interests weren't centred on poetry. Perhaps it was because she was too American and I was too Indian" (78).

Subsequently, all her writings, such as *Feminist Fables* (1981), *From the Bedside Book of Nightmares* (1984), and *The Blue Donkey Fables* (1988), explore her position as a lesbian feminist as well as this consistent tension between her "Indianness" and the omnipresent Western identity. This double marginalization first encouraged Namjoshi to express her politics in fable form. Sneaking into Northrop Frye's graduate lectures, she soon became enchanted with his literary universe. Yet she did not see any place for herself in this humanist domain, "except perhaps as one of the helpful animals in the mode of romance" (*Because of India* 28). As a perpetual "other," she could not be the prince, the princess, or the villain of the universal fairytale. Therefore, she constructed a realm of sexual dissidents and beasts in which both she and her readers could situate themselves outside the dominant order.

In Namjoshi's fable "The Creation: Plan B," a Parrot and a Tortoise set out to refashion the world. They agree that there will be continents like the patterns on the Tortoise's back, "lots and lots of parrots," and "an equal number of tortoises" (*The Blue Donkey Fables* 21). When the topic turns to the presence of humans, however, the Tortoise asks, "Do we have to have people?" and breathes a sigh of relief when the Parrot answers, "No." This misanthropy, a consistent theme throughout Namjoshi's work, derives from her dissatisfaction with contemporary gender and sexuality arrangements, further complicated by variables such as race and ethnicity. Heterosexual men, she writes in *The Conversations of Cow*, have created a male-centered universe by dividing society into "Class A" humans (men) and "Class B" humans (women), exiling every other creature to the position of "other": "Class A people do not wear lipstick, Class B people do. Class A people spread themselves out. Class B people apologise for so much as occupying space. Class A people stand like blocks. Class B people look unbalanced. Class A people never smile. Class B people smile placatingly twice in a minute and seldom require any provocation" (24). While women, as Class B citizens, are not considered to be "as human" as Class A citizens, their necessity to the reproduction of the race guarantees their place, albeit an inferior position, in the nation-state. By rejecting male sovereignty at the most basic level of sexuality, queers are deemed not-men, not-women, and thus not-human (see Wittig 9–20). They are exiled to the periphery of social discourse and practice and, when not rendered invisible, denigrated for their difference. Yet the solution to (androcentric) heteropatriarchy is not, according to Namjoshi, inserting the marginalized other into the dominant order of "death and destruction" (Hanscombe and Namjoshi, *Flesh* 41), but rather creating what Raymond Williams refers to as an "emergent" cultural system that offers an alternative that consequently undermines the hegemony of the dominant system.[3] Thus, in what may be seen as a play on Michel Foucault's "speciation" of homosexuality,[4] Namjoshi eschews the dominant heterosexual narrative by creating an imagined nation of animals and lesbians who exist on "the margins of the margins" of racial and sexual politics (Otalvaro-Hormillosa 91).

From Shakespeare's poem "The Phoenix and the Turtle" (1601) to Virginia Woolf's novella *Flush* (1933), animal tropes have historically connoted homoeroticism or homosexuality.[5] Indeed, the queer continuum on which Giti Thadani bases her argument for the "re-instatement" of sexual identities in India derives in part from the depiction of "lesbian" cows and mares in antiquated Indian texts.[6] For example, it is written in book 3, hymn 33, line 1 of the *Rig Veda*[7] that, "from the bosom of the mountain, desirous and content, two mares, like two bright cows as mothers licking, caressing and kissing" (qtd. in Thadani, *Sakhiyani* 25).[8] This "homosexualization" of animals may stem from the habitual association of animals with "natural," or instinctual, sexuality, as evident in the common vernacular of sexual discourse in which intercourse is sometimes referred to as "the birds and the bees" and animal classifications employed to connote sexual positions or genitalia.[9] The alignment of sexual alterity with animals may therefore "naturalize" these "unnatural" acts. However, Namjoshi's imagined nation of animals and lesbians is not based on the use of the former to validate the latter, but rather, on what she regards as the analogous "othering" of both by (heterosexual) men and their consequent kinship.[10] If queers are dehumanized on the basis of their sexual dissidence, animals, despite their "natural sexuality," are "not-human" and, therefore, are also exiled from the dominant order. (Namjoshi's hybridized animals—the blue donkey, the one-eyed monkey, the Brahmin cow—may even be seen to be doubly marginalized.) Through this dual marginalization, Namjoshi disintegrates not only the categories of "man" and "woman" but also those of "human" and "species."

In J. M. Coetzee's *Elizabeth Costello* (1999), the eponymous novelist shocks and offends a group of students and academics not only by drawing a comparison between the slaughter of animals for food and the mass genocide of Jews during the Holocaust but also by suggesting that the "degradation, cruelty and killing" of the former has "dwarfed" what even the Third Reich was capable of (65). Refusing the conventional arguments for man's superiority to other organisms, from St. Thomas's belief that man is made in the image of God and thus divinely superior, to the Platonic and Cartesian emphasis on the primacy of reason in the organization of species, Costello suggests that man has created an arbitrary "continuum that stretches from the Martian at one end to the bat to the dog to the ape," distinguishing gradients by some imagined "essential humanness" (76). The arbitrariness of these distinctions is epitomized by the facility with which (heterosexual, white) men have historically ascribed or removed the category of "human" even within what we currently define as "humanity." Indeed, prior to the abolition of slavery (and even afterwards), black men were regarded as animals and denied legal rights as such. This accentuated differentiation between "animals" and "humans" is, according to Namjoshi, a construct of the West:

> To me a beast wasn't "bestial" in the Western sense. To me a bird or a beast was a creature like anyone else. Hinduism is, after all, pantheistic; and the popular notion of reincarnation attributes a soul to everyone. This may sound odd to Western ears, but for me, it was familiar as it was unconscious . . . It is apparent to many women that in a humanist universe, which has been male-centred historically, women are "the other," together with the birds and the beasts and the rest of creation . . . but I don't want to be separated from the birds and the beasts, nor do I want to "humanise" them particularly. (*Because of India* 28–29)

By breaking down what she sees as a mere linguistic boundary between animals and humans, the boundary that in the West is considered the most biologically fixed, Namjoshi removes identity from the realm of heteropatriarchal social organization into the realm of the performative. Invoking a sense of play, costume, and artifice, her characters, such as Suniti and Cow in *The Conversations of Cow*, shift easily between the categories of "animal" and "human," "male" and "female," and "homosexual" and "heterosexual" to explore different notions of the self and therefore belie Judith Butler's assertion that shifting between (gender) identities is not as straightforward as "donning a coat for the day" (x). Identifications thus become a liberatory enterprise rather than a restrictive division of organisms into self and other, margin and center. "I can be anything, anyone," Suniti writes in *The Conversations of Cow*, "or no one" (76). While Namjoshi theoretically creates a nation of "others," gay men and even gay-male animals (with the exception of the Ugly Duckling in the fable "Happy Ending") are conspicuously absent from this realm (*Feminist Fables* 13). Presumably, for Namjoshi, their privileged status as men prevails over their marginalized sexuality.[11] Only women, therefore, can be truly "queer" and are able to "queer" border crossings between identities as they are always already marginalized.

Critics of Namjoshi's work have regarded her use and subversion of the fable form as a stylistic mirroring of this collapse of the boundaries and binaries of identity. Invoking fabulist traditions from the *Panchatantra* (c. 200 BCE) and Aesop (c. sixth-century BCE) to *Hitopadesa* (c. twelfth-century CE) and La Fontaine (seventeenth-century CE), Namjoshi is perceived as "reshap[ing] traditional literary forms, mix[ing] genres like the novel, fairy tale, fable and fantasy" in her creation of new gender arrangements (Steinisch 277). Despite its occurrence in almost all the titles of her work, Namjoshi's writing neither lends itself easily to the basic definition of fable as "a story invented to tell the truth" (Blackham ix) nor resembles our common understanding of realism. The simultaneous presence of elements from both genres suggests that the fundamental differentiation between reality and fantasy upon which the structure of the fable relies is yet another binary under scrutiny in Namjoshi's work. As evident in *Saint Suniti and the Dragon* (1981), it is often ambiguous whether the relationship of the author to her "animal" characters belongs solely to the realm of metaphor:

> Because the world seemed flat and fallen
> she conjured the creatures she had invented:
> the one-eyed monkeys, the shape-changing donkeys,
> and birds of divers sorts who hitherto

had flown at fancy's behest. "Wherein lies
wisdom?" she asked each of them. "In playing,"
laughed one. "In silence," said another. "In
purposely striving," offered a third.
And seeing she was vexed, they went away again.
"Am I a bird, a beast, a donkey?" she asked
the thin air. In the real atmosphere, no
bombs fell, plants still grew, and the planetary
soil was solid underfoot. "Cause for comfort?"
a voice suggested. Who said that? Dragon
or demon? Could she tell the difference? (*Feminist Fables* 29)

Although the narrator describes the animals as "invented" and "conjured," they maintain their own agency, providing answers to the narrator's questions, and leaving at their own will. The question of their fabrication is also rendered ambiguous by the intrusion of the unknown voice at the close of the stanza that, though possibly a "dragon or demon," is not depicted as the creation of the narrator, as well as by the shared name—Suniti—of the author and the narrator. This tension between the real and the phantasmagoric challenges Namjoshi's use of "invention" and, therefore, her work as fable. Namjoshi seemingly employs "invention" in the sense of imagining and creation. As she remarks in her article "Writing the Rag-Bag of Empire," "for me there is irony in the fact that sometimes the most exact descriptions, the most deeply felt griefs, are perceived by Western audiences to belong somehow to the realm of fables and poetry" (Hanscombe and Namjoshi 397).[12] This misapprehension of the real may be seen in the "fable" "By the River." Suddenly discovering that they are able to understand one another, a woman and her beautiful black mare look for something in their environment to explain this "fantastical" occurrence:

"Oh mare," said the woman while droplets fell from her wet black hair, "I understand you now. It must be the virtue of the water of this river."

"And I understand you," responded the mare, turning her head in a curve so graceful that had anyone seen her, his heart must have broken at the beauty of the gesture. "But it can't be the river. It must be the grass I've just eaten." (*Feminist Fables* 86)

However, the woman has not "nibbled so much as a blade of grass," and the mare protests that, "she herself hadn't stepped into the river" (86). The last line of the story offers as an alternative explanation for their sudden ability to communicate: "But would he [an observer] have noted that they liked one another?" (86). The mare and her mistress, Namjoshi suggests, can converse once they truly "see" and appreciate the other, while the male observer is marginalized to the periphery.[13] Thus, the lack of distinction Namjoshi makes between animals and humans is neither merely a stylistic device to allegorize the "real" world in fable nor a commentary on the arbitrariness of binary categorizations but an allowance for the genuine possibility of an imagined, rather than imaginary, nation of animals and queers.

In moving toward a nonconceptual, or literal, idea of "interspecies" communication, Namjoshi recasts her writings as alternative realities rather than fables. Just as men have employed and hierarchically arranged words such as "man" and "woman," "animal" and "human," and "fantasy" and "reality" to invent a world in their image, other worlds may just as legitimately be invented to contrast with and undermine this dominant reality. As Namjoshi writes in "Writing the Rag-Bag of Empire," "If you grow up in a traditional, liberal Hindu family, but are educated in English, then the constant awareness of the gap between the lived-in culture and the cultural load of the learnt language becomes a fact of life. This split reality is normal. Like a child playing off one parent against another you learn to look for and select what might suit you best. If two realities are possible, then the next thought, that perhaps multiple realities are possible, isn't far away" (Hanscombe and Namjoshi 391). Namjoshi, therefore, defines "reality" as a subjective method of organizing what one perceives as one's external environment, whether into a nation of "superior" men or an othered domain of animals and lesbians. As allusions in *The Blue Donkey Fables* to *A Midsummer Night's Dream* indicate, these "dream" worlds are permeable (35). While (heterosexual) humans (such as the lovers in the play) might try to order their experiences into "dream" and "reality," this boundary collapses with shifts in subject position. Thus "no Titania came to pronounce the Blue Donkey not only beautiful, but also beloved" (103). As pariahs in the pervasive "dream" of heteropatriarchy, queers and other beasts occupy a simultaneously denigrated and privileged space in the "forest" of society. Aligned with the fairies and the nymphs, particularly with Puck who orders the "realities" of the heterosexual couples (sexual dissidents may be seen as "ordering the reality" of heterosexuality as a signifier of what it is not), the queered animal nation is able to recognize that all "realities" may be perceived as "a dream and fruitless vision" (93) and are consequently at liberty to "play" with these categorizations. Thus, every organism is simultaneously a fabulist, sculpting its own universe, and the subject of someone or something else's fable.

Although Vikram Seth (born 1952–) and Suniti Namjoshi are both queer diasporic Indian authors writing in roughly the same time period, they occupy very different places in both Anglo-American and Indian literary traditions. While Namjoshi remains virtually unknown outside India for her plethora of lesbian-feminist fables, fairytales, poems, and novels, Seth has received numerous accolades for his writings in both India and abroad, from the Commonwealth Writer's Prize to the W. H. Smith Literary Award. However, unlike Namjoshi, reference to Seth's sexual alterity is glaringly absent from his popular "Byronesque" heterosexual romances (Perry 550). With the exception of a fleeting reference to the possible sexual relationship between Maan Kapoor and Firoz Khan, Seth's magnum opus, *A Suitable Boy* (1993), narrates the story of Lata Mehra and her search for a husband. In his later work, *An Equal Music* (1999), winner of the Ethnic and Multicultural Media Award for Best Book/Novel, a violinist is haunted by the memory of his former (female) lover. While *The Golden Gate: A Novel in Verse* (1986) depicts the same-sex relationship between a bisexual man and his gay lover among the dominant heterosexual couplings, sexual dissidence is displaced onto the white American protagonists, invoking the common claim that "there is no such thing (as homosexuality) in India" (Thadani, "Jami" 56). Moreover, the love between the two men fails due to the gay male's (Anglo-European) Christian guilt and his belief that sodomy is a cardinal sin. The bisexual man subsequently marries a woman whom he is not in love with and has children, thus reinstating the primacy of the heteronormative relationship.

As all of Seth's primary works are concerned principally with male-female desire, many of his readers were surprised by his mother's reference to his bisexuality in her recent memoir, *On Balance: An Autobiography* (see L. Seth). However, Seth's possible sexual alterity was not unknown to those who have read his poetry. Poems such as "Guest" and "Dubious" in the collection *Mappings* (1980) directly touch upon the author's love of both men and women, while *Beastly Tales from Here and There* (1992) may be read as allegories of homoeroticism. But despite publishing poetic works for more than a decade and receiving the Commonwealth Poetry Prize for the collection *The Humble Administrator's Garden* (1985), Seth's six books of verse have received little attention from a common readership and are absent from critical discourse. Seth's usual audience seems reluctant to embrace the verbal restraint and linguistic economizing of the poetic form from an author whose expansive verse resulted in the longest novel ever written in English (described by one critic as "three and a half pounds of perfection," *A Suitable Boy* reaches 1,359 pages). However, Seth's poetry may be regarded as some of his most daring work. While the novels allow themselves to be slotted neatly into thematic categories of

"Western" or "Indian," his verse as an oeuvre resists a single locational or national identity. Readers are taken on a narrative journey from Greece and China to India and the Ukraine, generating characters, as well as an aesthetic, that amalgamate multiple cultural variables including race, class, and sexual orientation. In Seth's bestial fables, this cosmopolitan journeying extends into the realm of the phantasmagoric. Both domestic and wild animals, including mice, goats, and dolphins, engage with the challenges of identity politics and, in particular, the social space and place of the diasporic Indian queer.

Like Suniti Namjoshi's "fables," Vikram Seth's "bestial" writings also eradicate the differentiation between humans and animals and offer the possibility of a more egalitarian relationship between the two "species." In the story "The Goat and the Ram," an old man and his wife are depicted as hosting a community of animals in their home, from a sow who "excelled at piano playing," to a gosling who "could predict the weather" (*Beastly Tales* 73), while on a grander scale, in "The Rat and the Ox," Seth literalizes the zodiac to suggest that both animals and humans participate in the organization of the universe. Yet the relationship of Seth's animals to homoeroticism is considerably more oblique than Namjoshi's "badge-wearing dyke" mice or lesbian-feminist wrens. In a possible mirroring of the author's public reticence concerning his own sexuality, same-sex desire is expressed primarily in implicit terms with gendered pronouns providing the only substantial evidence for its presence. For example, in the tale "The Mouse and the Snake," lesbian sexual intercourse is coded in the act of eating "illicit" grain (a common signifier of fertility and thus, female eroticism). Seth writes, "But the two [female] friends, unpoliced, / Broke in and began to feast; And their laughter fell and rose" (*Beastly Tales* 19). Just as his combination of the term "unpoliced" with a bacchanalian feasting suggests the habitual illicitness of same-sex practice, the rise and fall of the laughter invokes the rise (climax) and fall (anticlimax) of orgasm. Furthermore, the mouse is also a typical trope for female eroticism (Vanita, *Sappho* 236). However, unlike Namjoshi's writings, nearly all of Seth's allusions to homoeroticism or sexual alterity are confined to the subtextual realm, allowing for a desexualized reading.

According to Phaedrus, a freedman of the Emperor Augustus, Aesop invented the fable form in order to facilitate freedom of speech among slaves. Similarly, the codification of sexuality in fable has been employed in such a way that homosexual identification is possible while still retaining the façade of heterosexual moral rectitude. As Seth writes in *Beastly Tales from Here and There*, "myths of flexible dimension / Are apt to call forth less dissension" (129). Such obliqueness was necessary not only for the possibility of publication but also, prior to the repeal of most anti-sodomy laws in the 1960s, to avoid imprisonment. Thus, by invoking the tradition of these earlier texts and seemingly returning sexuality "to the closet," Seth's writings suggest his skepticism of a domain free from compulsory heterosexuality and queerphobia. As if in direct dialogue with Suniti Namjoshi, he writes in the story "The Elephant and the Tragopan":

> Someone suggested that we flee
> And set up our own community
> In some far valley
> Where no man
> Has ever trod—or ever can.
> Sweet to the mind though it may seem,
> This is, alas, an idle dream—
> For nowhere lies beyond man's reach
> To mar and burn and flood and leech.
> A distant valley is indeed
> No sanctuary from his greed. (*Beastly Tales* 104)

While Seth does allow for a possible rapport between animals and humans, he does not envision an alliance based on (queer) othering and a subsequent alternative reality. The dominant reality of heteropatriarchy pervades all other spaces and realities, setting up communities and social structures in its likeness. In "The Crocodile and the Monkey" (*Beastly Tales* 1–11), for example, a rewriting of the fable "The Monkey and the Crocodile" from the *Panchatantra*, the intergenus homosocial relationship between the monkey and the crocodile, Kuroop, is threatened by the crocodile's wife. Although she has continually benefited from the generosity of the monkey and his steady provision of mangoes to satisfy her appetite, Kuroop's wife decides one day that she would like to eat the monkey's heart, which she imagines is sweet from years of digesting mango pulp. She therefore commands her husband to bring the monkey to her, claiming that without this nourishment she will die filled with bitterness. Though Kuroop protests that the monkey is his friend (note that he is not presented as "their" friend) and has habitually referred to the monkey as "dearest" and his "sweet love" (2), he eventually cedes to the pressures of marital dissension and carries the monkey on his back under the guise of bringing him to his island home to reciprocate the monkey's unremitting liberality. This, however, is where the original fable and Seth's version of it diverge. In the *Panchatantra*, the crocodile informs the monkey of his wife's plans to give the monkey time to "pray to [its] favorite god" (301). The monkey subsequently convinces the crocodile that his own heart is forlorn and that he has another, sweeter heart stored in a rose-apple tree that would appeal even more to the crocodile's wife. But once the crocodile returns the monkey to land, the monkey runs away, laughing at the crocodile's foolishness in believing in the existence of two hearts. In Seth's account, however, Kuroop's confession of his true purpose is depicted as an intentional allowance for the monkey's possible escape, an encouragement for the monkey to fabricate a reason, any reason, to return to the shore. Thus, when the monkey offers the crocodile the ridiculous tale of the heart he has stored in a tree by his home, Kuroop "loses, then quickly finds his smile" (8) and promptly returns the monkey to safe land. However, despite the crocodile's collusion in the monkey's escape, the monkey refuses to pardon his friend for the initial betrayal of homosocial bonding for heterosexuality and throws mangoes on Kuroop's head as the crocodile watches him "with a regretful smile" (9). As Eve Kosofsky Sedgwick proposes in her work *Between Men: English Literature and Male Homosocial Desire*, in literature a marital and affective relationship between a man and a woman is often embedded in a triangle consisting of two men and a woman, in which erotic attraction between the two men is more significant than the relationship between either one and the woman (21). However, in a heteropatriarchal society, Seth suggests, the heterosexual union will always assert itself and weaken or destroy the homosocial-homosexual bond.

By refusing to develop a space for sexual alterity either inside or outside of the nation-state, Seth negates the possibility of a positive queer existence and reinscribes the queer subject into the legacy of suffering and grief embodied in Oscar Wilde's "The Nightingale and the Rose" and, indeed, in the figure of the artist himself, emerging from Reading jail to die alone and penniless. In her rewriting of Wilde's fairytale, Namjoshi employs the less emblematic iris and wren in place of the nightingale and the rose to suggest that the archetype of the suffering queer is an unnecessary romanticism. However, the pressures of heteronormativity inevitably defeat all of Seth's homosexualized beasts. To return to "The Mouse and the Snake," the entrance of the phallic snake, which swallows one of the lovers whole, quickly interrupts the homoerotic play of the two mice. Though the second mouse tirelessly fights the snake until it spits her lover's body back at her, the celebratory tone that the poet Chang (to whom the narrative is attributed) wishes to ascribe to his tale of the brave and faithful mouse is undermined by the final image of the mouse crying "Bitter tears for her who'd died. / Squeaking sadly, and bereft, / Corpse in mouth, she sobbed and left" (*Beastly

Tales 21). Unhappiness, suffering, and even death are portrayed as the inevitable consequences of same-sex desire.

A similar despair concerning the fate of sexual alterity may be seen in Seth's *Arion and the Dolphin: A Libretto* (1994). First commissioned by the Baylis Programme at the English National Opera as a libretto, and later revised into a children's story of the same name, *Arion and the Dolphin* rewrites the ancient Greek myth described by Herodotus in book 1 of *The Histories* and echoed in Plutarch's "The Cleverness of Animals." In Herodotus's brief recounting of the tale, Arion of Methymna, "the most distinguished musician of that date, and the man who first . . . composed and named the dithyramb" (10–11), decides to sail to Italy and Sicily to seek his fortune. After "making a great deal of money in those countries," he then chooses to return to Corinth from Tarentum in a Corinthian vessel as "he had more trust in the Corinthians than in anyone else" (10). However, his trust soon proves mislaid as the Corinthians, driven by greed, hatch a plot to throw Arion overboard and steal his fortune. Overhearing their plan, Arion begs for his life but to no avail; the sailors offer him the choice of either killing himself if he wants to be buried ashore or jumping overboard immediately. Arion selects the latter but asks that he be allowed to give the sailors one last song before he drowns. The sailors agree, and after playing a "lively tune" on his lute, Arion jumps in the ocean to be rescued by a dolphin that his music has summoned (10). The dolphin then returns him to Corinth where Periander, doubting Arion's tale of the heroic dolphin, keeps him under strict supervision until the return of the Corinthian ship. On their arrival, Periander sends for the sailors and asks whether they have anything to tell him about Arion. Hearing their reply of "Oh yes . . . we left him safe and sound at Tarentum in Italy" (11), Arion appears and the lie is detected. The story concludes with this discovery, though a passing reference is made to a small bronze figure of a man and a dolphin that Arion allegedly erects as an offering in a temple at Tarentum.

While Herodotus's story centers primarily on the betrayal by the sailors who throw Arion off the ship, Seth transfers the focus of the narrative to develop the relationship between Arion and the dolphin that saves him. The homoerotic undertones that pervade the entire libretto are established at the onset of the drama with the tyrant Periander's refusal to allow Arion to attend the singing competition in Sicily (the motivation for Arion's travels in Seth's version of the tale). Periander (who, according to rumor, has murdered his wife) begs Arion to "think of my court, of Corinth, and of me," reading Arion's desire to leave as a form of betrayal that is being planned behind his back (*Arion and the Dolphin: A Libretto*

10–11). He even attempts to elicit Arion's pity as a means of keeping the boy by his side, casting himself as a despised despot whose own children loathe him. It is only after Arion insists that his intention is to spread his lord's fame and his greatness and promises on his life that he will return that Periander allows him to go. The scene then shifts from Periander's courtyard to the shipboard where Seth anticipates the relationship between Arion and the Dolphin with the introduction of yet another homosocialized character: the Sea Captain. While the Captain is portrayed as a husband and father, the greater part of his time is spent among his crew whom he "cares for" and regards as "his family" (18). His attentions are soon turned toward Arion and, in what may be seen as an erotic gesture, the Captain affirms Arion's claim that he would not make a good sailor by taking the latter's hands in his own and says, "Those hands would grow callussed too quickly anyway" (16). His recognition of Arion's soft hands may be interpreted as an allusion to Arion's queer effeminacy, and his gift of the conch shell not only invokes the shell as a Buddhist emblem that signifies a prosperous journey but also may suggest the *s'ankha* (Indian conch shell) bangles an Indian bride is given to wear during her wedding and, consequently, their possible union.[14] Upon arriving on shore, the Sea Captain accompanies Arion into Sicily, where cheers of "welcome, Arion of Lesbos" greet them. While in Herodotus's version of the myth, Arion is also cited as being from Methymna on the island of Lesbos, the Sicilians' initial confusion about and lengthy discussion of Arion's origins in Seth's rewriting connote the more contemporary association of Lesbos with lesbianism, and thus queer sexuality. Although Arion asks him to stay to watch the competition, the Sea Captain regretfully refuses, claiming that he must leave to address "business before pleasure" (23). Arion, however, elects for "pleasure before business," choosing to accompany the Sicilians on "a proper booze-up" (24).

In scene 4 of the libretto, which depicts the music competition, a tired and hungover Arion endeavors to sing but can merely repeat the name "Periander" over and over again. On his second effort, he begins the song he has sung for the Captain on the ship—"Bright stars, bring comfort" (26)—but is unable to continue past this first line. These failed attempts at singing about Periander and the Sea Captain mark the end of his relationships with these two men. On his third and final try, however, Arion invokes the gods to "fill with your inspiration my empty shell" (27) and, hearing the sound of the sea and the dolphins in the conch, begins to sing. While it is the captain's conch shell that saves his life and secures his victory in the competition, the sound of the dolphins singing in his ear suggests a shift, and ironically, an evolution in Arion's erotic object choice. The Sea Captain and Periander pursue Arion while maintaining their primary kinship identifications of husband and father, thus remaining inside the dominant heteropatriarchal order. The dolphin, however, as doubly othered by virtue of being both an animal and queer, embodies sexual, rather than homosocial or homoerotic, practice and love. Thus, the possibility of interspecies love is evoked even before the dolphins save Arion's life.

As in Herodotus's narrative, Seth's Arion elects to return to Corinth on the Corinthian ship and is given the choice of suicide or death by jumping overboard by the sailors, with Arion choosing the latter. But before summoning the dolphins with his song, Arion returns the conch shell to the Sea Captain as a symbol of their "love . . . buried by gold dust" (34). Indeed, the song itself is an elegy of betrayal:

> My voice was loved, myself I cannot tell.
> A hollow voice cried out from every shell.
> Those who gave friendship I least understand
> Who, when I needed love, let slip their hand.
> But so it was, and I am glad I leave
> No friends to mourn, no family to grieve. (35)

The singing has an unsettling affect on the sailors, and they begin to quarrel. Some attempt to guard Arion with an oar or a sword, others to charge him. But at the height of the chaos, Arion, having been deceived by everyone around him, leaps into the waves.

Although Arion initially believes that he has died, he quickly realizes that a company of dolphins and one dolphin in particular, Dolphin (the name of Arion's dolphin lover is capitalized), has saved him. In what may be interpreted as homoerotic sport or courtship, he is "buoyed up by dolphins, danced and *played with*; and carried along (holding a fin, *riding on a dolphin's back*) at a wonderfully *rapid rate*" (37; emphasis added). While the term "play" connotes a general tenor of sexuality, "riding on a dolphin's back . . . at a rapid rate," specifically suggests male-to-male intercourse. However, the relationship between Arion and the dolphins is not exclusively sexual. The day is spent discussing music and the habits of dolphins, breaking "bread" (or raw fish), and exploring the history of human-dolphin relations through masquerade. Though all the dolphins participate in the feeding and the performance, dialogue is confined to the Dolphin and Arion and culminates in a musical declaration of their mutual love:

DOLPHIN.

I love Arion, and would like to be
Bound to his voice and him eternally . . .

ARION.

The days pass one by one,
I feel my life has only just begun—
And, for the first time, I am having fun!

ARION AND DOLPHIN.

In air and water both, our voices part and blend,
And I/you, who never sought a friend
Have found one in the end. (46)

One by one, the other dolphins depart, leaving Arion and the Dolphin alone with their love to swim toward Corinth.

Once Arion and the Dolphin reach the shores of Corinth, Arion endeavors to convince his friend to depart as he recognizes that "my part is here above, and yours below—/ I where the winds, you where the waters flow" (48). Interspecies love is equated with what Oscar Wilde referred to as "the love of things impossible" (Wilde, *Letters* 185). But in contrast to Periander, who expresses his adoration of Arion through possessiveness and threats of death, and the Captain, who betrays his love of the musician for his (heterosexual) family's well-being, the Dolphin refuses to leave Arion's side, claiming that if he and Arion part they will never meet again and he "would die of loneliness and pain" (48). Arion's warnings, however, prove prophetic. While Periander imprisons Arion for seemingly lying about the animal's ability to speak (though this act could also be read as jealousy), the Dolphin is turned into a circus act, in which he is forced to jump through hoops and leap for dead fish. Seth thus suggests that queer love, when not punishable by law, is reduced to heterosexual spectacle. Refusing to eat, the Dolphin eventually dies with the name of his lover on his lips. Arion mourns and the depth of his grief compels Periander not only to free him from his jail but also to erect a tomb for and provide a procession in honor of the deceased Dolphin. In the midst of the procession, the Sea Captain and his crew return to Corinth. When questioned by Periander about the whereabouts of Arion, the weeping Captain insists that Arion left for Lesbos to see his native coast but refuses to swear on his mother's (or the Dolphin's) tomb that this is the truth. Arion then reveals himself and the Captain once again expresses his love for the boy, claiming that he has "been thinking of [Arion] night and day" and that his melodic "voice has crept through [the Captain's] heart's maze" (58). But although Arion persuades Periander to defer the sentence of the Captain and crew for a day, the only love Arion will sing is for his deceased:

> I hear your voice sing out my name by night,
>> By dawn, by evening light.
> I mourn for you, yet, Dolphin, to my shame,
>> I never asked your name.
> Your element protected me, but mine
>> For you proved far too fine.
> Dolphin, it was from your marine caress
>> That I learned gentleness.
> May music bind the sky, the earth, the sea
>> In tune, in harmony.
> Dark sea, protect all voyagers whose home
>> Rests in your ring of foam.
> Warm earth, teach us to nourish, not destroy
>> The souls that give us joy.
> Bright stars, engrave my dolphin and my lyre
>> In the night sky with fire. (59)

By casting him as nameless, Seth codifies the Dolphin as "the love that dares not speak its name" that is doomed to failure. While same-sex eroticism may exist between men and beasts, lived out in the spaces between the dominant (heterosexual) kinship structures, an overt sexual alterity can exist only in the realm of the unreachable, as embodied in the constellations of Delphius and Lyra in the night sky. Thus, according to Seth, the place of the queer (whether human or animal) in contemporary society is in the "gutter," always "looking to the stars" (Wilde, *Lady Windermere's Fan* 56).

"Words invent the world," Suniti Namjoshi and her life-partner, Gillian Hanscombe, write in their anthology *Flesh and Paper*, "and then the invented world invests language with images of itself. In turn, we see and hear the emerging world with words" (1). Though the world she has "inherited" is structured so that she occupies the lowest rung on Gayle Rubin's sexual hierarchy, Namjoshi's depiction of animals in fable points toward multiple emergent cultural systems, continuously rewritten to undermine the dominant order.[15] From the unlikely friendship between a human and a cow to the love between a mare and its mistress, a queered, despeciated nation is feasible for those who are willing to envisage and embrace the Blue Donkey (or the diasporic Indian lesbian). In Vikram Seth's fables, however, animals and humans may coexist, but words cannot be disengaged from their dominant origins. An invented world will always be a residual system mirroring the dominant humanist order, and there is no place in either for homosexuals, whether among the humans or the animals.[16] Thus, the dominant order must be restructured with words from within.

But if words do "invent the world" and we are free to fashion our realities as we see fit, then what are the implications of creating a world composed of animals and queers in which the former half of the population are denied access to the dominant, or indeed any common discourse? Ignoring the practicalities of how an integrated, despeciated nation might function, it is important to recognize that the animals Namjoshi and Seth wish to embrace in the creation of a society composed of "others" bear little resemblance to the creatures that they empirically encounter. Rather, the beasts invoked are what Wendy B. Faris refers to in a different context as "autogenerative": they engender their own lives and others beyond themselves, independent of their referential worlds, yet remain bound to the "metaphorical register" (164). Whether conversing with the author in flawless English (Namjoshi) or saving the narrator from drowning (Seth), these simultaneously "real" and "allegorical" animals are completely without agency, and reliant upon the authors to speak for them (recalling other unreliable proxies, such as white women speaking for all women in second-wave feminism or Orientalists speaking for the subaltern). The supposedly "queered" border crossings of Seth and Namjoshi therefore repeat the hierarchical structures of heteronormative patriarchy the authors critique continuously in their work, insisting on the mutual marginalization of animals while engaging in the anthropomorphism that they eschew. Their new, posthumanist communities do not extricate themselves from the hegemonic framework of patriarchal society but emulate it in a peripheral microcosm, as power and individualization are still equated with moving oneself from a marginalized position at the periphery of the nation to the dominant and dominating center. Thus, Suniti Namjoshi and Vikram Seth cross and subsequently queer the border between "animals" and "humans" without queering their (and our) understanding of what these identities are meant to convey or recognizing that not all queers (whether animal or human) or forms of queering are the same.

NOTES

1. Theocritus's third-century-BCE poem, "The Idylls," is made up of 30 "idylls," seven of which are homoerotic (Norton).

2. "Bat Boy," an animal-human hybrid first described in the *Weekly World News* in the early 1990s, periodically appears in the tabloid papers (Goldstein 24). When the phenomenon of "Bat Boy" was transformed into a popular off-Broadway play in 2001, gay men in particular applauded this drama of acceptance and inclusion (Goldstein 37).

3. Emergent cultural systems are "new meanings and values, new practices, new relationships and kinds of relationships" that are substantially alternative to the dominant system (Williams 123).

4. Foucault writes, "Homosexuality appeared as one of the forms of sexuality when it was transposed from the practice of sodomy onto a kind of interior androgyny, a hermaphroditism of the soul. The sodomite had been a temporary aberration, the homosexual was now a species" (43).

5. In her analysis of "The Phoenix and the Turtle," Ruth Vanita reads the interspecies coupling of the turtledove and the phoenix, traditionally gendered female, as an act of same-sex female desire (*Sappho* 239–40). She also reads *Flush* as a homoerotic text. Though *Flush* describes the love of Elizabeth Barrett-Browning's (male) dog for its owner, male dogs are common signifiers of female eroticism (217–28).

6. According to Thadani and others, the introduction of Section 377 of the Indian Penal Code terminated, and erased, a flourishing tradition of alternative sexualities in Indian writing prior to colonialism. Recently, scholars such as Vanita and Thadani have begun to (re)create a queer Indian continuum, "excavating" nominations, philosophies, and cosmologies, such as *bhangni* (female erotic bonding), *sakhi* (female companion), and *jami* (twin), which, they claim, were "desexualized" and subsequently "heterosexualized" during the period of British colonization.

7. Composed between approximately 1700 and 1100 BCE, the *Rig Veda* is a collection of Sanskrit hymns, incantations, and rituals that are among the most ancient religious texts.

8. Although Thadani provides a plethora of "evidence" for the establishment of a queer genealogy in precolonial India, it is important to recognize how current (Western) queer discourses inform her "excavation" of ancient Indian identities and practices and her agenda in "queering" these tropes.

9. In his 1913 novelette *Ermyntrude and Esmeralda*, Lytton Strachey describes girls who refer to the male genitalia as "bow-wows" and the female genitalia as "pussies," the latter still existing today as a pejorative term in colloquial speech (Vanita, *Sappho* 217).

10. Namjoshi refuses to hold heterosexual women responsible for the marginalization of queers. For example, in the fable "All Right, Call Them Another Species," the universal heterosexual woman is depicted as "charmed and enthralled" by homosexuality until the universal man arrives (Hanscombe and Namjoshi, *Flesh* 41).

11. While Namjoshi's emphasis on the originary marginalization of women is unsurprising, it is also problematic. By representing womanhood as a prerequisite for citizenship in the posthumanist nation, and, essentially, for the

queering of identity boundaries, she reasserts a hierarchical binary between male and female (albeit an inverted one) and undermines her emphasis on identity as "play."

12. Salman Rushdie has also noted the distinction between Western and South Asian audiences. In a 1987 interview, he remarked that his novels are often read as fantasy in the West and as realistic narratives in India and Pakistan (Suleri 176).

13. "By the River" recalls the story in the *Matsya Purana* (also recounted in the *Ramayana*) in which King Ila, wandering in a forest, enters a grove in which Shiva and Parvati are sporting. To please Parvati, Shiva has willed that any male who enters this grove will be turned into a female. So Ila is turned into a beautiful woman and his horse into a mare (Vanita, "Introduction" 18).

14. The tradition of wearing *s'ankha* bangles goes back to 6500 BCE as is evident from the discovery of *s'ankha* bangles among the grave ornaments in a woman's tomb in Mehergarh ("Lakshmi Conch Report").

15. Rubin suggests that (Western) society has set up a sexual hierarchy that draws an imaginary line between "good" (read "monogamous," "heterosexual," "reproductive," and one might argue, "white") sex and "bad" (read "promiscuous," "queer," and "nonwhite") sex. For example, sex between monogamous homosexuals is "better" than sex between men who cruise but not as "good" as sex between promiscuous heterosexuals (282).

16. Raymond Williams defines residual cultural systems as thus: "Certain experiences, meanings, and values which cannot be expressed or substantially verified in terms of the dominant culture, are nevertheless lived and practised on the basis of the residue—cultural as well as social—of some previous social and cultural institution or formation" (122).

WORKS CITED

Blackham, H. J. *The Fable as Literature*. London: Athlone, 1985.

Butler, Judith. *Gender Trouble: Feminism and the Subversion of Identity*. 1990. New York: Routledge, 1999.

Byatt, A. S. "Permenides and the Contemporary British Novel." *Literature Matters* 21 (1996): 6–8.

Coetzee, J. M. *Elizabeth Costello*. 1999. London: Secker, 2003.

Faris, Wendy B. "Scheherazade's Children: Magical Realism and Postmodern Fiction." *Magical Realism: Theory, History, Community*. Ed. Wendy B. Faris and Lois Parkinson Zamora. Durham: Duke UP, 1995. 163–90.

Foucault, Michel. *The History of Sexuality*. Vol. 1. 1976. Trans. Robert Hurley. London: Penguin, 1998.

Goldstein, Judith L. "The Origin of the Species." *differences* 15.1 (2004): 23–47.

Hanscombe, Gillian, and Suniti Namjoshi. *Flesh and Paper*. Charlottetown: Ragweed, 1986.

————. "Writing the Rag-Bag of Empire." *Engendering Realism and Postmodernism: Contemporary Women Writers in Britain*. Ed. Beate Neumeier. Amsterdam: Rodopi, 2001. 391–406.

Herodotus. *The Histories*. 1954. Trans. Aubrey de Sélincourt. London: Penguin, 1996.

"Lakshmi Conch Report." *Planetary Gemologists Association*. 28 May 2004. <http://www.p-g-a.org>.

Namjoshi, Suniti. *Because of India: Selected Poems and Fables*. London: Onlywomen, 1989.

————. *The Blue Donkey Fables*. London: Women's, 1988.

————. *The Conversations of Cow*. London: Women's, 1985.

————. *Feminist Fables: Saint Suniti and the Dragon*. 1981. London: Virago, 1994.

————. *Saint Suniti and the Dragon, and Other Fables*. London: Virago, 1994.

Norton, Rictor. "A Critique of Social Constructionism and Postmodern Queer Theory." *Rictor Norton Homepage*. 17 July 2006. <www.infopt.demon.co.uk>.

Otalvaro-Hormillosa, Sonia. "Racial and Erotic Anxieties: Ambivalent Fetishization, from Fanon to Mercer." *Postcolonial and Queer Theories: Intersections and Essays*. Ed. John C. Hawley. Westport: Greenwood, 2001. 87–111.

Panchatantra. Trans. Arthur W. Ryder. New York: Limited Editions, 1972.

Perry, John Oliver. "World Literature Review: Indian." *World Literature Today* 65.3 (1991): 549–51.

Rubin, Gayle. "Thinking Sex: Notes for a Radical Theory in the Politics of Sexuality." *Pleasure and Danger: Exploring Female Sexuality*. Ed. Carole S. Vance. London: Pandora, 1992. 267–319.

Sedgwick, Eve Kosofksy. *Between Men: English Literature and Male Homosocial Desire*. New York: Columbia UP, 1995.

Seth, Leila. *On Balance: An Autobiography*. New Delhi: Penguin, 2003.

Seth, Vikram. *An Equal Music*. London: Phoenix, 1999.

————. *Arion and the Dolphin*. New York: Dutton, 1994.

————. *Arion and the Dolphin: A Libretto*. London: Phoenix, 1994.

————. *Beastly Tales from Here and There*. 1991. London: Phoenix, 2000.

————. *The Golden Gate: A Novel in Verse*. London: Faber, 1986.

————. *The Humble Administrator's Garden*. Manchester: Carcanet, 1985.

————. *Mappings*. New Delhi: Viking, 2005.

————. *A Suitable Boy*. London: Phoenix, 1994.

Shakespeare, William. *A Midsummer Night's Dream*. 1967. Ed. Stanley Wells. London: Penguin, 1995.

————. *The Poems: Venus and Adonis, The Rape of Lucrece, The Phoenix and the Turtle, That Passionate Pilgrim, A Lover's Complaint*. Ed. John Roe. Cambridge: Cambridge UP, 2006.

Shuttleton, David. "The Queer Politics of Gay Pastoral." *De-Centring Sexualities: Politics and Representation beyond the Metropolis*. Ed. Richard Phillips, Diane West, and David Shuttleton. London: Routledge, 2000. 125–46.

Steinisch, Sabine. "Subversive Fabulations: The Twofold Pull in Suniti Namjoshi's Feminist Fables." *Engendering Realism and Postmodernism: Contemporary Women Writers in Britain*. Ed. Beate Neumeier. Amsterdam: Rodopi, 2001. 265–78.

Strachey, Lytton. *Ermyntrude and Esmeralda: An Entertainment*. London: Blond, 1969.

Suleri, Sara. *The Rhetoric of English India*. Chicago: U of Chicago P, 1992.

Thadani, Giti. "Jami or Lesbian?" *Amazon to Zami: Towards a Global Lesbian Feminism*. Ed. Monika Reinfelder. London: Cassell, 1996. 56–69.

———. *Sakhiyani: Lesbian Desire in Ancient and Modern India*. London: Cassell, 1996.

Theocritus. *The Idylls*. Trans. R.C. Trevelyan. Cambridge: Cambridge UP, 1947.

Vanita, Ruth. "Introduction: Ancient Indian Materials." *Same-Sex Love in India: Readings from Literature and History*. Ed. Ruth Vanita and Saleem Kidawi. Basingstoke: Macmillan, 2000. 1–30.

———. *Sappho and the Virgin Mary: Same-Sex Love and the English Literary Imagination*. New York: Columbia UP, 1996.

Wilde, Oscar. *Lady Windermere's Fan*. London: Methuen, 1964.

———. *The Letters of Oscar Wilde*. Ed. Rupert Hart-Davis. New York: Harcourt Brace, 1962.

Williams, Raymond. *Marxism and Literature*. Oxford: Oxford UP, 1977.

Wittig, Monique. *The Straight Mind and Other Essays*. New York: Beacon, 1992.

Woolf, Virginia. *Flush*. Oxford: Oxford UP, 1998.

Chapter 9

Genet among the Palestinians

Sex, Betrayal, and the Incomparable Real

James Penney

Massacre and Subjectivation

Beginning in October 1970, at the invitation of Mahmoud el Hamchari, the Paris-based Palestinian Liberation Organization (PLO) leader whose 1972 assassination at the hands of the Mossad, the Israeli secret service, Steven Spielberg depicts in his film *Munich* (2005), Jean Genet spent a total of 11 months among the Palestinian refugees and resistance fighters in the northwest corner of Jordan. Following Israel's illegal 1967 annexation of the West Bank, Gaza, the Sinai peninsula, and the Golan Heights, the Palestinian refugee community expelled from these regions organized an armed guerilla resistance to the Israeli occupation. Approximately 5,000 Palestinian fedayeen took up positions in a handful of camps on the hills of the Jordan River's east bank between Amman, the Jordanian capital, and the Syrian border.

While officially endorsing the Palestinian struggle, the Jordanian Hachemite monarchy grew increasingly wary of the refugees' powerful presence in the kingdom after the Six Day War. King Hussein feared that the political destabilization occasioned by the Palestinian presence would lead toward a military coup establishing Palestinian sovereignty in the kingdom. Under intense diplomatic pressure, Hussein, in concert with Egypt, signed in August 1970 a U.S.-sponsored peace accord with Israel, which the Palestinians understandably viewed as a betrayal of their cause. Jordan then instigated a brutal crackdown on the Palestinians, which culminated in the infamous massacres of Black September 1970, during which the Jordanian army, at this time composed mainly of Bedouin soldiers, decimated the camps around Amman and Zarka, killing at least 3,000 Palestinians. Genet arrived in Jordan roughly a month after these attacks. Thus was inaugurated Genet's new persona as Palestinian revolutionary fellow traveler, a persona that would fuel the fires of his literary and political passions for the remainder of his life. In this persona Genet would compose his most radical texts, which compellingly articulate how sexuality's counteridentitarian power forces us to reset the terms of comparative literary and cultural study.

The massacres of Black September motivated Genet to return to West Asia for the first time since his late teens, when he had been stationed in French-mandate Syria in his nation's foreign legion. But an even more infamous tragedy put an end to the ten-year period of creative procrastination that followed Genet's first Palestinian sojourn. Foreseeing the Palestinians' dark destiny in the Lebanese war—his instincts on political developments in the region were nothing if not prescient—Genet returned to Beirut in September 1982. There he witnessed firsthand the events leading up to the massacres in the Palestinian camps of Sabra and Chatila, where armed fighters, outfitted in the uniforms of Israeli-allied right-wing Lebanese Christian Phalangist militias, slaughtered a significant portion of the refugee population, most of which had been forced to relocate from Jordan to Lebanon in the aftermath of the Black September massacres 12 years before.

Prior to the attacks on Sabra and Chatila, the Israeli Defense Forces had put in place a military installation at the camps' entrances to monitor the goings-on within. Though the extent of Israeli involvement in the massacres has never been incontrovertibly established, it is clear that Israeli soldiers stationed at the installation observed the carnage and did nothing to intervene or to sound the alarm. Witnesses also reported that the Israelis lit up the sky above the camps with flares, likely to facilitate the slaughter occurring below. Outrage at Israel's complicity arose even within Israel itself. "The connection with the I[sraeli] D[efence] F[orces]," Israeli historian Ilan Pappe observes, "was clear enough to convince 400,000 Israelis to protest against the massacre, and led to the establishment of a commission of inquiry." Israel's own Kahan commission eventually "dismissed several senior officers involved," Pappe dryly adds, "and ruled that [Ariel] Sharon, [then Israeli] minister of defense, was unfit to serve in such a high position" (223).

As Robert Fisk notes in his monumental *Great War for Civilization*, the commission went so far as to hold Sharon "personally responsible" for the killings (505). Fisk underlines how Sharon spuriously proclaimed PLO responsibility for the assassination of Phalangist leader Bashir Gemayel, who had just been elected Lebanese president, directly before issuing his directive to the Christian militias to enter the camps (604). The number of dead at Sabra and Chatila, which the most reliable sources estimate at around 1,500 ("up to 1,700 Palestinians" perished; Fisk 505), remains indeterminate today. The Israeli army controlled the camps' entrances in the days following the killings, preventing authorities from assessing the carnage precisely. Not until 19 September, three days after the massacres, did Genet, posing as a journalist, manage to enter the camps, becoming the first Westerner to do so. Wading through a devastated landscape littered with corpses rotting under a blistering sun, Genet spent an afternoon observing the massacre's gruesome outcome. He then immediately returned to Paris where, in a sudden spurt of creative intensity, he spent the month of October writing the harrowing and unforgettable "Quatre heures à Shatila," which first appeared in the *Revue d'études palestiniennes* the following January. Relieved, it would seem definitively, of his debilitating depression, Genet at last set to work on what would eventually become *Prisoner of Love*, a text he had envisioned during his return to West Asia 12 years earlier, which he had been urged to write by no lesser a figure than Yassir Arafat, the recently departed leader of Fatah and tarnished post-Oslo symbol of Palestinian aspirations.

With surprisingly few exceptions, *Prisoner* has received scant attention, particularly among critics writing in English. If we speculate on why this has been the case, a variety of factors can be mentioned, including widespread support for Israeli foreign policy in the dominant English-language media; the thoroughgoing delegitimation of Marxian revolutionary movements since the collapse of the Eastern bloc; the ideological overdetermination, especially since the World Trade Center attacks and consequent Anglo-American occupation of Iraq and North Atlantic Treaty Organization presence in Afghanistan, of engagements with the Arab and Muslim worlds; and finally, perhaps especially, the literary difficulty and historical density of the text itself. In this light, comparative criticism's intrinsic insistence on both decentering any privileged national point of view and broadening the historical horizon against which a text is interpreted lend themselves especially well to the task of reading *Prisoner of Love*. A genuinely comparative method can help attenuate the prejudices and preconceptions that to date have hindered the reception of Genet's ultimate literary work.

The attention that *Prisoner* has managed nonetheless to receive largely confirms the unsettled response that Genet's numerous scandalous crossings have elicited from a bien-pensant reading public since the appearance of his earliest work. For the boundaries that Genet sets himself the task of transgressing are not merely the ones whose subversion is ordinarily celebrated in comparative literary and cultural studies, namely, those between cultures, ethnicities, and "races," socioeconomic classes, languages or dialects, and sexualities. Rather, like Lacan's Antigone, Genet sets himself the task of crossing the line that demarcates the field of intelligibility of life as such, the line that implicitly establishes the very terms by means of which cultural comparisons are normatively drawn. Indeed, the crossings effected by *Prisoner*, along with the rest of Genet's late texts, violate so systematically the hegemonic Western identity formation's frontiers—white as against nonwhite, Occident as against Orient, male as against female, civilization as against barbarism, freedom as against fraternity, order as against violence, sexuality as against incest or perversion—that the very conditions of possibility of this identity, along with the multiple differentiations that form its ground, are torn asunder. Genet's violations thus reveal the acts of ideological and epistemological violence that take place, unrecognized, before the work of standard-issue comparative cultural studies can even begin.

The difficulty with comparativism as a method of literary and cultural analysis is that it is logically bound to posit a term of comparison, which inevitably sets the parameters of any path of inquiry. Historically, the discipline of comparative literature has failed in its duty to give an account of itself—to acknowledge explicitly, that is to say, its frame of comparison. To the extent that this failure remains unrecognized, comparative method must remain ignorant of the critical terrain that it must implicitly but necessarily cordon off. One is tempted to take the history of the discipline of comparative literature as an example. Though, in principle, it exhibited admirably globalist ambitions, early paradigmatic work in the area—one thinks of figures such as René Wellek, for example—remained, in practice, alarmingly Eurocentric, not in some banal politically correct sense, but rather in its reluctance to acknowledge how the concrete histories of European colonialisms and imperialisms surreptitiously informed the discipline's methodological foundations, more specifically the terms of its comparative points of reference.

Genet's transgressions succeed in exposing these blind spots. Indeed, they articulate an ethics of revolt so challenging that even those most sympathetic to his project, notably biographer Edmund White and the late Edward Said, have felt obliged to maintain their distance from specific aspects of his work. Commenting on a 1971 Genet essay in a French photography magazine published in tandem with Bruno Barbey's images of Palestinian refugee camps, White concludes that "although the editors of *Zoom* were careful to point out that Genet was anti-Zionist but not anti-Semitic, the question remains an open one" (558). As becomes quickly apparent in his biography of Genet, White's overly familiar position on Israel implies that an anti-Zionist argument can only with extreme difficulty, if at all, be extricated from charges of anti-Semitism. Brought to its conclusion, this logic dismisses outright the legitimacy of any Arab claim to historical Palestine, a logic that, like the ambient and cynical postholocaust blackmail from which White fails to extricate himself, can, in my view, be correctly qualified as racist.

But a closer look at White's commentary is no doubt necessary here. Paraphrasing Genet's *Zoom* article argument, he writes that "after two thousand years of the humiliating Diaspora and ten years of the Nazi extermination campaign, Jews ha[d] taken on the inhumanity of their former masters," adding that, for Genet, "although Israel was conceived as a refuge for European Jews, it ha[d] become the bastion of Western imperialism in the Middle East" (558). White goes on to take issue with Genet's contentions, averring that such views result from what he calls Genet's "highly coloured version of Jewish history" (558). Conveniently, White's comment exonerates him from the obligation of actually considering the substance of Genet's perfectly legitimate criticism of political Zionism's self-justifying manipulation of the holocaust's terrible tragedy, as well as its consistent complicity with European, and more recently American, strategic interests in the region. This history goes back most significantly to the days of the post-Ottoman British mandate, of which the generally friendly policies toward Zionist colonization—the notorious 1917 Balfour declaration is the best example—were surely a historical condition of possibility for the creation of the Israeli state.

As is widely recognized, Said's work on Palestine represents one of the best and most heroic attempts to defy the manipulative *Denkverbot* that finally prevents White from accounting with integrity for Genet's position. His laudable article "On Jean Genet's Late Work" is chock full of illuminating insights on the singular courage shown in both Genet's embrace of progressive politics in the Arab world and the literary manifestation of this politics not only in *Prisoner* but also in his last dramatic piece, *The Screens*. Said's essay is, without question, literary criticism of the highest order. Yet even though he proves himself unusually penetrating in his analysis of the uncompromising negativity and anti-identitarianism of Genet's concept of betrayal, in part by carefully distinguishing Genet's always sociopolitically situated ethics of revolt from a conservatively and metaphysically nihil-istic doctrine, in one particular passage Said awkwardly and violently minimizes the weight of Genet's challenge by qualifying his ethics as "dubious, even repellent, on moral and political grounds." Though he warmly identifies Genet as an effective advocate for the Palestinian cause, Said ultimately proposes the confinement of Genet's underlying idea of betrayal to the decidedly bourgeois and "tolerable" terrain of an "aesthetic or rhetorical credo" (237).

There is something deeply symptomatic about the contradiction between, on the one hand, Said's sensitive and more or less ringing endorsement of Genet's partisan enthusiasms for Algerian and Palestin-ian sovereignty and, on the other, his cagey self-distancing from Genet's desire to systematize his musings on ecstatic betrayal and the import of evil into a sort of ethical conceptuality. Genet's concrete positions on Arab-Israeli and Arab-European politics are one thing, but his general conceptual-poetic framework, it would seem, quite another. Indeed, Said proves reluctant to take on the full consequences of Genet's disruptive sensibility, as if doing so might commit him to undefined causes and positions that might compromise the respectability of his own work. One surmises that Said might have wished to reproach Genet for what he calls his "solitude." Indeed, the Frenchman's ethics of revolt proves tricky to reconcile with any familiar notion of collective anticolonial national sov-ereignty, or even arguably of "national culture" in the properly Fanonian sense. For Fanon, we recall, "national culture is the collective thought process of a people to describe, justify, and extol the actions whereby they have joined forces and remained strong" (168). Doubtless Genet would endorse Fanon's valorization of the transformation of cultural forms resulting from the counterimperial struggle for sovereignty. Yet Fanon's contention that it is a "mistake" to "miss out on the national stage" of cultural development (179) emphasizes the importance of the state form in a way that is foreign to Genet's thinking, and this is so even when the state is defined, as it is in Fanon, in rigorously nonethnicizing and anti-culturalist terms. Curiously, however, Said's underdeveloped reservations never reach such a substantive level, and his reader is left with the nagging sense of a promising opportunity missed.

THE REAL OF COMPARISON

As a Frenchman, albeit one definitively alienated from his nation and its traditions, Genet engages with the Arab-Muslim world in the wake of a long and by now exhaustively interrogated tradition of European Orien-talisms and exoticisms. As is well known, Said's rightly acclaimed work on this topic, along with the entire critical tradition that it has helped to inspire, has spelled out how European representations of non-European realities have served to justify claims to Western cultural identity and its inherent superiority and thereby to grant specious ideological legitimacy to centuries of intensely exploitative imperialisms and colonialisms. In response to this unseemly history, critics have justifiably striven to produce more contextually situated analyses of "other" cultural artifacts. More specifically, in the best examples of comparative work in this tradition, complex patterns of cross-cultural, transnational, cosmopolitan, and interlinguistic influence have been suggestively charted and theorized.

Yet I want to argue that Genet's Palestinian calling is borne of a different desire, one that surely calls into question a predominantly culturalist assumption that underlies much of even the most sophisticated comparative work. According to this assumption, the crossings of cultural travelers such as Genet dissolve borders between cultural contexts or systems, which in spite of their varying degrees of complexity and internal antagonism or even self-contradiction, remain more or less fully chartable and available to comparative knowledge. Numerous "diagnostic" claims about Genet's Arab adventures could be made here. Disgusted with French and Judeo-Christian traditions, Genet seeks to reinvent himself, along with his literary initiatives, in alien cultural territory, seeking inspiration or renewal in radical otherness. A more critical version of this same view might run as follows: In the rejection of his French childhood and adolescence, Genet turns to Palestine in a gesture of compensatory revolt, failing in the process to appreciate, through projection or ignorance, the authentic cultural nuances of his new surroundings.

The more obvious shortcoming of the brand of comparativism that produces such (admittedly far from irrelevant) insights is that it culturalizes what is first and foremost a patently *political* mode of solidarity or affiliation in Genet. To be sure, late Genet is rife with pronouncements on the repressiveness and hypocrisy of a surely undernuanced notion of "Judeo-Christian morality." Yet Genet is at bottom as little concerned with the cultural or racial identity of the Black Panthers (though he is certainly intrigued by their politico-aesthetic mobilization of blackness) as he is with some putative Arab essence of the Palestinian community, except insofar as these can be negatively mobilized as weapons against racializing colonialist European universalisms. Never is Genet "anthropologically" fascinated by cultural, ethnic, or religious differences for their own sake; never do such differences become a key component of his political thought.

In addition, however, a second and, in my view, more crucial drawback of the culturalist-comparativist approach that I have sketched out here is its inherent inability to recognize that what captures Genet's interest within his political movements—the Palestinian resistance and the Black Panthers, but also very importantly Baader-Meinhof (the German Red Army Faction)—what transforms him into a *captif amoureux* (the English translation fails to convey the sense of capture or captivation), is their radically immanent yet negative-impossible status within the political contexts in which they erupt. Crucially, the events occasioned by these groups momentarily uncover the repressed, unthought, unconscious, "constitutively outside" element of the sociopolitical situations from which they are inevitably forcibly excluded, the element that very precisely *cannot be thought* within available cultural and ideological systems.

Now this reference to the unconscious, psychoanalysis teaches us, leads inexorably onto the terrain of sexuality, a thematic that is surely inextricable from Genet's singular ethico-political orientation. Despite his iconic status as a twentieth-century homosexual writer, on the biographical level Genet's influential and, in many ways, pioneering imaginative exploration of marginal sexualities notably failed to lead him to adopt a "political" view of homosexuality, a view comparable to those that emerged during the post-Stonewall decades, from the activisms that arose in response to the HIV/AIDS pandemic, to the elaborate and politically questionable deconstructive-*cum*-Foucauldian posturing of queer theory.

There is little question that Genet's sexual sensibility, so dramatically shaped by his experience in the French correctional system's so-called colonies, impacts heavily on the political engagements that mark his maturity (indeed Genet himself repeatedly spells this link out). Yet it is equally clear that the logic of Genet's work firmly resists any attempt at rendering his treatment of sexuality as anything remotely programmatic, as a substantive category of difference, for instance, featuring either necessary or desirable political consequences. On the contrary, Genet appears to have considered sexuality not as a function of psychological identity, and therefore as a term through which claims for recognition might be made within a liberal political conceptuality, but rather as the mode of this identity's impossibility and consequent unavoidable failure. In this precise sense, sexuality acquires in Genet a properly ethical dimension: it signals the terrain of the unthinkable, the unintelligible, the excluded, and for this reason plays a privileged role in his assault on hegemonic power and its properly metaphysical pretensions.

This brief consideration of Genet's theory and practice of ethico-political rupture also allows for a reconfiguration in precise psychoanalytic terms of the reception of *Prisoner of Love*, for it would be a grave mistake to link this text's multiple idiosyncracies—sudden spatiotemporal shifts, the absence of a dominant narrative thread, and the complex interweaving of political and historical analysis with oneiric-surrealistic and mythopoetic passages—with a subjective, or more properly psychological, function. Indeed, what motivates these numerous apparently postmodernist techniques is rather a thoroughgoing authorial self-expropriation, a process whose superficially subjective machinations dissimulate a fundamentally antipsychological—objective, concrete, sociohistorical—intentional core. To be sure, this self-expropriating textual movement closely parallels the development of the notion of the end of analysis in the later Lacan, according to which the analysand is called heroically to traverse the unconscious fundamental fantasy that undergirds its entire sociosymbolic reality and to withstand the traumatic and disorienting jouissance of the subjective destitution it brings.

In addition to being a careful, albeit idiosyncratic, contextualization of the Palestinian resistance at two specific moments of its history, *Prisoner* is thus in a crucial sense a record of Genet's analysis of his object-relation, that is to say of the very unconscious fantasy-kernel that ignites his literary and political passions. Indeed, the text performs a kind of self-analytical work analogous to the one mobilized by Freud in *The Interpretation of Dreams*. The perhaps surprisingly psychoanalytic tenor of his textual practice is in fact what permits Genet to divest himself of the transferential demand that he would otherwise place on his privileged political agents, from the graceful Palestinian fedayeen to the provocatively attired Black Panther militants. Genet grants himself in the process the capacity to view them through a lens only minimally distorted by the idealizing deformations of desire.

"A begging bowl made of flesh"

Genet explores in *Prisoner of Love* the dynamic tension that animates the relation between the ego-predicated ideality underpinning claims to determinate hegemonic identity and the subjective destitution resulting from what he describes as the at-once-treasonous-and-ecstatic relinquishing of those claims. Echoing Fanon's memorable depiction of the Manichean spatial organization of the colonial capital (implicitly Algiers), Genet evokes an imaginary cityscape, which he presents as Amman circa 1970, when the Jordanian capital was beset by increasing political tension between the exiled Palestinian resistance fighters and the Hashemite monarchy, which had begun to align itself more closely with Israel and the United States. While Amman at this time may not have featured a *quartier réservé*—no disreputable neighborhood of brothels, illegal gambling halls, and black markets—Genet features such a neighborhood in order to illuminate the underlying phantasmatics of colonial power and class oppression and spell out the means by which they tend to give rise to their own self-defeating identitarian negations.

Genet describes an urban space divided into two distinct zones: first, a luxurious palatial quarter inhabited by King Hussein, his Bedouin and Circassian military supporters, and other members of the Jordanian elite; and second, a teeming, insalubrious shantytown housing an assemblage of the desperate and the weak, including significantly the most subaltern segment of the Palestinian refugee population. My claim here will be that Genet's disturbing oneiric imagery figures the polarizing logic by which an assertion of identity supported by colonialist power creates a realm of social abjection that may then succumb to the temptation of issuing a defensive but only pseudosymmetrical (because issuing from powerlessness) counteridentitarian response. In consequence, Genet suggests, what we can precisely term a *screen* emerges in the liminal space between the two antithetical identities—the hegemonic and the potentially revolutionary—on which the spectacle of unconscious colonialist fantasy may then be projected. This spectacle not only betokens the function of the exoticized repressed as an excluded object of desire for the hegemonic social class but also presents for both sides the possibility of what Genet throughout his work consistently calls *betrayal*: the traumatically pleasurable dissolution of identity's alienating specular quality, that is to say, the disorienting abandonment of the ego's sociosymbolic anchorage.

For the privileged members of the Jordanian elite, the shantytown offers the promise of an escape from "moral and aesthetic effort"; it is the place where tribal leaders, landowners, high government functionaries, and their attendant wannabes go slumming (60). Adventures here provide an earthly release from demanding ideals of morality, religion, and decorum. Genet makes clear that the underlying attraction of such frolic is the means it offers to divest oneself of the symbolic accoutrements of membership in the privileged classes. Outside palatial space, one can throw off "the pride of self" that comes along with "having a surname, a family tree, a country, an ideology," Genet writes (61). In Lacanian terms, the shantytown's brothels and gambling dens provide access to the self-expropriating experience of the symbolic order's suspension, the intoxicating feeling of liberation from the burden of social visibility that usually accompanies positions of material privilege. The courtier therefore succumbs to the part of jouissance excluded from the terms of membership of the elite; the great sociosymbolic Other reflects back to the deserving tribal elder an image of his enviable status that disintegrates under the shattering force of proscribed pleasures. Genet emphasizes, however, that this excessive pleasure is secured only at the cost of temporarily disappearing from one's own psychical map.

On the other side of the boundary, by contrast, everyday life is marked by precisely this kind of official nonexistence, an invisibility that gives rise to a desire for the same repressive legitimacy from which the privileged seek relief. Crucially, the material anguish of deprivation is compounded by a psychical desire for recognition, which cannot entirely be reduced to a properly socioeconomic marginalization. This is the realm of the Marxian *Lumpenproletariat*, that great aggregate of subjects whose vague existence lies beneath the threshold of historical and political representability, but whose revolutionary potential in the (post)colonial mode of production, fuelled equally by material need and sociosymbolic invisibility, Fanon firmly defends against Marxist orthodoxy (which by omission reduces the latter to the former). The palace's ceremoniousness and formality issue to the socially abject the prospect of sanctioned *being*: the self-assurance guaranteed by a social position recognized by the Other and reassuringly reflected back upon oneself.

The force of this legitimizing power is what leads Genet to evoke the symbolic value of commodities signifying social position and prestige. The "scarves, shirts and watches" (58) that circulate in the shantytown are acquired by those applicants to the royal court who wish to graduate to more comfortable life circumstances; they are more than willing, Genet makes explicit, to offer up voluptuous erotic transgression in exchange for access to the presumed refinements of the court. The paradigmatic, indeed symptomatic, quality of the Manichean social organization that both Genet and Fanon find in protorevolutionary colonial space is no doubt attributable to what here appears at first glance to be a smooth exchange of equivalent values in enjoyment: the slumming Hachemite courtier is accorded a fleeting release from the demanding renunciations of elite social identity; and the ambitious but subaltern Palestinian arriviste is granted at least the tokens of social recognition within the hegemonic class.

Intriguingly, Genet's evocation of Amman's sociospatial structure focuses specifically on the question of the body and its image. Indeed, the passage lends itself to interpretation through the lens of Lacan's well-known idea of the specular construction of an alienated body image in the space of the Other. The Lacanian reference will allow us to see that what appears to be an equivalent exchange veils what in reality is an entrenchment of political asymmetry. Whereas the young Arab men of the shantytown discover, according to Genet, a completed image of their own bodies in the desiring reflections of the Jordanian court, the participants in the sexual exchanges in the shantytown brothels, in sharp contrast, have a very different corporeal experience, one that proves to be unmediated by the specular and in consequence becomes disassembled and decomposed. Indeed, Genet's depiction of sexual life on the other side offers a dense and disturbing weave of images evoking body parts and secretions: erotic intensities grafted onto corporeal fragments disaggregated from any discrete shape or bodily whole. While the body image of the ambitious Palestinian boys betokens the ideality and personhood of the corporeal ego, among the shantytown's less-respectable denizens we find only disembodied organs and desubjectivized pulsations that begin to converge with the nonhuman organic matter lying beneath:

> The shanty town, a medley of monsters and woes seen from the Palace, and in turn seeing the palace and its woes, in turn knew pleasures unheard of elsewhere. One went about on two legs and a torso, around dusk—a torso from which a wrist stuck out with a hand on its end like a stoup, a begging bowl made of flesh that demanded its mite with three fingers you could see through. The wrist emerged from a ragged mass of crumpled, worn-out, dirty American surplus, merging ever more completely with the mud and shit until it was sold as rags, mud and muck combined.
>
> Further on, also on two legs, is a female sex organ, bare, shaven, but twitching and damp and always trying to cling on to me. Somewhere else there's a single eye without a socket, fixed and sightless, but sometimes sharp, and hanging from a bit of sky-blue wood. Somewhere else again, an arse with its balls hanging bare and weary between a pair of flaccid thighs. (59–60)

This arresting vision of social and sexual abjection pays testament to the mutual implication of poverty and the bodily ego's fragmentation or dissolution. The commercialization of sexual exchange in the shantytown, in other words, deprives its residents of the luxury of idealization that frames erotic life in the palace and entrances those who succumb to its lure. It is not to be denied that there is a sociological point to be made here: Without a doubt, Genet wishes to draw his readers' attention to the intimate link between material desperation and the depersonalization that occurs in tandem with the sex trade as it develops in such circumstances of desperate material hardship.

Yet I want to argue that Genet's emphasis in fact lies elsewhere, namely on the symbiosis, to use a biological metaphor, between the two locales: on the lack of "friction," as Genet himself puts it, between them. Considered as a totality, the palace and shantytown function for Genet as a kind of ecosystem in which a libidinal balance, however fragile or deceptive, is achieved through the apparently equal exchange of phantasmatic energies that I have already spelled out. What is crucial to note, however, is that whereas the exchange itself is fair in the sense of bidirectional—a quantity of (presumptive) jouissance travels from one side of the screen to the other both to and fro—the contents of the exchange are logically contradictory. This ensures that the encounter between courtier and hustler will be *missed*: the conspicuous visibility that the shanty-dweller seeks in the palace is for the courtier the source of the demanding "sublimation" that he must escape; conversely, the ecstatic self-dispossession that the courtier seeks in the brothel is for the shanty-dweller the source of his social nonrecognition and material plight.

Not unlike Hegel, it must be said, in his celebrated dialectic of lord and bondsman, Genet underscores the dependence of each constituency on a view of life on the other side. The inhabitants of each locale become entranced by what they (imagine they) lack, such that Genet can write that "the two powers [are] so evenly balanced you wonder if it wasn't a case of mutual mesmerism, that familiar, flirtatious but bitter confrontation linking the two [places]" (58–59). Also like Hegel, however, Genet implies that the relationship between the two parties is only deceptively symmetrical, for he stresses in another, apparently contradictory passage that "the splendour of the Palace is a kind of poverty," its status "purely mythical" (61). What disrupts the exchange of libidinal equivalents between naughty nobleman and provocative hustler is the immanence of disintegration, which Genet evokes as the "inexplicable lull" deflecting the mirror reflections that bounce back and forth between the two places. This lull corresponds to a distinctly negative and nonspecular spatiotemporal paradigm in which, Genet asserts, "nothing survive[s] but bodily functions" (60). All subjects lose their self-images, however tenuously constituted or well established, and corporeal wholeness disintegrates not into some Deleuzo-Guattarian body-without-organs, but rather into a nondenumerable sequence of organs that precisely *cannot* be unified within a recognizable bodily shape and resists therefore all logics of figure or form.

Genet's presentation of the relation between the two spaces ultimately privileges not one or the other but rather highlights a specific kind of ecstatic, self-expropriating encounter that effectively sabotages the self-interested commercial exchange between their inhabitants. I say "sabotage" because the eruption of jouissance in the shantytown so memorably evoked by Genet not only reveals the palace's glamorous lure to be an empty sham but also qualifies as vain the efforts of the ambitious to penetrate palatial space by means of sartorial conformity or erotic seduction. Genet evokes for example the "beauty" of "a few handsome" shantytown boys whose desire for social mobility comes into being through an act of identification that Genet explicitly qualifies as alienated and virtual. When given as children mirror fragments in which "they trap a ray of the sun and reflect it into one of the Palace windows," the boys "discover bit by bit their faces and bodies," thereby anticipating, through these reflections, a corporeal wholeness seemingly denied them by material hardship and the pain of exile (62). In this way Genet formulates a notion of corporeal perfection or completion that takes the form of a specular reflection posited in the space of an idealized Other. Asserting that the palace "consumes a great deal of youth," Genet ensures that his reader is not misled as to the destiny of these beautiful Arab boys (62). Captivated by an illusion, they lose themselves amid the corrupt machinations of court life, lured by the empty promise of conspicuous wealth and devoured by the socially invisible sexual appetites of the powerful.

A thesis of sorts emerges: both the courtier and the subaltern see their ambition of transcendence from constriction and deprivation come to naught before the immanence of a self-expropriating ecstasy that causes all boundaries organizing social and psychical identities—here the focus is on a construct of class complicit with European colonialism—to collapse. For all the intensity of its abject imagery, then, Genet's vision of 1970 Amman would remain disappointingly descriptive if we were to conclude that what I called its ecological dimension is its final word. What is required here is a return to Genet's key notion of betrayal, for it becomes possible in this context to understand this notion as the subversion of the false harmony between the two locales, as the shattering of the specular binary that is upheld by each side's anticipatory captivation by a jouissance to be had on the other side. "Anyone who hasn't experienced the ecstasy of betrayal knows nothing about ecstasy at all," writes Genet and, referring to the Abbot of Cluny's desire to understand Islam by ordering the translation of the Koran, he links this ecstasy to the kind of desanctification that occurs in consequence of the fact that "in passing from one language to another the holy text [can] only convey what can be expressed just as easily in any tongue—that is everything except that which is holy" (59). Translation, transgression, betrayal, *déclassement*—each of these motifs in Genet's text evokes the scandal of disintegration that occurs when the fantasy propping up a structure of social meaning falls asunder. Just as the fascination the abbot harbors for the Islamic faith evaporates with the translation of its holy text into familiar, pedestrian French, so does the ambition of the Arab boy who, upon gaining entry into the palace's confines, is consumed by the cynicism of aristocratic sexual and political intrigue.

But at this point a crucial nuance must be added. For Genet is surely not attempting to persuade his reader that the inevitable frustration of the desires fuelling social ambition and erotic fantasy should lead the inhabitants of his Manichean Amman simply to stay home. Rather, Genet wants to *valorize* the moment of voluptuous negation that subtracts the subject from its own identity coordinates without furnishing any subsequent redemption; without, that is to say, the materialization of the dividend in enjoyment that caused the subject's desire to betray in the first place. The release of jouissance, Genet implies, takes place not in the comforting propping up of psychosocial identity, but rather in this identity's coming to ruin. Genet's point can be clarified with reference to Lacan's differentiation of desire and drive: Whereas the subject derives its *raison d'être* (desire) from a phantasmatic idealization of a forbidden but impossible enjoyment, its satisfaction (drive) can only occur by means of a radically decentering self-dispossession, one that staunchly resists all attempts at integration within the realm of possible social meaning.

Genet's concept of betrayal thus merits the epithet *ethical*: Indifferent to any communicable maxim of morality, the ethics of betrayal enjoins us not only to inhabit the space of radical social abjection and invisibility but also to resist the temptation to domesticate this space, to render it respectable by integrating it within the terms of an intelligible discourse or ideology. It is in this light that we should understand Genet's numerous claims in *Prisoner of Love* that he will abandon, *betray* the Palestinian cause when it becomes fixated on territoriality and nationhood—clearly Genet was able to discern already in the 1970s the signs of this now-familiar development—after it becomes, in other words, something more normatively positive than a radical negation of the values of Euro-American capitalist-colonialist modernity and its dutiful political-Zionist offspring. Not coincidentally, the concepts of nationhood and territoriality functioned as conditions of possibility of comparative literature as a discipline and to this day animate the practice of "area studies" in its various geopolitical incarnations. As far as West Asian politics is concerned, today one needs to go far into the Marxist margins of the Palestinian resistance—beyond Hamas, Islamic Jihad, and even Fatah—to find elements that remain faithful to the specific cause that Genet embraced.

Of Grey Hair and Treachery

The import of what we might call *Prisoner's* Manichean Amman passage surely lies in its suggestion of a kind of psychodynamic sociology of colonial space. Genet uncovers not only how the specular logic that undergirds colonialist social relations rests significantly on the identification of the oppressed with an image, pregnant with fantasy, of the power that oppresses but also how this logic is inherently vulnerable to collapse, a collapse catalyzed by the ecstatic passions of betrayal. Yet the strange power of a different but associated motif overshadows the reading of *Prisoner of Love*. Indeed, despite the scattered and insubstantial space that its account in the text takes up, Genet's remembrance of his encounter with a young fedaï and an elderly Palestinian woman—Hamza and his mother, as they are referred to in the text—plays the most powerful role in Genet's assessment of his attachment to the Palestinians and their cause. These two figures become the very cornerstone of Genet's autobiographical architecture; they take center stage in the drama of the author's curiously disaggregated memorial reconstruction of his experiences in the Jordanian camps.

The recurring image of Hamza and his mother functions in a manner analogous to the Freudian screen memory, though one that has been identified as such and already analyzed. Situated at the very nexus of the sociohistorical and the psychical, this hybrid memory-fantasy both protects Genet from, and threatens to expose him to, the real of his desire vis-à-vis the Palestinians. The properly psychical dimension of this image—its function, very precisely, as an index of the fundamental fantasy's structuring power—reveals itself most strikingly when Genet makes the patently illogical claim that its construction predates his Jordanian experience. It is as if, in other words, the image of Hamza and his mother retroactively compensates for Genet's abandonment at the hands of his own biographical mother to the care of the French public services. Linked in the text, naturally enough, to the Pieta tradition in Christian art and iconography, this "incestuous" textual image of Hamza and his mother is therefore the signifier that knots together Genet's psychical structure. This knot is the place where the subjective specificity of Genet's fantasy—one that, no doubt unsurprisingly, gives pride of place to a phallicized maternal figure—grafts itself onto sociohistorical objectivity, that is to say, onto the concrete vagaries of the political struggle that defined the last two decades of his life.

In its function as the hinge of Genet's psychic life, the various iterations of the image of Hamza and his mother features all the ambivalence that, as psychoanalysis consistently argues, characterizes the love object's essence. In the light of narcissistic idealization, the image stands for the paradoxical transgressive purity of the revolutionary impulse as Genet perceives it, a purity characterized by a combination of elements:

the self's sacrifice to the good of a fraternal cause; the absolute negation of bourgeois materialism, or more precisely the triumph of ludic, death-defying spontaneity over the calculated discipline of joyless productivity; and, perhaps most crucially, an incest-tinged enjoyment linked to a youthful and homoeroticized sociality placed under the sign of not a paternal, but rather a maternal, normative instance. Indeed, as if to underline his marginal status within his fantasy-memory of mother and son, Genet makes reference to Hamza's father only once in a minor, relatively insignificant passage.

It is not until "reality" intrudes—Genet upon his 1982 return to Jordan obtains Hamza's telephone number in Germany, where he is now married and works in a factory of the Ruhr—that the sublimity of this emblem of insubordinate Palestinian dignity crumbles under the weight of exile and dispossession. Though Genet inserts scattered intimations of Hamza's fate throughout the text, it is not until its final pages that we get a more-or-less straightforward narration of this crucial conversation. In keeping with the merciless analytic acumen of *Prisoner of Love*, Genet reveals himself to be deeply conscious of his depiction's phantasmatic element, to the point where he explicitly questions in the text's final paragraphs whether it was "a light of [his] own that he threw" on the two central figures (374). To be sure, this unflinching self-criticism leaves its mark on the entire portrayal of the resistance movement. On several occasions, for example, Genet comments ironically on the disjunction between his homoerotic figuration of the sexy young fedayeen—Genet's homosexuality seems more than anything to be the object of playful teasing among the fighters, most of whom, incidentally, are portrayed as devout Muslims—and the fedayeen's own (mainly but not exclusively) heterosexual and patently adolescent romantic yearnings.

On *Prisoner*'s narrative level, Genet's account of his return to the camps a full ten years after his initial sojourn is shot through with the anticipation of his reunion with Hamza and his mother. Given my argument thus far, however, it will not come as a surprise to learn that what Genet eventually finds in Irbid contrasts sharply with the too-perfect image that, as he readily admits, is more akin to an imaginary construction than a reliable recollection. In a general sense, the insistent linkage of Hamza and his mother with the techniques repeatedly used by Genet to subvert authorial mastery conveys his cognizance of the impossibility of autobiography: the unavoidability of the supplement that fantasy adds to fact. Yet Genet's intention here moves far beyond this postmodernist banality. More consequentially, Genet shows his awareness that the recognition, indeed the *betrayal* of this fantasy—the traversal that produces what

Lacan calls subjective destitution—is a necessary condition of possibility for the ensuing, deeply insightful (auto)critical evaluation of both the cause's vicissitudes and Genet's investment in them.

Thus, in a second light Hamza and his mother become in *Prisoner of Love* metonyms for the resistance's various treacherous compromises of its revolutionary ideals, first nationalist and bourgeois, then later Islamist. Before narrating his reunion with the mother at long last, for example, Genet evokes a number of rumors that were circulating among his Palestinian contacts concerning the destiny of the son, all of which—torture, imprisonment, assassination at the hands of Israeli intelligence—carry strong suggestions of heroic martyrdom. When he evokes his phone conversation with Hamza, however, now securely exiled on German soil, Genet remarks that his young friend's voice is "full of real despair." Asked if he anticipates ever being able to return to his "own country," a country beside which his refugee mother of course still resides in destitution, Hamza responds with a despondent "which country's that?" adding, in a movingly desperate attempt to conjure a sense of hope, that his own son in some vague future will return to Palestine on his behalf. Devastatingly, Genet informs his reader that "the despair in [Hamza's] voice was greater still" in this last response, which betrays for Genet the guilty, mutedly exasperated melancholy of a revolutionary dream crushed under the weight of Zionist propaganda and U.S.-Israeli military power. To be sure, the contrast could not be starker between the youthful, exuberant Hamza of 1970, who disappears in the middle of the night to join a dangerous commando offensive on the other side of the Jordan in Israeli-occupied territory, and the older, mournful, exiled Hamza, who complains that he's "done for," casually referring to "grey hairs" that suggest premature old age (330).

This crucial motif recurs in Genet's climactic narration of his return to Hamza's camp, specifically when he relates his awkward reunion with Hamza's mother, whose hair has now lost all its former color. The motif's repetition is likely a symptom of the quasi-incestuous intimacy that permeates what Genet explicitly frames as his own deeply subjective literary representation of mother and son. More certainly, however, Genet's text explicitly links Hamza's abandonment of the Palestinian resistance—albeit after imprisonment and torture at the hands of not the Israelis, but the Jordanians, as Genet finally discovers from his informants—not only with the mother's marked despair at the resistance's protracted decline but also with her mounting hopelessness in the face of Israeli intransigence and military might. The grey hair shared by mother and son therefore hints at a sense of guilty complicity imperfectly buried. Though by all accounts both did everything "humanly possible" to resist the occupation—to the point, in Hamza's case, of being subjected to torture—one senses that the vitriolic hatred that Hamza's mother directs toward the Israelis is partly directed against herself. It is as if the limits of the humanly possible dissimulated another, only vaguely discernible possibility, one that would effectively negate, against all odds as it were, the Israeli negation of Palestinian humanity.

Offered directions by a friendly young refugee, Genet immediately recognizes the courtyard of the house in which he had been a guest over a decade before. There he meets "a frail woman whose white hair [is] just visible" (349) and concludes that she is in fact Hamza's mother. When she asks Genet whether he brought a camera to this initial visit, Genet senses that the question is in fact a test, telling us that he remembers full well that he had no camera with him at the time. Now apparently secure in the knowledge of her European visitor's identity, the mother grabs Genet by the hand, leading him into the bedroom where he had slept and pointing out the "hole" in the wall in which Genet was to have hidden in the event of an attack by Hussein's Bedouin soldiers and Circassian generals. Despite the apparently hospitable reception that greets both him and his translator-companion, however, Genet detects a strange reticence in the old woman when she insists, for instance, that it was tea, and not coffee, that she brought him during the night. Compounding this impression of ambivalent suspicion are the repeated interjections of one of the old woman's grandsons, who joins the group midinterview to learn of any news of his uncle that Genet might have brought, and who proceeds sharply to scold his grandmother for her seeming cooperation with outsiders whose motivations, Genet surmises, surely at best seem unclear.

As the conversation unfolds, Genet gains a sharper sense of the depth of Hamza's mother's bitterness. Moreover, he begins to discern the resentment with which she responds to his attempts at recapturing, through an act of collective reminiscence, a time when the resistance, still ingenuously referred to as a revolution, was young, carefree, and hopeful. Twelve years prior to this moment, the Palestinian movement was no doubt rationally cognizant of the slim odds of victory against the massive weight of U.S.-backed Israeli military power and the seductive pull of Zionist ideology in the wake of the Jewish holocaust. But this realism during the earlier era was nonetheless superseded, Genet implies, by the anything-can-happen zeal of what he wants to depict as an authentically revolutionary moment. Though Genet assures himself that the woman before him is indeed Hamza's mother, the radical change in her appearance—she was once the spry, gun-toting paragon of militant Palestinian femininity, surely idealized, as Genet himself intimates, through the synchronous and inextricable agencies of memory and fantasy—has unveiled a hardened and argumentative old woman whose hair is so white and thin that a casual glance reveals henna stains on her scalp. Indeed, the transformation is so thoroughgoing that it calls into question for Genet the trustworthiness of the subjective representation of his entire Palestinian adventure:

> After it's been used in the bath for a long time and dwindled to half its original size, a piece of soap, amazed at the change in itself, might exclaim, "It's not possible!"
>
> Before, my memory had been firmly imprinted with the image of a woman strong enough to carry a gun, and to load, aim and fire it. Her lips weren't thin in those days, nor faded to the same pallor as the trace of henna on her dandruff. I hadn't been present at the debacle; I could measure its effects all the better. Hamza's mother had become as thin and flat as all the other two-dimensional shapes you saw in Jordan. (407)

In passages such as this, Hamza's mother clearly becomes for Genet an icon that represents the destiny of the entire Palestinian resistance. What is most significant about Genet's consideration, however, is that he is so acutely aware of the dangers of succumbing to the cardboard nostalgic reverie that had settled over the Jordanian refugee camps at the time of his return. Indeed, the paradox of the Hamza and his mother motif is that the depressing realism of Genet's evocation of the Palestinians' bitter destiny is precisely what allows him to maintain his fidelity to that aspect of the resistance that he wishes so passionately to defend. Genet's militant sobriety prevents him from demanding, in a symptomatic manifestation of the transference, that the youthful and heroic image come together with the tired and cynical one in a reinvigorated but pseudorevolutionary idealism, hopeful but ultimately empty. In effect, the memory-images of the despairing Hamza in his pathetic German exile and his balding mother in her anti-Jewish vitriol become through his textual self-analysis the true objects of Genet's love, the true cause of his authentically revolutionary desire. In Lacanian terms, Genet keeps separate his I and his *a*, his ego ideal and his partial object. No doubt it is this success that made it possible for Genet finally to complete, after a decade of neurotic procrastination, what is surely the most arresting, challenging, and politically disciplined memoir in all of twentieth-century literature. The radical ethical challenge and self-expropriating analytical intricacies of *Prisoner of Love* deserve to inform the practice of comparative criticism for decades—and centuries—to come.

WORKS CITED

Fanon, Frantz. *The Wretched of the Earth*. Trans. Richard Philcox. New York: Grove, 2004.

Fisk, Robert. *The Great War for Civilization: The Conquest of the Middle East*. London: Fourth Estate, 2005.

Genet, Jean. *Prisoner of Love*. Trans. Barbara Bray. New York: New York Review, 2003.

———. *Un captif amoureux*. Paris: Gallimard, 1986.

Pappe, Ilan. *A History of Modern Palestine: One Land, Two Peoples*. Cambridge: Cambridge UP, 2004.

Said, Edward. "On Genet's Late Works." *Imperialism and Theatre: Essays on World Theatre, Drama and Performance*. Ed. Ellen J. Gainor. London: Routledge, 1995. 230–42.

White, Edmund. *Genet: A Biography*. New York: Vintage, 1994.

Afterword

Comparisons Worth Making

Valerie Traub

Comparatively Queer heralds an ambitious intervention. The editors aim to queer comparative studies while destabilizing its Eurocentrism and to comparativize and decolonize queer studies while challenging its presentism. What are the means by which this is to be done? Through a range of conceptual border crossings and comparative "intersectionalities" that enable us to explore the space "in between." Further, the editors propose that the project of comparatively queering is, in the end, "queerly redundant" (2) because queering and comparing not only necessitate and "enhance" (6) each other but also perform closely aligned versions of almost the same thing.

Such bold pronouncements initially gave this "noncomparativist" pause. If they are to persuade, it will be because both *queer* and *comparative* have undergone the radical reformulations that this volume proposes to enact (including, it would seem, the dismantling of my own identity as a "noncomparativist"). It is with the prospect of such an ample reconstruction in mind that I begin by seeking the contours of *queer* and *comparative* as deployed in the essays themselves. Although the editors highlight the analytical potential of crossings and intersections, my strategy is to focus on the oscillating views that come into and out of sight as themes, tensions, conflicts, and questions rub up against and merge into and out of each other. By articulating some of the logics, both explicit and implicit, offered here, my remarks, coming *after,* are meant to sharpen some of our angles of vision as well as return us to the inaugural question posed by the editors: "*when* is a comparison worth making?" (1).

Neither *comparative* nor *queer* names a fixed entity, and in a volume dedicated to elucidating what Canadé Sautman calls "forms of blurring and crossing: across national cultures, borders, language barriers, genders and across a range of performances and ascriptions to 'art'" (92), we should expect the prospect they provide to continue to fluctuate and move. *Comparative* and *comparativism* come under intense scrutiny, in part because one disciplinary formation that they designate and in which many of the contributors work, comparative literature, remains in the process of a paradigm shift. The mission and contours of their discipline (and the related field of area studies), including the proposed deconstruction of those self-other boundaries that initially constituted it, are up for grabs. As they grapple with the legacies of nation, language, race, ethnicity, gender, and sexuality within the context of a transnational world and all its attendant power asymmetries, the methodological question, "*how shall we compare?*" becomes limned with the force of an imperative.

Describing the traditional use of *comparative* in the disciplines of anthropology (for cross-cultural work), history (for viewing multiple temporalities), political theory (for assessing capital development), and literature (for reading across language "worlds"), Arondekar points out that "these early appropriations of the comparative model relied primarily on axes of similarity and difference and rarely interrogated the Eurocentricity of the normative categories that founded the very grounds of comparison" (115). Yet, she argues, "the recent focus on transnationalism" (113) has made comparative projects (including the "conversation between area studies and sexuality studies"; 113) "more pressing, but also more difficult than ever before" (113). Difficult indeed, in part because they are inflected with what Arondekar calls "comparative imaginaries" (113)— "the incursions of temporality, . . . the 'politics of time' that emerge in our desire for knowledge and in our ethical stances toward otherness" (113). It is one of the strengths of this volume that the "politics of time" (113, 124) is also constantly reiterated in relationship to questions of space— not only of geographical space, but also of normative boundaries of inclusion and exclusion. Indeed, despite their diversity, the contributors seem to be unified in the belief that transgression of the discipline's traditional borders provides the reason for comparison in the first place.

But given the difficulties, how *do* we compare? As the editors emphasize, across geocultural space, across time, and across identities—and it is in terms of identity that the alignment of comparativism with "intersectionality" is most evident. But there are other modes of comparison—and noncomparison—operative here as well. Most of the contributors employ a cultural studies method: examining a range of discourses and taking little note of distinctions between literary and nonliterary texts. With a couple of exceptions, they also tend to work within a single historical period, however broadly construed (the medieval, the Victorian, the present). Most focus on printed texts as their primary materials of analysis, and in only one chapter (Lanser's) is the distinction between print and manuscript deemed salient. Although all of the chapters address social and political formations, only those by Canadé Sautman and Penney push the meaning of comparison inward, toward subjects' "daily experience" (Canadé, 108) of norms and their exclusion from them.

It is worth noting that most of the chapters assume that comparison involves two terms, rather than, for instance, three (Lanser again is an exception). The chapters focused on a distant past keep "modernity" in their lines of sight, while those exploring the present moment tend to gaze, either directly or over their shoulders, at the "West." Given their emphasis on crossings and intersections, it is not surprising that none explicitly propose triangulation as a possible mode of comparative queering. If the meanings of *comparative* and *comparativism* are scrutinized, then, the methodological choices involved in different acts of comparison are the subject of less pointed articulation.

The meaning of *queer*, in contrast, seems to function less as a point of contention than a form of working assumption—standing in, as it often does, for nonnormative erotic acts and identities in general and same-sex ones in particular, as well as for nonnormative performances of gender and, in Canadé Sautman's phrase, "differenced bodies" (93). Canadé Sautman's appraisal *that* queer "float[s] between recognition of gender transgression and the space of the homoerotic" (107) provides an apt metaphor for the relatively diffuse application of *queer* within and across the chapters. In search of greater precision, we might want to contrast Ha's apparent understanding of *queer* as primarily a matter of gender practices rather than eroticism; Armbrecht's comparison of gender *to* sexuality as discrete yet related concepts in his comparison of *parité* and PaCS; and Canadé Sautman's vision of a "queer potential" that, while erotic, does not depend on specific sexual acts or identities and disperses across a particular physical locale. Indeed, Canadé Sautman's vision of *queer* is of something "always in process, shifting, and redeployed in contact with other instances or moments of queer potential" (92).

As much as this vision brings new possibilities into view, I wonder whether there is, as Canadé Sautman maintains, "an *endless* concatenation of 'queer possibility,' . . . located in a space of constant motion, reconfiguration, and multiple border crossings" (92; emphasis added). As several of the other chapters imply, the horizon of queer possibilities would seem to be delimited by specific, historically wrought configurations of gender and sexuality—ones that can be improvised upon but are not necessarily subject to "constant motion" (92). Further, this vision of *queer* might fail to address the queer *impossibility* embodied by someone like Genet, for whom sexuality, according to Penney, was conceived "not as a function of psychological identity . . . but rather as the mode of this identity's impossibility and consequent unavoidable failure" (200).

Two temporally and methodologically disparate readings of French discourses of "homosexuality" help clarify some of what is at stake in these different approaches to "queer possibility" and its relations to cultural intelligibility and historical specificity. A focus on particularities, as well as the very *meaning* of particularity as a political discourse, informs Armbrecht's comparison of French and U.S. "discussions of homosexuality" (154). While acknowledging how the specter of "a Western European-American queer hegemony" (154) productively unifies diverse acts of resistance around the globe, he nonetheless maintains that "it is a mistake simply to lump" (154) France and the United States together. Leaving the nation-state analytically intact in order to trouble the larger monolith of "the West," he argues that cultural and social differences, going to the very core of how each nation imagines itself, render their concepts of sexual identity incommensurate, not least in terms of their respective commitments to universalism and communitarianism. Exposing the chiasmic structure of French efforts to legislate PaCS and *parité*—a logic internally incoherent yet politically "progressive"—Armbrecht shows the crucial role played by gender binaries in the dismantling of the homo-hetero binary while also demonstrating how very "French" this strategy was.

Armbrecht's concluding gesture toward a future in which "sexuality might lose its universal meaning, and queer will be a modus operandi instead of a modus vivendi" (167) provides an avenue to approach Campbell's mapping of male "homosexuality" back into medieval France. Campbell persuasively demonstrates "a tradition that conflated language, genealogy, and sexuality and gender" (27) in "the inception of the European vernaculars (a precondition for the existence of a Western comparative literature)" (26). However, having invoked only to reject the Foucauldian distinction between sodomy as acts and homosexuality as being, he does not persuade that the conflation he reveals gives rise to something we might term *homosexuality*. Nor does the more diffuse *queer* necessarily settle the historical question. Without confronting the lack of fit between pre- and early modern and contemporary formations of desire, *homosexuality* and *queer* function as vague placeholders for the various erotic acts and gendered positions alluded to in *De Planctus Naturae, Roman de la Rose*, and *Roman de Silence*. I am not the first to worry that the very capaciousness of *queer*—often seen as its unique promise as an analytical category—might obscure as much as it enables historical understanding. This concern becomes all the more pressing when queering and comparing are proposed as coincident—if not quite isomorphic—activities; if the forms of *comparison* require precise delineation, so, too, do the forms of *queer*.

The distinction between a mode of living and a manner of operating can be both great and small. The measure of this difference is one issue at stake in the redeployment of *queer* to describe cross-species identifications and intimacies. Facing the challenge thrown up by increased recognition of humanity's historical and ongoing relation to other species, Freccero's and Jackson's queering of animal studies seem to move in counterposed directions, implicitly exposing an interpretative contradiction in the emerging investments and dynamics of this new subfield. Is the goal of queering across the species divide, as Jackson implies in her analysis of the fables of Namjoshi and Seth, to articulate parallels between the treatment of animals and queers? Faulting these fabulists for unwittingly repeating "the hierarchical structures of heteronormative patriarchy" (188) by denying animals "access to the dominant" (188) discourse, Jackson links these authors' inability to "extricate themselves from the hegemonic framework" (188) to their failure to recognize "that not all queers (whether animal or human) or forms of queering are the same" (188). Her acknowledgement of noncoincidence leads me to wonder whether the very attempt to "*align* . . . queers and beasts" (172; emphasis added) analytically is necessarily the best strategy to confront our different histories or negotiate our common future.

In contrast, Freccero's "figural historiography" of human-canine relations injects a dose of skepticism into the fantasy of equity that can animate the desire for a cross-species rapprochement. Her approach to this "companion species relation" (55) "does not privilege only the human or the nonhuman as the site of subjectivity and agency but implicates both in a consequential becoming" (48–49) constituted by "shared histories of predation and oppression, dominance and submission" (58). Focused on the figure of "the devouring dog" (47, 59) and its corollary, the cynocephalic and cynanthropic cannibal, she charts the "transspecies habitus" (48) of dogs and humans, demonstrating how, in the violence of colonialism and the contemporary prison-industrial complex, dogs and humans become ontologically blurred. This reading of the "conundrum of dog-human 'natureculture'" (55) implicates race, racism, transnational capital, virile masculinity, queer heterosexuality, and lesbian domestic relations in a complex affective network that resists "any progressive, ameliorative rational accounts of historical process" (61). Freccero's deconstruction ends, not with a political assertion of what is to be done, but with an ethical appeal to all of us "to figure out how to survive" (62) the evolutionary "crime" of our cross-species relations.

Part of that "figuring out" involves situating subjects in a more "promiscuous" relationship to temporality. A major impulse of Frecerro's reading of pre- and posthumanist cross-species relations is to disrupt the logic of temporality itself—an aim she shares with several other contributors. Ever since the integration of postcolonial critique into queer studies, the recognition of the tight conceptual link between modernity and a tendentious idea of progress—or inversely, premodernity and, in the words of Arondekar, "the time(s) of the primitive in a postcolonial world" (125n2)—has given renewed urgency to the critique of the developmental, coming out model of lesbian and gay history insofar as chronological history is assessed to be necessarily "progressive, teleological, and generative" (Freccero 46). The problem is astutely described in Arondekar's assessment of the logic of temporality that, she argues, underwrote Indian activists' attempts to overturn Section 377 of the Indian Penal Code: "For sexuality studies, the emphasis on transnational approaches has provided . . . a cautionary tale, a haunting reminder of the colonial genealogies that found the very languages of its articulations" (114). Arondekar, in seeking "to understand how the languages of contemporary legal reform are constantly deflected by, if not into, a revisionist comparative framework produced and institutionalized by certain forms of nationalist and queer historiography" (116–17), attempts "to push against the stabilizing of time's corpus, toward a historiography of sexuality that settles into uncertainty as the very possibility of return" (124). Working with very different materials, Freccero expresses a similar desire; approaching historical trauma phantasmatically (as persistence and repetition), she fashions a historiographic method that "works through" the complex and incomplete legacies of both modernity and history writing.

Freccero's "comparatively queer" mediation between distinct temporalities provides one strategy to defy teleology. Ha's and Arondekar's attempts to track the logic of asymmetric temporalities offer another. Analyzing "Hong Kong gender practices . . . [that] partake simultaneously of two distinct cultural formations of the body—the Western biomedical one and the Chinese cosmological one" (140), Ha's exploration of a phenomenology of temporality that is not "disenchanted" (139) refigures modernity as an uneven synchronicity. Just as Arondekar enacts "a shift to thinking of locations of difference (west vs. east, north vs. south, metropole vs. colony) as conceptually commensurate" (115), Ha sees within Hong Kong understandings of the gendered body a practice of health, a "tactics," that disrupts "the otherwise seamlessly homogenous surface of the hegemonic Western worldview" (144). Whereas, following Armbrecht, we might note the current pressures bearing down on that worldview (as witnessed by the global market in alternative medical therapies, California's legalization of medical marijuana, and the push in the United States for insurance to cover alternative medicine), Ha's goal "to articulate a research framework that would enable [the Chinese] to stay with [their] own heterogeneities and resist the universalizing impulse of Western theories" is grounded in an incisive, almost sociological, understanding of "heterogeneities" (146).

These deliberately methodological chapters recognize, in the words of Arondekar, that sexuality studies have "a sedimented politics of time" that "often reproduces subjects, critical genealogies, and methodological habits that duplicate the very historiographies we seek to exceed" (124). But their rejection of chronological history, it turns out, is not the only way to resist teleology. Lanser provides a salient alternative. For Lanser, "sapphic subjects" name a "flashpoint" in the inauguration of sexual modernity, a "spatiotemporal *position* rather than . . . a form of being" (78; emphasis added). In describing the "use of female same-sex desire" (70) as "the very *signifier* of modernity" (71), Lanser tells a "story of modernity itself" (72). Aiming "to flip the scholarly coin from the *history of sexuality* to the *sexuality of history*: from the premise that sexuality is historically constructed to the claim that history is also sexually constructed" (72), Lanser scrupulously parses the historical contingencies of sapphic subjects, focusing here on their status as topics of discourse, and sequencing this to the social categories and constituents of subjectivity addressed in her larger project. Delineating the specific geographic locations in which these contingencies become manifest, Lanser asks "why some locations seem to be comparatively queerer than others" (72), attempting to make sense of France's location as the European vanguard of such representations as well as the role of "western*most* Europe" (84) in this discursive proliferation. Integrating social specificity into an argument of much broader sweep, Lanser offers a temporally focused synchronic analysis in the service of a diachronic one, along the way pointing to how the history of sapphism (and not just its historiography) is inextricably bound up with narrative ("the imperative of action" that reveals itself as *plot;* 77). The effect is a careful balancing act: chronological and sequential, but neither progressive nor teleological—and about as far from heteroreproductive as it is possible to be.

A signal success of this volume, then, is the extent to which its contributors use the postcolonial critique of modernity's troubled relation to "othered" pasts and "othered" locales to develop new methods that extend beyond critique, and which are adequate to the complexity of sexuality's history. Whether tracking the incommensurate synchronicities of East and West (Ha and Arondekar), theorizing, by historicizing, modernity itself (Lanser), or flouting that division by continually trespassing it (Freccero), these chapters proffer strategies to address some of the central questions currently challenging not only comparativists and queer studies scholars but also postcolonialists and historians of sexuality.

As the angles of vision offered by *Comparatively Queer* converge and change, we turn from questions of historicity to questions of geopolitical and intersubjective space. One of the more startling juxtapositions that thus slides into view is the site of the circus and fair in nineteenth-century Western Europe and the Palestinian refugee camp before and after the first intifada. The nineteenth-century fair, according to Canadé Sautman, "made the oddness of body transgression oddly familiar and its erratic production of fear and abjection a passionately desired cultural experience" (94). Much the same could be said of the Palestinian refugee camp, as depicted in Penney's reading of Genet's *Prisoner of Love*. Regarding the erotic exchanges between "the slumming Hachemite courtier" (203) and the "subaltern Palestinian *arriviste*" (203), Penney emphasizes "the dependence of each constituency on a view of life on the other side" (205). As locales organized via a spectral economy of illicit eroticism, affect, and violence that depends on a mutually sustaining, if asymmetrical, mirror of bodies, desires, and power relations, the fairground and the refugee camp both embody, to use Canadé Sautman's phrasing, "open, transnational borders, crossed by uncertain and borrowed identities and unstable notions of home and place" (100). Notwithstanding these similarities, there are dangers to comparing these spectral economies across such divergent geopolitical terrains. How far would we want to take this comparison and what would it mean to linger in that overlapping space? In *Prisoner of Love*, "Genet sets himself the task of crossing the line that demarcates the field of intelligibility of life as such, the line that implicitly establishes the very terms by means of which cultural comparisons are normatively drawn" (196). Might this recognition of dissimilar fields of intelligibility be a place to test the limits of the editors' assertion that "the heart of comparison . . . lies somewhere *between* almost totally different but not quite and almost the same but not quite" (1)? For it is here that one faces the incommensurability of the abject—not a hierarchy of oppressions, but a radical distinction in the register of what Penney calls the "incomparable Real": poverty, political dispossession, and recurrent massacres.

However much we are drawn to celebrate border crossings—temporal, spatial, geopolitical, and psychic—it is the ethics of our engagement, including the ethics of the comparisons that enable and derive from such crossings, that are of ultimate concern. If this volume analytically conjoins crossings and intersections in order to infuse new potentials into the act of comparison, it also demonstrates that discrete forms of identity, social location, and historical time both create borders *and* inform our desires to conjoin, trespass, or defy them. Further, along with intersections and crossings, there are sure to be bypassings and parallel lines—including asymptotic curves that, however closely they veer, never meet. Some acts of comparison might not lead to crossings or intersections, but toward greater recognition of the analytical limits of this organizing trope.

This caveat is as relevant to this afterword as to the volume as a whole. However transtemporal, transnational, intersectional, and interdisciplinary we tutor ourselves to be, intellectual training, personal investments, and disciplinary sites matter—perhaps nowhere more than in the acts of encountering, characterizing and assessing the work of others. If, because of this volume's success in refiguring the meanings of comparison, I am now less likely to think of myself as a noncomparativist, my location within particular configurations of knowledge production continue to inform my preferences for certain kinds of work: namely, that which is informed by meticulous historical understanding, that which attends scrupulously to the precision of its analytical categories, and that which articulates what is at stake in the questions it asks and the methods by which it proposes to answer them. Whether these will become the primary criterion by which comparatively queer scholarship will judge the impact of its own future contributions remains to be seen. But what this volume makes clear is that the project of *comparatively queering* is worth doing precisely because the comparisons to which it is dedicated are worth making—and not only for the sake of comparativism and queers.

Contributors

Thomas J. D. Armbrecht is an associate professor of French at the University of Wisconsin, Madison. His book *At the Periphery of the Center: Sexuality and Literary Genre in the Works of Marguerite Yourcenar and Julien Green* was published in 2007, and he has translated and introduced Eric Jourdan's novel *Wicked Angels* (2006). He has also written on homosexuality in Turkey, the intersection of rhetorical and architectural tropes in Pierre Loti, and Jean Cocteau's cinema. His current project is a monograph on fractured identity in Loti, Cocteau, and Guibert.

Anjali Arondekar is an associate professor of feminist studies at the University of California, Santa Cruz. Her research engages the poetics and politics of sexuality, colonialism, and historiography in South Asia. She is the author of *For the Record: On Sexuality and the Colonial Archive in India* (2009) and has published most recently in *GLQ, Journal of Asian Studies, Interventions, Victorian Studies, Feminist Studies*, and the *Journal of the History of Sexuality*. She is currently working on a second book-project, provisionally titled *Subject to Sex: Caste and Community Formation in Colonial Western India*.

Kofi Campbell is an associate professor of English at Wilfrid Laurier University's Brantford campus, and a member of the graduate program in Cultural Analysis and Social Theory at its Waterloo campus. He has published on medieval, postcolonial, and queer literatures. His book, *Literature and Culture in the Black Atlantic: From Pre- to Postcolonial*, focuses on the constructions of blacks and Africans in medieval and early Renaissance literature and on the continuing effects of those constructions on postindependence Caribbean literature. His current research focuses on same-sex love and lovers in the literature of the Caribbean diaspora and on the process of nationalism in medieval England.

Francesca Canadé Sautman is a professor of French at Hunter College and The Graduate Center of the City University of New York. She has published in medieval and early modern studies, Francophone literature, folklore, ethnic studies, gender and queer theory, including an essay in the period she discusses in this volume, "Invisible Women: Retracing the Lives of French Working-Class Lesbians, 1880–1930" (1997). She is the author of *La religion du quotidien: Rites et croyances de la fin du Moyen Age* (1995), the coeditor of *Same-Sex Love and Desire among Women in the Middle Ages* (2001) and of *Telling Tales: Medieval Narratives and the Folk Tradition* (1998), and was a member of the editorial board at Gale Macmillan for the *Encyclopedia of Sex and Gender* (2007), as well as editor for several journals of folklore and folktales.

Carla Freccero is a professor of literature, feminist studies, and history of consciousness and the director of the Center for Cultural Studies at University of California, Santa Cruz, where she has taught since 1991. Her books include *Father Figures* (1991); *Popular Culture* (1999); *Queer/Early/Modern* (2006); and the coedited *Premodern Sexualities* (1996; with Louise Fradenburg). Her essay in this collection is part of a book project titled *Animate Figures*.

Marie-Paule Ha teaches in the School of Humanities at the University of Hong Kong. Her research interests are gender and postcolonial studies. Her current project investigates the colonial experiences of French women in Indochina. Her recent publications comprise numerous articles, as well as her book, *Figuring the East: Segalen, Malraux, Duras, and Barthes* (2000); an edition of *Homme jaune et femme blanche* by Christiane Fournier (2008); and a coedited special issue for *Research in African Literatures* on multiculturalism.

Jarrod Hayes is an associate professor of French and Francophone studies at the University of Michigan, Ann Arbor. His research focuses on the intersection between queer theory and postcolonial studies. He is the author of *Queer Nations: Marginal Sexualities in the Maghreb* (2000) and is currently working on a book manuscript titled *Queer Roots for the Diaspora, Ghosts in the Family Tree*.

Margaret R. Higonnet, a professor of English and comparative literature at the University of Connecticut and cochair of the gender study group at Harvard University's Center for European Studies, has written on the intersection of feminist theory with comparative literature, which she addressed in the collection *Borderwork* (1995). Past president of the American Comparative Literature Association and of the American Conference on Romanticism, she has addressed romantic theory, nineteenth-century British women poets, Thomas Hardy, and gender in the literature of World War I.

Bianca Jackson obtained her DPhil from Wadham College, University of Oxford, in 2008, examining the representation of the queer subject in postindependence Indian Anglophone literature. She has coedited the reference book *Defining Moments in History: Over a Century of the People, Discoveries, Disasters, and Political and Cultural Events That Rocked the*

World (2008) and is currently pursuing a graduate degree in law at Lucy Cavendish College, University of Cambridge, with a view toward fusing legal theory and English literature.

Susan S. Lanser, a professor of English and women's studies at Brandeis University, is a comparatist who works in the areas of feminist theory, narrative theory, the history of gender and sexuality, and the French Revolution. She has held fellowships from the American Comparative Literature Association, the National Endowment for the Humanities, the Folger Library, and the Radcliffe Institute. In addition to her numerous articles and editions of women writers, she has published *Fictions of Authority: Women Writers and Narrative Voice* (1992) and *The Narrative Act: Point of View in Prose Fiction* (1981).

James Penney teaches in the Department of Cultural Studies at Trent University, Canada. He is the author of *The World of Perversion: Psychoanalysis and the Impossible Absolute of Desire* and is currently finishing his second book titled *The Structures of Love: Art and Politics beyond the Transference.*

William J. Spurlin is a professor of English and the director of the Centre for the Study of Sexual Dissidence and Cultural Change at the University of Sussex. His most recent books are *Imperialism within the Margins: Queer Representation and the Politics of Culture in Southern Africa* (2006) and *Lost Intimacies: Rethinking Homosexuality under National Socialism* (2009). He has written extensively on such comparative areas as postcolonial queer studies, and feminism and queer studies; his most recent work is at the interface of queer theory and biomedicine.

Valerie Traub is a professor of English and women's studies at the University of Michigan, Ann Arbor. She is the author of *Desire and Anxiety: Circulations of Sexuality in Shakespearean Drama* and *The Renaissance of Lesbianism in Early Modern England. Gay Shame*, coedited with David Halperin, was published in 2009. Her most recent publications include "The Joys of Martha Joyless: Queer Pedagogy and the (Early Modern) Production of Sexual Knowledge" in *The Forms of Renaissance Thought: New Essays in Literature and Culture*, "The Past is a Foreign Country? The Times and Spaces of Islamicate Sexuality Studies" in *Islamicate Sexualities*, and "The Present Future of Lesbian Historiography" in *A Companion to Lesbian, Gay, Bisexual, Transgender, and Queer Studies*. She is currently working on two books: *Mapping Embodiment in the Early Modern West: Anatomy, Cartography, and the Prehistory of Normality* and *Making Sexual Knowledge: Thinking Sex with the Early Moderns.*

INDEX